THE BUSINESS OF CIRCUMFERENCE
A Kaleidoscope

Other Works by Joseph Gallagher

The Story of Baltimore's New Cathedral
Universal Press: 1959

The Documents of Vatican II (Translation Editor)
America/Association Press: 1966

The Christian under Pressure
Ave Maria Press: 1970

Painting on Silence (Poems)
Exposition Press: 1973

The American Catholic Who's Who (General Editor)
Bicentennial Edition: 1976

The Pain and the Privilege (Memoirs)
Doubleday Image Book: 1983

The Symphony of Two Worlds
by Dom Helder Camara (English Translator)
Pastoral Press: 1984

Voices of Strength and Hope for a Friend with AIDS
Sheed and Ward: 1987

The Business of Circumference

A Kaleidoscope

by JOSEPH GALLAGHER

Introduction by
BRADFORD JACOBS
Editorial Page Editor (1968–79)
The Baltimore Evening Sun

Christian Classics, Inc.

POST OFFICE BOX 30, WESTMINSTER, MARYLAND 21157

1988

First Published, 1988

© 1988 by Joseph Gallagher

Library of Congress Catalogue Number: 88:70217

ISBN: 0-87061-145-3

Printed in the United States of America

DEDICATION

To the magic circle of my Friends
who bandage the dark and crown the light
especially Frank, Judy, Guz, Paul, Gene,
Mike, Ruth, and Charlotte

EPIGRAPHS

Gloria Patri: My Business is Circumference.

EMILY DICKINSON

Et Filio: What I like best about the world is
that it's round.

TEILHARD DE CHARDIN, S.J.

Et Spiritui Sancto: To turn, turn, will be our delight
'Till by turning, turning, we come
'round right.

SHAKER ELDER JOSEPH BRACKETT

Introduction

by BRADFORD JACOBS

Editorial Page Editor, *The Baltimore Evening Sun* (1968–79)

BECAUSE newspaper editors are impatient, deadline-haunted people, they snatch feverishly for the heart of the thing. That's what makes Joe Gallagher almost as much headache as blessing. You're laying out the day's journalistic smorgasbord—a little of this, a lot of that, hit that topic hard, cater to the damn reader's supposed taste—but what's this thing Joe Gallagher's up to today?

Automatically you go for the place where you guess his heart beats: you go for sanctimony. Joe Gallagher being a man of the church (in his own special fashion), you go for the predictable sermon. What then is our editor's surprise when no sermon appears? God's there, about as often as not. Sanctimony never—unless you count a glimpse of it fleeting past the corner of the eye.

Take a day when what you need is maybe a pious little lecture, something to cool down a corner of some pretty hot politics you whooshed up on the editorial page. What do you get from Joe Gallagher? Not piety. What you get is an exhilarating pursuit of Abe Lincoln, into his own Illinois, a fresh perception of the Lincoln offspring, a neglected grave site.

Lincoln himself didn't think much of newspaper editors. He would have chuckled at Joe Gallagher's disconcerting leap out of the smarmy footsteps of sanctimony. So, you guess, would others. You print it. Then what? More Lincoln? Other probes into secular history?

No. Now comes an almost demure parade, saint or saintly, each on his or her appropriate day—Mother Seton, John Neumann, Valentine, Patrick, Aquinas, Francis of Assisi. Each piece brings the saint to vibrant life, not the dutiful rumble half-heard from some bemused pulpit. Joe Gallagher, perhaps capriciously, even tosses in a defense of atheism beyond the eloquence of most atheists. Alas for editors fond of straight edges.

Alas again when, seized by still another vagrant mood, off trots our man on a twisting highroad to almost everywhere: to Mexico, pre-invasion Grenada, England at Jubilee time, Ireland of course, Jerusalem, Constantinople, Rome . . . On the move, typewriter humming, Joe Gallagher trails behind him the suspicion that, upon arrival on Mars, the first astronaut afoot there will find, tucked in some pinkish niche, a Gallagher vignette setting forth a Martian's view of earth.

Setting it forth, what's more, in prose so polished you can see your face in it—or, better, see straight through it. Here, in his style, along with the psychedelic choice of subjects, is where the Gallagher book shines brightest. It's a style so stylish it doesn't cry out to the reader—See? Style! It's more an amiable, rambling chat—low-keyed, sweet-tempered—from a man personally at home among stylists from Virgil to T. S. Eliot to John Kennedy. What emerges overall—simply, clearly— is simple clarity. Joe Gallagher talks to you usually with a sunny smile, occasionally with a troubled frown, but always in language and syntax chosen with care to tell you exactly what he means.

There's one tiny, delightful quirk: Joe Gallagher is a lover of words themselves. For the life of him he can't stop himself from plucking at their roots. Years of training in Latin and Greek, more years of French and German give his English a special depth. In mid-sentence—mid-thought, even—he will stop to reflect momentarily on where a word comes from, thus perking up an idea otherwise humdrum with a fresh bouquet. The net of this is not the cuteness that the spelling of it out here may suggest. It is the Gallagher way of cramming more meaning into writing than most writers, then of squeezing more meaning out.

I came to know Joe Gallagher in the late 1960s when, a restless new editor of *The Evening Sun*'s editorial page, I began hunting for pieces livelier than what a predecessor called "belaboring the obvious." Joe popped in one morning, gloomy clericals and a sort of all-day five o'clock shadow illuminated by an apparently inextinguishable Irish smile.

Uneasily, even uncertainly, I called him "Father Gallagher"— uneasily because I am a Protestant, uncertainly because I wondered if he shouldn't be called "Monsignor," which as former editor of Baltimore's *Catholic Review*, he really was. I needn't have worried. Not five minutes passed before, bouncing grins and jokes around the office like ping-pong balls, this monsignor had two secretaries giggling, a passing editorial writer charmed, and me fascinated by a handful of un-belabored, non-obvious essays he was offering.

Joe gave us a bravura performance that day. Despite his own desperate illness, the shattering early death of his politically promising elder brother, and a head-on collision on policy with the church he deeply understands and loves, the bravura has never faded in the last twenty years.

Anyway, Joe Gallagher came to ornament the editorial page of *The Evening Sun* and, later, the new-born page set aside for "Other Voices." It amused me that H. L. Mencken, sulphurous scourge of "parsons," had once—if briefly, almost catastrophically—been editor of this very page upon which Joe Gallagher now spread his twinkling insights. Secretly, I suspect, this improbable pair would have seen much eye to eye. They never met, so far as I know, but wouldn't Mencken have relished the Gallagher distaste for monolithic thought? Wouldn't Joe Gallagher, compulsive word-dissector, have delighted in the author of *The American Language*. Wouldn't they have joined hands in casting a little light of irreverence into self-reverent corners?

Mencken was the more formidable personage, Gallagher the more whimsical and, in his own gentle way, the more sympathetic to the plight of his fellow man. And yet a linkage exists. If separated by their respective generations and by other, larger oceans of difference, here are two men who nevertheless recognize life as a delicious enterprise needing urgently to be pinned down by the pen.

Joe Gallagher's "message" here—and I suppose all clergymen must have one—may be a little ambiguous. At the center is his church—to which he cleaves in his special way, and with which, on occasion, he differs respectfully. Still he freely and zestfully ventures into that other world beyond holy walls. The overriding point is this: Joe Gallagher is worth following wherever he leads.

Preface

IN JULY, 1862, pursuing one of the century's most famous correspondences, Emily Dickinson declared to her newly chosen poetry mentor: "My Business is Circumference." She was so fascinated by the idea of circumference that there's a book about her entitled *Circumference and Circumstance* (by William R. Sherwood, 1968). The word appears in a number of her poems, where, for example, she speaks of it as "the Bride of Awe," and "the Ultimate of Wheels." She also insisted that "Success in Circuit lies."

In her special use of the word, circumference refers to the farthest reach of knowledge that anyone can gain about reality or any of its parts. Human awareness stands at the center of encircling mysteries. Our human task, especially the poet's, is to push out as far as possible, in all directions, the circumference of comprehension.

As one of her best biographers put it, Dickinson's purpose was "to encompass the truth of life, the whole range of human experience" (Richard B. Sewall). Playing on prepositions, we might say that the poet's task and ours is not merely to understand our circumstances, but to circumstand them; not merely to get a handle on them, but at least a fleeting embrace, if not a bear hug.

Any essayist treating of a host of serious ideas and serious personalities may be said to be engaging, however modestly, in *The Business of Circumference*. By coincidence, the essays chosen for this volume proved agreeable to being catalogued into various groups of circles.

So here is one searcher's report on various charmed circles he has been blessed enough to make the rounds of. The kaleidoscope invented in 1816 by Scottish physicist Sir David Brewster was meant to give the viewer a "beautiful/shape/to see" (*kalos/eidos/skopein*, in Greek words). His toy revealed what you could do with some pieces of glass. As fragmentary as these essays may be, may the truth and beauty and goodness of what preoccupies them provide the curious and receptive reader with some satisfying shapes.

The specific pieces gathered into this volume were written over a span of nearly a quarter of a century (from 1963 to 1987). Most were published in eight journals: nationally, in *The New York Times*, *The National Catholic Reporter*, *America* Magazine, and *The Lincoln Herald*; and in Baltimore's *Evening Sun*, *Sunday Sun*, *Sun*, and *Catholic Review*.

A few of the entries appear here for the first time. Some of the pieces have been slightly edited for their book appearance. The *America* article on Pius XII and the Holocaust has been expanded. Because these articles were published piecemeal over the years, some repetitions are unavoidable in their collective embodiment. A prize awaits the reader who discovers the most instances.

This volume reflects a lifelong fascination with history and with people who are, from one point of view, no longer with us. G. K. Chesterton had a comment worth citing on the kindred matter of tradition: "Tradition means giving votes to the most obscure of all classes, our ancestors. Tradition refuses to submit to the small and arrogant oligarchy of those who merely happen to be walking around." He was making the needed distinction between the dead hand of the living and the living hand of the dead.

May the history-loving reader relish finding herein some occasions for nostalgia, or for comparative remembering of events like the deaths of Pope John XXIII, President Kennedy, and Dr. Martin Luther King, Jr.; or for some instructive recollecting of how current preoccupations were viewed at earlier stages—*e.g.*, the Vietnam War, the post-Vatican II upheavals in U.S. Catholicism, and the abortion controversy.

Historically, this is an apt year for a book of essays. Though ancient authors such as Cicero, Marcus Aurelius, and Plutarch wrote what might now be called essays, it was just four centuries ago (1588) that the beguiling Frenchman Michel de Montaigne first published the full text of his famous musings on subjects such as love, death and friendship. Regarding them as distractions from the death of a close friend, he called them *Essais* and thereby created a modern category of writing.

Not long afterwards, in the England of 1597, Francis Bacon gave the same name for the first time in English to a series of his own observations. Bacon's "essay" and Montaigne's *essai* go back to the French verb *assayer*, which was in turn derived from the Latin verb *exigere*—antique words which carry the notion of "trying" or "weighing."

In an essay a writer wants to weigh a thought, an opinion, an experience, to circumstand some circumstance. So he gives it a try. Often, part of that try is trying to convince the reader that something is worthy of his attention or belief or devotion. That try, that essaying of a literary goal, that assaying of a topic, is usually brief—a relative term, admittedly. Being brief, it typically focuses on a single point or item.

A gathering of essays reaching back over a quarter of a century and remembering back over half a century provides a welcome and unique occasion for saying thanks—to my official teachers of readin', 'ritin' and ratiocinatin': especially the School Sisters of Notre Dame at the elementary level, and my twelve years of seminary teachers, Sulpicians and others (like Fr. Richard Ginder). Later, Elliott Coleman and Michael Lynch were inspiriting teachers in the Creative Writing Seminars at Johns Hopkins University.

Thanks also to Archbishop Francis P. Keough and Lawrence Cardinal Shehan, my publishers and superiors when I wrote for Baltimore's *Catholic Review*; and to Archbishop William Donald Borders in more recent years. And to professional fellow editors who taught me much: Gerry Sherry, Dave McGuire, and Ed Wall at *The Catholic Review*; at *The Evening Sun*, Brad Jacobs and Gwinn Owens. For his delightfully extravagant introduction to this volume I am in even deeper debt to Mr. Jacobs.

As I think of the sacred dead who enriched me in special ways, there comes to memory "a festival of hidden faces": especially my gallant-hearted mother Nellie; my brother Frank—gifted to a dazzle and too soon dead; friends like Sara and Lou Azrael, Cy Brunner, Kathy Cooper, Fr. Jack Hooper, Joe Keeney, Mary Meyer, Millie and Joe Nunes, Victorine Key Robertson, Dr. Buck Schaffer, Belva Thomas, Dr. James Whedbee, Msgr. Tom Whelan and cousin Anne Williams.

As for resident earthlings: thanks for various kinds of kindness to Fr. John Abrahams, Ron Allen, Dr. Gene Barenburg, the Barthelmes (niece Mary Ellen, "Country" and Anne Kelly),

Margaret Beckwith, Sr. Bernarde, Rick Berndt, Dom Bilotto, Mike and Angie Bornemann, Mike and Nancy Brady, the Burdells (my sister Mary Jo, Bill, Pat and Mary), Lenora Burgan, Greg and Pat Bruce, the cousins Carolan, Sr. Catherine, Rich Cassara, Classmates of St. Ann's Class of 1943, St. Charles College Class of 1949, and St. Mary's Seminary Class of 1955, the Wexford Corcorans, the cousins Doyle, Ruth Eger, Msgr. John Tracy Ellis, Sr. Emmanuel, Jackie Evert, Don Farley, Beverly Fine, Fr. Jack Franey, Fr. Ed Frazer, Russ and Julie Forrester, Jack and Nancy Furlong.

Also, the Gallaghers of Philadelphia, Wildwood and Baltimore (especially brother Tommy and nephews Frank, John, Pat and Jim), Pete and Fran Garthe, Ann Gearhart, Bishop Joe Gossman, John and Gerri Gray, David and godchild Susan, Amy Greif, Fr. Ed Griswold, Fr. Jim Gutting, Dennis Hand, Fran Harris, Jim Harrison, Dave and Cindy Henry, the Steve and Sandy Herricks, Sr. Anne Higgins, the Detroit Hoffmans (Guz, Tess, Dorothy, and godchild Jesse), Fr. John Hynes, Josephine and Eric Jacobsen, Sally and Cal Jenkins and family, Fr. Bernie Keigher, the Kelly families, Steve Kepics, Sr. Charlotte Kerr, Jerry and Janet Klarsfeld, Pat Kossmann, Karl Kunz, Jerry and Marlyne Kwasek, the cousins King and Langmead, Mike and Pat Laverriere, Tom and Theresa Lester (and namesake Joe).

In addition, Clinton Macsherry, Laura Malick, Dr. Abdul Malik, Tom and Charlotte Mancine, Stephen Mann, Dr. William Martin, Larry Mayer, Barbra McCune and Ed, cousin Judy McGinn and family, Msgr. Dan McGrath, John McHale, Mary Mehegan, the Mercy Sisters of Villa Maria and Mercy Medical Center (especially Sr. Mary Thomas, Sr. Helen, and the Pastoral Care staff), Annie Meyer, Fr. John Mike, the Mission Helper Sisters, Ernie Moncada, Mary Moore, Fran and Domenica Moroney, the Morris families, Frances and Bill Mueller, and Bishop Frank Murphy.

As well as Bill and Pat Nagle, Fr. Bob Newman, Dr. Catherine Neill, Dr. Riva Novey, Dr. Tom Oglesby, Rick Paolini, Earl Parrott, Fr. Paul Philibert and Bea, Denny Pinkerton, cousin Marita Podder and family, Roxie Powell, Carrie and John Ramsay, Jim Redding, Ike Rehert, Dr. Bill Richards, Dr. Bill Rinn, Bob Rivenbark, Drs. Frank and Mark Roberts, Henry Romoser, the Rosiers (especially Charlotte and Walter, Ellen and Ron),

Fr. Charlie Saglio, Ruth Schaffer, Diane Scharper, Forrest Schoenbachler, Teri and Devon, Fr. Mike Schmied, Kate Serio, Dr. William Sharpe, Fr. Rusty Shaughnessy, Chris Smith and family, Sue Sommers and Jim, Regina Soria, Eleanor and Bob Sprankle, John and Roberta Standafer, Fr. Tom Sullivan, Dr. Nelson Sun, Mil and Bicki Thompson, Rick and Marian Vessels, Steve Vicchio, Joe Walker, Fr. Gene Walsh, Ned and Pat Ward, Eunie Williams, Jim and Pat and Jeannie Winders, John Woods, Dr. Hiltgunt Zassenhaus, Steve Zinicola and all the unnamed others—benign and cheering—who, when occasion permitted, became associate members of the magic circle of friends and friendly folk.

Contents

Part Two: Around the World

Part Three: Literary Circles

Part Four: Religious Circles

Part Five: Church Circles

Part Six: A Round of Timely Topics

Part Seven: Private Circles

THE BUSINESS OF CIRCUMFERENCE
A Kaleidoscope

Part One

The Year Round

1. Happy New Year, So to Speak; and Why Today Isn't Thirteen Days Ago

The Baltimore Sun: December 31, 1987

TODAY begins a new year, and if you "shouted" your "Happy New Year" last night you were acting quite historically. For our word "calendar" comes from the Latin word "to shout," and recalls the ancient Roman days when a religious public official—time is sacred!—raised his voice to proclaim that a new moon and therefore a new month (moonth) had begun. One of these shouted month-starting days (called "calends") was also a year starter.

But it would be wildly unhistorical to think that January 1 has any rock-hewn claim to being New Year's Day. For in any given year the most popular and influential work of fiction is the calendar we now use. After all, today inaugurates a new year A.D. Since A.D. stands for *anno Domini* in Latin, or "in the year of the Lord" in English, one might sensibly wonder why Christmas isn't New Year's Day.

In point of fact, our Anglo-Saxon ancestors did start their year on December 25 up until around A.D. 1220. (That December date approximated the winter solstice—another kind of beginning.) Then they adopted the practise of starting it on March 25—nine pregnant months before Christmas. The March date celebrated the springtide conception of Christ, i.e., his incarnation or enfleshment. Because that epochal event occurred when the angel Gabriel announced God's plan to Mary of Nazareth, March 25 is also called Annunciation Day and Lady Day.

That means that the Englishmen who "founded" Maryland on March 25, 1634 thought they were doing so on New Year's Day. If they had dallied until 1753, they wouldn't have thought so. In 1752 Parliament decided to fall in step with other European countries and make January 1 New Year's Day. That was the same day on which—probably for practical reasons, since new consuls were installed on that day—the ancient Romans had decided to celebrate New Year after they moved it from March 1. In the Roman climate, Mother Nature was, by the start of March, showing springtide signs of a new year after the dead of winter. When some Christian localities later started their new years on Easter, they were making the same poetic statement on the spiritual level.

March 1's stint as New Year's Day explains two curious things: why leap years add a day to February (that would once have been the year's final month); and why September, October, November, and December take their names from the Latin words for seventh, eighth, ninth and tenth, whereas they are now months number nine, ten, eleven, and twelve.

But why is this 1988? Ancient peoples had various ways of dating their years, e.g., from the founding of the city of Rome (753 B.C.) or the start of the Olympic Games (776 B.C.) Even today the Jewish calendar dates itself from the year of creation (3761 B.C., according to Biblical reckoning), and the Muslim calendar from the year of Mohammed's historic flight (Hegira) from Mecca (A.D. 622).

A Roman monk named Dionysius Exiguus ("Denny the Tiny") gets the credit for the idea of using Christ's age as a way of numbering the years. He worked out that notion around what we now call A.D. 525. But scholars figure that his figuring was a bit off, and that Jesus was probably born in the final years of B.C. (Before Christ) or B.C.E. (Before the Common Era, as some non-Christian countries prefer to abbreviate that era.) Curious, how A.D. abbreviates two Latin words, while B.C. abbreviates two English ones.

Such head-spinning confusion! But most of this calendrical complication flows from these few natural facts: we reckon time by three spins: the earth around itself (days), the moon around the earth (month), and the earth around the sun (year). But, alas! these spins don't neatly coincide. The moon doesn't complete its circle or phases around the earth in an exact number of days, nor does the earth its circle around the sun. Other unneatnesses: months have a varying number of days, and the year doesn't have an even number of weeks.

In 46 B.C. Julius Caesar, by decreeing the sun-based Julian calendar, tried to improve the very messy moon-based Roman calendar with Egyptian ideas. (Dating tips from Cleopatra?) That year of 46 B.C. was extended an extra ninety days and became known as "the year of confusion." For the next forty-eight years the new rules were misinterpreted and the calendar stayed mixed up until into the A.D.s, though no one yet knew that the A.D.s had arrived. Incidentally, the Romans had a superstitious fear of even numbers. They didn't fuss too much about a February with an even number of days since that dreary month was already dedicated to the infernal gods.

A key problem remained. Caesar's new rule about an extra day every four years (leap year) still made the average calendar year eleven minutes and fourteen seconds too long. Over the centuries the calendar year kept getting farther and farther behind the natural year.

By 1582 spring was arriving on March 11. Pope Gregory XIII decreed that ten days be dropped that year, so October 4 was followed immediately by October 15. Catholic countries went along with the Gregorian reform sooner than England did. That's why Shakespeare and Cervantes died on the same historic day but on diverse calendar days.

When England and its colonies went Gregorian in 1752, their calendar was eleven days behind nature. So at age twenty-one George Washington, who thought he was born on February 11, became born on February 22 (New Style). And since the year now began on January 1 instead of March 25, he found himself born in 1732 instead of 1731! Prior to 1753, an English baby could be born in April and die in February "of the same year," as a burial stone in Salisbury Cathedral chronicles one sadly brief life. Some folks in 1752 England who believed one's date of death was fixed and fated felt short-changed by the dropping of eleven days. They took to rioting.

When atheist Lenin adopted the papal calendar, Russia was thirteen days behind. That's why the October 25 Revolution is now celebrated on November 7. There's a place in the Carolinas which still refuses to celebrate New Year's until mid-January.

But if Pope Gregory's reform merely dropped ten days, the calendar would still get about three days behind every four centuries. What's an easy way to ditch those three days? Just don't have a leap year in a centennial year unless it is evenly divisible by 400. Thus, A.D. 2000 will leap, but 1900, 1800 and 1700 didn't—although, being evenly divisible by four, they should have. Nobel Poet George Seferis was born on February 29, 1900. When his native Turkey and ancestral Greece later adopted the Gregorian calendar, his birth date was very prosaically annihilated.

There's one part of the Gregorian reform we haven't yet used. Even with the dropping of three leap years every four hundred years, the calendar will still get one day behind every 3,323 years. Gregory's farsighted solution? Even if a year is evenly divisible by 4 and 400 (like A.D. 4000), it still won't be counted a leap year if it is evenly divisible by 4,000. That rule will pretty much take care of that pesky one-day lag you get every thirty-three centuries or so.

Paradoxically, another lag probably explains the "leap" of a leap year. In a non-leap year, a given calendar date comes one weekday later than it did the previous year. Thus if your birthday came on Sunday last year, it would normally fall on Monday this year. But thanks to the insertion of an extra day at the end of February, from March 1 onward in a leap year a given date comes two weekdays later than it did the previous year— that is, it "leaps" over the next, expected weekday and falls on the following one. But a leap year could just as sensibly be called a lag year.

These may be weighty thoughts for New Year's Day. But for Auld Lang Syne's sake, we should lift a cup each year to all those ghosts of New Years past that came on other days in other years. For we are the children of our past, a past as colorful and precious and messy as human nature itself and as all the patchwork ways we've tried to measure our breathless hegiras through the dizzying spirals of time. For what is life, asks Dante, but a race to death? And races have to be clocked.

2. The Correlation of Elizabeth Ann Seton (Feast: January 4)

The Baltimore Sun: September 17, 1975

RECENTLY I heard a youngster refer to the "correlation" of Mother Seton, who was canonized three days ago. No doubt about it: canonization, the addition of someone's name to the fixed list (canon or measuring rod) of official Christian saints, wasn't a household word for him.

As for saint, that is a household word of sorts among Americans of all religious faiths and of none at all. After all, Saint Nick, Santa Claus, St. Valentine, and St. Patrick are well-known members of the calendar. San Francisco, San Diego, and St. Louis are well-known places. Dog lovers know their St. Bernards. Doctors deal with St. Vitus's dance. Actors perform G. B. Shaw's *Saint Joan*. Musicians play Camille Saint-Saens. And fans of *The Little Prince* are grateful to Saint-Exupéry.

But saints as people, saints in the traditional sense — aren't they largely out of date in the last third of the twentieth century?

Even among Roman Catholics, who were once preeminent for naming their children, their churches, their cities, their statues, and their holidays after some saint or other, devotion to the saints has been on the decline since the Second Vatican Council. And in this age of personality development, it is hardly reassuring to recall the definition of a martyr as someone who lives with a saint.

So, are saints out of date? Different people will naturally have different answers to that question.

My response would pivot on the meaning of the word saint. For instance, even by strict Roman Catholic reckoning, Mother

Seton is not the first U.S. saint. She is, rather, the first native-born citizen of the United States to have her "holiness" recognized officially by the Church.

Translated into the Christian vision of life, this recognition affirms that at the time of her death, this brave wife, widow, and mother was extraordinarily "in love" with God and His creatures, and that she has had that love fulfilled by the secure and deathless possession of God's own Self. That means she is a truly happy human being and that she will stay that way.

The annual feast of All Saints on November 1 is the Church's official recognition that there are plenty of unrecognized saints. There have always been quiet heroes of courage and generosity and self-giving of whom the official Church has known little or nothing, much less the organs of worldly power and publicity. Gerard Manley Hopkins wrote: ". . . good grows wild, and wide,/Has shades, is nowhere none"—and he might have been writing about sanctity, both inside of Christianity and outside of it.

Last year an article appeared in a new journal, *Synthesis*, which bore the fetching title, "The Repression of the Sublime." In it the author recalled Sigmund Freud's thoughts concerning the unconscious repression of sexual and aggressive energies. The author then proceeded to argue that the fear of hardship or of being thought "different" causes many of us to repress another deep and fundamental "instinct": the call to truly generous and dedicated behavior.

He noted that this call to the sublime often grows strongest after a person has fully indulged himself in all other available pleasures and learned that the heart's hunger for fulfillment goes above and beyond whatever a human being can grab for himself. Then may come an intoxicating whiff of the joy experienced by those who let themselves be taken over by something (Someone?) larger than their self-seeking and self-centered selves.

By coincidence I was also reading at this time a biography of the poet John Keats, a man who knew how to be generous. He believed ardently in the poet's need for a "negative capability"—the power to negate his own noisy, pushy ego and to allow realities outside of that ego to enrich his awareness with the gift of themselves. The two themes meshed remarkably well.

The words in the *Synthesis* article about disillusionment as the preface to a breakthrough of the sublime recalled for me Walter Pater's literary axiom: the way to perfection is through a series of disgusts. The great Augustine of Hippo and, to a lesser extent, the universally beloved Francis of Assisi could attest to the rightness of that axiom in the moral area.

Other saints, like Mother Seton, seem to gravitate from birth toward goodness and graciousness. Persons of this type (and I've met quite a few in my own life, usually where not many people were looking) strike me as "moral miracles."

They support the argument that genuine goodness of spirit is something that a person receives as a gift. Disdainful self-righteousness therefore is out of place in the "righteous." The fact that the word "saint" is a passive past participle is another supportive fact. A saint is one who has been *made* holy.

This means, at the practical level, that genuine sanctity will draw people closer together by muting their competing, divisive egos. On that basis alone, sainthood would come well recommended in this, the fourth decade of the atomic age.

The poet Philip Larkin wrote that ". . . someone will forever be surprising/A hunger in himself to be more serious." Persons in that mood take heart from other human beings who have answered the call to the sublime and done something beautiful and beautifully for God and man—to paraphrase the title of Malcolm Muggeridge's book on Mother Teresa of Calcutta.

If canonization leads hard-pressed and discouraged human beings to focus closer attention on as appealing and as successful a human being as Mother Seton, then I think sainthood will always be in style, no matter what the style of its expression; and my young friend's interest in her "correlation" will be fully justified and surprisingly apt.

3. John Neumann: The First U.S. Male Saint (Feast: January 5)

The Baltimore Evening Sun: July 27, 1976

THE United States will soon have its first male canonized saint in the person of John Nepomucene Neumann (1811–1860), the fourth bishop of Philadelphia.

Born in what is now Czechoslovakia, near the West German and Austrian borders, this son of a Bavarian stocking weaver read stories in his early twenties about German immigrants to the United States who acutely lacked spiritual leaders. Inspired by the ideal of St. Paul as a missionary, he resolved to devote his life to being a priest in America. He began adding English to the German, Czech, French, Spanish, Italian, Greek, and Latin he already knew.

With his seminary studies finished, but still unordained, he arrived in New York in May, 1836—friendless, with only a dollar in his pocket. The bishop of New York ordained him the following month and sent him to the Buffalo area for four years of exhausting work.

While recovering from a physical collapse in September, 1840, Neumann sent a letter to Baltimore, where the superior of the Redemptorist order was then residing. Expressing his need for the support of a religious community, he was accepted and sent to a Redemptorist house in Pittsburgh, where he became the first novice of that order in America.

The Redemptorists had been founded in 1732 by the Italian St. Alphonsus Liguori. As members of the Congregation of the Most Holy Redeemer (C.SS.R. in the Latin initials), they had arrived in the United States in 1832 and were busy with missionary work, especially among German immigrants.

In 1840 the Baltimore parish then known as St. John's, at Park and Saratoga, was put under the care of the Redemptorists. To this parish Neumann was sent in May, 1841, to continue his novitiate. In the ensuing months, St. John's was torn down and replaced by the present St. Alphonsus, the first major Gothic Revival Church in Baltimore and the first important commission for its architect, Robert Cary Long, Jr.

In the interim, Neumann and his confreres lived at another Baltimore parish lately confided to them, St. James on Aisquith Street. There, on January 16, 1842, Neumann became the first Redemptorist to take his vows in America. He stayed on at St. James until he was sent back to Pittsburgh as a pastor (1844–47). Here his health failed again, and he was ordered back to St. Alphonsus, only to learn that he had been appointed superior of all the American Redemptorists, then numbering about forty.

During his two years as superior (1847–49), his headquarters were in Baltimore. Here, in 1848, he became a U.S. citizen. He persuaded the School Sisters of Notre Dame to establish their motherhouse in Baltimore, near St. James; and he saved the Oblates of Divine Providence, a Baltimore-founded sisterhood of Negro nuns, from disbanding.

Replaced as superior, he continued as pastor of St. Alphonsus until 1852. Meantime, the new archbishop of Baltimore, Francis Patrick Kenrick, had chosen Neumann as his spiritual adviser and would walk from the Basilica rectory to St. Alphonsus to make his confession. One day, while Neumann was absent from his rectory, the archbishop left a ring and a pectoral cross on the Redemptorist's desk—Kenrick's way of telling the stunned Neumann that he had been appointed by Pope Pius IX to be bishop of Philadelphia, one of the largest dioceses in America.

Later that month, on March 28, 1852 (his forty-first birthday), Neumann was consecrated a bishop at St. Alphonsus. A few days later, he was off to Philadelphia for eight laborious years before his sudden death on one of the snowy streets of that city. During those years, he maintained his contact with Baltimore, attending important church councils there and laying the cornerstone of another Redemptorist church, St. Michael's on Wolfe Street, in 1857.

Neumann was declared venerable in 1896 and beatified on October 13, 1963, during the Second Vatican Council. He was canonized on June 19, 1977. Like Mother Cabrini (another naturalized immigrant) and Mother Seton (a native American), whose ranks he has now joined as American canonized saints, he had a vigorous personality well worth special scrutiny. His January 5 feast day occurs on the anniversary of his death in 1860.

4. Should Auld Aquinas Be Forgot? (Feast: January 28)

The Baltimore Evening Sun: March 7, 1974

SEVEN centuries ago today, on his way to the Fourteenth Ecumenical Council, Thomas Aquinas died. The Dominican friar was about fifty years old and belonged to the Italy that produced Francis of Assisi and Dante. He was about two when Francis died; Dante was nine when Aquinas died.

Aquinas has the habit of dying in various fashions. Within a decade of his physical death, some of his teachings were condemned by one bishop of Paris and two archbishops of Canterbury. Within Catholicism, his writings have undergone several periods of decline and revival. Martin Luther regarded him as "the greatest chatterbox" among the scholastic theologians and had doubts about his salvation.

As the Twenty-first Ecumenical Council was ending nine years ago, the official and almost monopolistic sway of Thomism in Catholic teaching appeared once again to be in decline. He is mentioned only twice in the body of the council's 103,000 words of decrees, declarations, and constitutions. (Two councils earlier, at post-Reformation Trent, his works kept the Bible company on the altar.)

A humorist suggested that the bishops should have filed out at the end singing, "Should Auld Aquinas Be Forgot?"

Meantime, Aquinas still enjoys the rare distinction of being one of the authors in the Great Books Program; indeed, he is one of only four world authors who are represented by more than one volume in that series. Two volumes were needed to present the bulk of his masterwork, the *Summa Theologica* or

Theological Summary. The opus is sometimes called *Summa Theologiae*.

Still incomplete at his death, the *Summa* was Aquinas's attempt to provide young students with an orderly and simplified handbook of Catholic theology. He saw it as a kind of "milk for babies"—though one commentator noted that the milk is still in the cow and you have to work for it.

Reflecting his neat, patient, subtle, and richly furnished mind, the *Summa* is composed of three major parts, which are broken down into 38 treatises, which are subdivided into 611 key questions, which are further developed by some 3,000 articles. In the course of this work, he calmly and succinctly presents about 10,000 objections to the viewpoints he himself espouses.

Though he insisted that in strictly philosophical matters the argument from authority is the weakest of all, he respected the wisdom of tradition in matters of faith. So it isn't surprising to find him quoting in the *Summa* from nineteen church councils, forty-one popes, fifty-two "ancient" fathers of the church, and forty-six philosophers and poets. He is said to have known the Bible by heart; one edition of his works takes eighty small-print columns to list the Bible texts he cites. In another edition, his total writings require 10,000 columns of print.

It is the quality of such quantity that counts, of course. Harvard's Crane Brinton finds Thomism "a marvelously balanced system, holding the middle way in all the great problems of philosophy . . . with the ease of supreme skill." Of another of Aquinas's *Summas* (the *Contra Gentiles*) agnostic Bertrand Russell wrote: "Even if every one of his doctrines were mistaken [it] would remain an imposing intellectual edifice." Of this same work, the fashionable Herman Hesse wrote in poetry: "Whenever we entered the temple of Aquinas . . . A new world greeted us, sweet, mature . . . There all seemed lucid, Nature charged with Mind . . ."

As with other eminent medieval thinkers (including the masterful Jewish scholar, Moses Maimonides), Aquinas set himself the task of harmonizing the conclusions of "pure reason" with the claims of Biblical faith. In his respect for the dignity of the intellect and for the sense data that feed it, Aquinas found an ally in the then recently rediscovered works of the pagan Aristotle. This openness to all other thinkers, this trust in reason and this fondness for the physical universe shocked many of his contemporaries. And not only them.

Yet his "worldliness" was theologically grounded. As a believer, he held that God is good, His creation is good and noteworthy, the human intellect is respectable, as is every man who tries to say what he honestly sees. Hence, Aquinas felt there must be room for everything, things must somehow fit together.

The tensions between Creator and creature, grace and nature, faith and reason, flesh and spirit, time and eternity, providence and free will must not be viewed, he held, as irreconcilable. Consistently, Aquinas regarded philosophy—the search for wisdom—not as an ego trip permitting one man to show how wrong everybody else is, but as a family effort of the human race. It was an effort requiring attentiveness, good will, and humility.

These qualities he admirably embodied. Though repeatedly accused of exaggerating the power of reason, he knew that "all the effort of the human mind has not succeeded in exhausting the essence of a single fly." Never unaware of the mystery of existence, he had a mystical experience at the end of his life that made him view all his vast and laborious writings as "a heap of straw."

Though less than most men, perhaps, Aquinas was a man of his time and shared some of its limitations. His admirers have at times harmed him by blindly idolizing him and violating his own spirit of openness. And no thirteenth century intellectual synthesis can be literally transported, body and bones, to the twentieth century.

As one, however, who believes that auld Aquinas should not be forgot, I plan to remain inspired by how he searched for wisdom. With G. K. Chesterton, I hope to stay inspired by his "broad and virile appetite for the very vastness and variety of the universe."

5. A Pilgrimage to the Land of Lincoln

The Baltimore Evening Sun: February 15, 1982

I F, IN the world beyond, you get to meet anyone of your choice, Abraham Lincoln will be among my top choices. (I would have said "Abe," but Stephen Oates's 1977 biography insists that Lincoln disliked that abbreviation.) In the meantime, I had visited the site forty miles south of Louisville where he had been born, on the very same day as Charles Darwin. I had visited the scenes of his assassination and death in Washington, and his stately memorial there. But making my pilgrimage to his home and grave in Springfield was a dream deferred—until last summer, when I was teaching 170 miles from the Illinois capital.

As president-elect, Lincoln left Springfield for the last time on the day before his fifty-second birthday. I arrived the week after my fifty-second birthday. The little railroad depot from which he departed still stands. Outside, a sign bears his celebrated farewell remarks: ". . . Here I have passed from a young to an old man." I smiled a coeval smile.

Springfield is now a city of 100,000. As a state legislator, Lincoln led the move to change the capital from Vandalia to the more centrally located Springfield. Even so, Springfield was one hundred times smaller than it now is when Lincoln, newly admitted to the bar and carrying seven dollars in his pocket, arrived to settle there on April 15, 1837. He was twenty-eight. Twenty-eight years later, to the day, he died in the nation's capital, 800 miles due east.

While a resident of Springfield, Lincoln:
— met and married Mary Todd, a fellow Kentuckian living with her married sister. Lincoln joked that God spelled His name with one "d" but the Todds required two . . .

- begot his four sons and buried one, the three-year-old Eddie . . .
- bought and enlarged the only home he ever owned . . .
- began his law practice and served as a partner in three firms, all within a block of the Capitol . . .
- finished his final term as a state assemblyman in the then-new Capitol (1840–41) . . .
- was elected to a single term in the House of Representatives (1847–49) . . .
- was nominated to the U.S. Senate and gave his famous "House divided against itself" speech in the state Capitol. He lost . . .
- was nominated for the presidency and elected, in 1860 . . .
- was laid in state at the Capitol and buried in the public Oak Ridge Cemetery.

Today Lincoln's two-story wooden house is a national historic site in the heart of downtown. He bought it in 1844 for $1,500 from the Episcopal minister who had officiated at his marriage two years earlier. Though most of the major furniture was sold to the president of the Great Western Railroad and destroyed in the Chicago Fire of 1871, the house is furnished as Lincoln would have known it. To discourage souvenir hunters, the guards will not identify original items in the house.

On the parlor wall hangs the front page of Frank Leslie's *Illustrated Newspaper* for March 9, 1861. It shows the parlor as the departing Lincolns left it, and carries a story about the rumor of a Baltimore plot to kill Lincoln, and Mr. Pinkerton's protective insistence that the entrained president-elect be spirited in disguise through Baltimore ahead of schedule.

The Lincoln family church (the First Presbyterian) is two blocks away. Though Lincoln himself never joined the church and was not a frequent church-goer, the family did rent a pew, which is still draped and set aside. A nearby plaque that lists former pastors reveals that from 1857 to 1864 the Lincolns' hometown pastor was named John Brown.

Another four blocks west stands the Old State Capitol. It is now a museum, restored and furnished as Lincoln would have remembered it—down to ashes under the stoves and mid-nineteenth century newspapers strewn on the desks of the legislators. In the summer, the Capitol houses one of the few copies of the Gettysburg Address in Lincoln's own spidery handwriting. Also nightly during the summer, a historical light and sound show is presented outside the building, which is credibly described as a perfect example of Greek Revival architecture.

Elsewhere throughout this clean and inviting city, I found links with the Great Emancipator, including his final law office across from the Old Capitol, and a large statue of the departing Lincoln in front of the impressive new Capitol, which was opened in 1889.

An easy mile or two north of these two proximate Capitols lies Oak Ridge Cemetery. In its center rises a 117-foot monument in which Lincoln was placed six years after his death. In 1876 thieves tried to steal the body by way of demanding a ransom of $200,000. Earlier his remains had reposed in two temporary vaults.

Today you enter the tomb at ground level, underneath the commanding obelisk. Until 1930 you could climb to the top of the obelisk, but now the entrance is sealed with a stone from Rome's Servian Wall (578 B.C.). Just before his death, Lincoln received this stone from the people of Rome, who compared him to their ancient liberator king, Servius Tullius—who was also assassinated.

The ground level corridors that lead to the rear crypt are adorned with small statues of Lincoln and bronze copies of his most famous speeches. In the semicircular crypt itself, an elegant marble stone bearing Lincoln's name and dates marks the site of his underground burial vault. Over a window behind the stone are inscribed the words: "Now He Belongs To The Ages."

Behind the marble are flags from states in which Lincoln and his ancestors lived. By coincidence the Virginia flag is nearest the head of the marble, and I saw with a jolt that the state motto on the flag was nearly touching the sarcophagus. It is *Sic Semper Tyrannis* ("Thus Always to Tyrants")—the words shouted by the assassin Booth and possibly the last words heard by Lincoln.

Behind you as you gaze at the sarcophagus are the crypts of his wife and the three sons who died before they were twenty. Two of these predeceased their father, and three their mother. The first-born son, Robert Todd, lived to be eighty-two, served as U.S. secretary of war and minister to Great Britain, and lies buried with his childless only son in Arlington National Cemetery.

Just twenty miles northwest of the cemetery, I found the reconstructed village of New Salem, where Lincoln lived for six decisive years before settling in Springfield. Never housing more than twenty-five families, New Salem died out shortly after Lincoln left, but was restored in 1906, thanks largely to William Randolph Hearst.

The only original structure there is the barrel-maker's shop where Lincoln read late by the fire of wood shavings. To this village Lincoln came as a flatboatman, and there he worked as a store clerk, store co-owner, postmaster, and deputy surveyor. From there he went off as a company captain in the brief Black Hawk War. One of his fellow soldiers urged him to study law and later became his first partner in Springfield.

In the meantime, as Paul Horgan details in his captivating *Citizen of New Salem*, Lincoln had been twice elected to the Illinois legislature. In his first newspaper campaign notice, the twenty-three-year-old candidate wrote: "I have no other ambition so great as that of being truly esteemed by my fellow men, by rendering myself worthy of their esteem." He lost that time.

While at New Salem, I saw a spirited and moving outdoor drama under the stars, *Your Obedient Servant, Abraham Lincoln*. A corps of young actors tell Lincoln's story with gusto and sensitivity. On alternate summer nights, another presentation is given, *Abraham Lincoln Walks at Midnight*. This play focuses on three Illinois poets who felt the force of the Lincoln legend: Vachel Lindsay, Carl Sandburg, and Edgar Lee Masters.

If you take Illinois highway 97 from Springfield to New Salem, you can stop at a roadside cemetery called Farmers' Point and visit the grave of Mentor Graham, Lincoln's influential teacher at New Salem. Graham, who lived until 1886, said that out of his four to six thousand students, Lincoln was "the most studious, diligent, and straightforward young man in the pursuit of knowledge and literature." Graham died and was originally buried in South Dakota, but a teachers' association arranged to have him reburied here in 1933 next to his wife.

Another New Salemite was Ann Rutledge, Lincoln's legendary sweetheart who died at nineteen. Her grave is in Petersburg, two miles from New Salem, but I wasn't aware of that fact during my visit.

When it was time for me to catch my bus for the return trip through Peoria to Davenport, I returned my hotel key to the desk clerk. I had been required to make a five dollar deposit, and now she repaid me with a Lincoln bill. As I looked at that strong, compassionate, and melancholy face, I found the bill emblematic of my visit. Lincoln had indeed been given to me— though in a way that money could never measure.

6. The Sons of Father Abraham

The Baltimore Evening Sun: February 11, 1983

I F YOU stand behind the Lincoln Memorial in Washington, gaze across the Potomac and look just to the right of the main entrance to Arlington National Cemetery, you may see a small cluster of trees shading a pink granite sarcophagus. That's where Robert Todd Lincoln is buried. He was the eldest son of Abraham Lincoln, the last of his four children to die, and the only one to beget children.

Robert's only son was Abraham Lincoln II. He died in London at the age of sixteen, and with his death in 1890, the future of the Lincoln name expired. Since 1930 he too has been buried on that knoll, though namelessly.

All four children of Mary and Abraham Lincoln were born in Springfield, Illinois between 1843 and 1853. As with Mahatma Gandhi, all four were sons. Robert Todd was named after Mary Lincoln's father. Eddie was named after Edward Baker, a political friend of Abraham. Willie Wallace was named after the family physician. Thomas was named after Lincoln's father; but Abraham thought he looked like a tadpole at birth, so he became Tad.

The second son, Eddie, died in the Lincoln home when he was three—possibly from diphtheria. The third son, Willie, died in the White House when he was eleven. The cause was something like malaria or typhoid. The fourth son, Tad, was sick at the same time, and not expected to recover.

This Tad seems to have had the largest share of his father's disposition. At the end of the Civil War, Iowa's Senator Harlan stood by Lincoln's side and addressed a crowd outside the White House. "What shall we do with the rebels?" he asked.

Answering his own question he shouted, "Hang them!" "No," protested eleven-year-old Tad, "hang *on* to them." A pat on the head from his father. Tad's brother Robert later married Harlan's daughter.

Later that week, Tad was at Washington's National Theater watching a magic lantern show when word came that his father had been shot. When the Lincolns left the White House, Tad and his mother lived for several years at numerous addresses in Chicago. They returned to Chicago after a thirty-month stay in Europe. Two months later, the eighteen-year-old Tad died of pleurisy.

Robert's life was marked by a number of curious coincidences. He once suffered a mishap as he was boarding a train and might have been killed. A fellow passenger yanked him from danger. It was Edwin Booth, the brother of John Wilkes. Over his mother's protest, Robert joined the Union Army and served as a captain on Grant's staff. As Lee surrendered at Appomattox Court House, the president's son stood by on the porch.

Arriving at the White House on Good Friday, 1865, the young captain pleaded fatigue when his parents invited him to join them that night at Ford's Theatre. Robert sat chatting with his father's secretary, John Hay, when Booth aimed his small derringer over the empty chair behind the president. That empty chair haunted Robert, who wondered what difference it might have made if he had been sitting in it that fateful night.

He was with his father, though, when he died the next morning in the Petersen boarding house across from Ford's. In 1881, he saw President Garfield shot in Washington's railway station, and was on hand when President McKinley was shot in Buffalo in 1901.

After leaving the White House, Robert had gone to Chicago with his mother and brother. There he was soon admitted into the Illinois bar and became a partner in a newly formed law firm.

President Garfield named him secretary of war. Later, President Harrison appointed him minister to Britain. There he dined with Queen Victoria in Windsor Castle. She found him "very pleasant and sensible." He was invited to be a pallbearer at Tennyson's funeral, but couldn't make it.

Off and on for forty years, Robert was mentioned as a possible presidential candidate, but he was never interested in that "gilded prison" of a White House. In 1897, however, he did become president of the Pullman Company. By 1912, this son of a man born in a log cabin was a millionaire and moved to 3014 N Street in Georgetown. He had a summer home in Manchester, Vermont, and there he died on July 26, 1926, in his eighty-third year.

7. A Namesake Grandson Gets His Own Lincoln Memorial

The Baltimore Evening Sun: March 5, 1984

ON THIS day in 1890 a charming, bright, and handsome boy of sixteen died in his father's home in London. His father was Robert Todd Lincoln, the sole surviving son of the Civil War president. The previous year President Benjamin Harrison had named Robert U.S. minister to Britain.

With him to England went his only son, who bore the arresting name of Abraham Lincoln II. Actually, he was the third such Lincoln, if you count the president's grandfather as the first—the man who was killed by Indians in the sight of the president's father Tom.

Within his family, where he had an older sister Mary (1869–1938) and a younger sister Jessie (1875–1948), Abraham Lincoln II was known as "Jack." He wanted to enter Harvard as his father had done, so he went as a tourist to France to begin learning French.

Toward the end of 1889 he developed a carbuncle under his arm. An operation was performed, but blood poisoning set in. As his condition worsened, his father hastened to France and took the boy back home to London. There he died nearly a century ago. Since he was the president's only grandson, the future of the Lincoln named died with him.

Later that year, Robert sailed for the United States with the body of his son. He traveled to his own native Springfield, Illinois, and there, in Oak Ridge Cemetery on November 8, he buried his only son in the monument that already held the remains of his father, his mother, and his three younger brothers: Eddie, Willie, and Tad, who had died at ages three, eleven, and eighteen, respectively.

For nearly forty years, Abraham Lincoln II rested near his illustrious grandfather. Then in 1930 he was disinterred and reburied on May 27 at the site of his own father's grave in Arlington National Cemetery. There is a mystery here. Robert Lincoln had intended to be buried with his six family members in Springfield. But after he died on July 26, 1926, at his vacation home in Vermont, his wife had him buried in a nearby vault. She then obtained a site in Arlington and had him buried there in 1928. Two years later, she had their son buried next to him. Another seven years later, she was herself buried there.

Prior to her death, Mrs. Lincoln arranged for a large, rosy granite sarcophagus to be placed on the shady plateau that now contains the three bodies.

In January of 1983, while preparing a Lincoln's Day article on the four Lincoln sons for *The Baltimore Evening Sun*, I paid my first visit to this sarcophagus. On one side were the name and dates of Robert Todd Lincoln: 1843–1926; on the other, of "Wife" Mary Harlan Lincoln: 1846–1937. But I was perplexed to find no mention of their son. The cemetery historian, Ben Davis, was also puzzled by this glaring omission. Within view, just across the Potomac, Abraham Lincoln's name was splendidly enshrined in the Lincoln Memorial. Over here, his namesake lay in a nameless grave. (On my second visit I found, beneath dirt and grass, a small marble stone marked "A.L.II"—but these few square inches weren't much of a memorial.)

I wrote to Maryland Senator Paul S. Sarbanes about this unworthy anonymity. His office contacted the Department of the Army, which on May 12 sent this explanation: "At that time inscriptions for minor children were not allowed under Army regulations . . . something which would be permissible today." Moreover, "Lincoln survivors could be privately sought out and prevailed upon to alter the present monument situation."

My next problem was to find a Lincoln survivor. A 1976 clipping in the *Sunpapers* files told of a divorce granted to Robert Todd Lincoln Beckwith, the great-grandson of the president.

The article mentioned his Washington lawyer, Elizabeth Young. Sure enough, there was such a name in the D.C. phone book. She told me that she had been associated with legal affairs of the Lincoln family since 1935, and that Beckwith, the son of Abraham Lincoln II's sister Jessie, was the sole family survivor.

Beckwith's only sibling Mary had died childless on July 10, 1975. His only cousin Lincoln Isham, the son of Jessie's sister Mary, had died childless on September 1, 1971. Thus Beckwith is the last of the president's three great-grandchildren. Born on July 19, 1904, Beckwith has been thrice married but has no children. Young agreed to inform her ailing client of the possibilities regarding his uncle's grave.

In early September, Beckwith wrote to his lawyer: "I think it a crying shame that this matter has not been brought to my notice long ago . . . Of course the answer is yes. By all means put the name and dates on the sarcophagus."

A few more hurdles remained. I delivered word of Beckwith's reply to an Army official in Alexandria, Virginia. But the Army still required an affidavit that Beckwith was indeed a Lincoln descendant and that the request was truly his. Lawyer Young was able to see to this. Meantime I tracked down a stonecutter, Scotty Kinnaird, from Thurmont, Maryland, who had been recommended to me. We arranged to meet at the sarcophagus on the twentieth anniversary of the death of President Kennedy, who is buried nearby. Then Kinnaird and his son had to make a design and have it approved by the Army. This authorization was finally signed on December 29, 1983.

Since the stonecutting had to be done on site, the carvers had to wait for promising weather. Because of his Parkinson's disease, Beckwith would not be able to attend, but his present wife, Margaret, wished to do so in his name, and her schedule had to be accommodated. Finally, after one postponement, the date of February 9 was chosen, largely because of the proximity of President Lincoln's 175th birthday.

At 9 A.M. on that chilly winter morning, Scotty Kinnaird began attaching a rubber-base stencil to the blank, river-facing side of the sarcophagus. Then his son John donned his protective goggle-suit and started sandblasting through the openings in the stencil. By noon of what turned out to be the day of

Soviet Premier Andropov's death, these simple words rescued a winsome boy from a nameless grave: Their Son/Abraham Lincoln II/1873–1890.

The project had taken nearly a year. But now, on each side of the Memorial Bridge that spans the Potomac, each of two Abraham Lincolns had been given a memorial. In the words of one of them, spoken at another cemetery, all those connected with the project felt it was "altogether fitting and proper that we should do this"—to see that President Lincoln's only grandson and namesake should at long last have an explicit and plainly visible inscription of his own.

Postscript

The Baltimore Evening Sun: April 24, 1984

I mentioned that it is a mystery why Robert Todd Lincoln was not buried with his parents, brothers, and son in Springfield, Illinois. I have in the meantime been contacted by Mr. Irving Babb of Milwaukee, Wisconsin. His father was a boyhood chum of Abraham II, and later the president of the Allis Chalmers Manufacturing Company.

Babb says his father told him that it was Robert Lincoln's wife Mary who contravened her husband's wishes. She feared that just as Robert had been overshadowed in life by his famous father, so would he be in death if they were buried together. As a Civil War veteran and former secretary of war, Robert was entitled to be buried in Arlington, so she decided to inter him there in 1928.

Two years later, when she made the decision to move their only son to the side of her husband, she asked Babb's father to oversee the transfer of the remains. This project required a special act of the Illinois Legislature and the consent of a special commission in charge of Lincoln's tomb. At the time, poet Carl Sandburg was the head of the commission.

Babb's father noticed that the plate on the young boy's coffin had the wrong date of birth. He knew the proper date because he had attended his friend's birthday parties nearly half a century earlier. The plate was corrected.

To express her thanks, President Lincoln's only daughter-in-law gave to Mr. Max Babb the autographed copy of *Artemus Ward: His Book*, which author Charles F. Browne had sent to Lincoln in 1862. "Ward" was the president's favorite humorist. On occasion, Lincoln would begin Cabinet meetings by reading a chapter from this book—as he did just before presenting his draft of the Emancipation Proclamation. The Babb family has since made a gift of this book to Yale's Beineke Rare Book Library.

8. A Great-Grandson Dies: The Last Lincoln

The Baltimore Evening Sun: December 27, 1985

THE LAST descendant of President Abraham Lincoln died on Christmas Eve in his eighty-second year. Naturally I am recalling my sole, hour-long visit with him in tidewater Virginia on August 9, 1983. At that time, the ailing Robert Todd Lincoln Beckwith was living on Woodstock Farm along the Piankatank River near the town of Saluda. Last April, *Life* magazine carried a story picturing him in the Saluda nursing home, where he died.

I had driven down Maryland Route 103, crossed the Potomac River Bridge into Confederate Virginia, shortly turned left on Virginia Route 17 (just beyond the Rappahannock River), passed signs pointing to the birthplaces of George Washington and Robert E. Lee, and arrived at Saluda, fifty-five miles southeast on Route 17.

Had I continued on Route 17, I would have come to Yorktown, near Williamsburg. Instead I traveled another ten miles down a side road to the small town of Hartfield. A couple of helpful teenagers showed me the way from Saluda. I wondered whether those descendants of Johnny Reb knew whose great-grandson lived on Woodstock Farm.

Beckwith's mother, born Jessie Lincoln, and married to Warren Beckwith in 1897, bought this large waterfront property around 1919. Her father was Robert Todd Lincoln, the president's eldest son and the only one of the four presidential offspring to marry and produce children. Jessie Lincoln had an older sister, Mary, and an older brother, Abraham Lincoln II. It was this boy, who died in 1890 at the age of sixteen, who was putting me in touch that day with Lincoln's last descendant.

Early in 1983, I had discovered that because of a technicality, the young boy was buried in a nameless grave in Arlington National Cemetery. He was interred with his parents, whose names were carved on an elegant granite sarcophagus, but not his. The U.S. Army said that his name could now be inscribed if a relative so requested. I tracked down Beckwith's lawyer, who wrote him about the situation and told me where he lived.

That summer, I was on my way to visit friends in Virginia Beach and seized the occasion to stop by Woodstock Farm, even though Elizabeth Young, Beckwith's Washington lawyer, felt that her client might be too sick to entertain visitors. I proceeded up the mile-and-a-half driveway to the old brick mansion with its two white pillars framing the main entrance.

It was about 4 P.M. when I knocked on the screen door and was greeted by a seven-year-old girl who turned out to be Elizabeth Hoverson. She is the granddaughter, by a previous marriage, of the third wife of Beckwith, whom the youngster called "Uncle Bob." This wife, Margaret Hogan by birth, was born on Beckwith's seventeenth birthday. Her first husband was born on Lincoln's birthday. Shortly the little girl's mother, Lenora, joined her at the door with two even smaller children in tow. Thanks to my clerical outfit and the letter already received from Beckwith's lawyer, the young mother recognized me.

When I inquired after Beckwith's health, his stepdaughter replied: "He's fine. Would you like to see him?" I was gratifyingly startled. We walked about fifteen paces across the main floor to a bedroom on the far left. There Beckwith lay stretched out at an angle across a daybed next to a high four-poster. (Just a month earlier, I had visited the Petersen house in Washington and had gazed at the too-short bed where the dying president had been laid at an angle until his death.)

Dressed in a plaid sports shirt, white shorts, and tennis shoes, Beckwith rose and shook my hand. After Mrs. Hoverson explained, he seemed to know who I was and said something about wanting to discuss my letter with his wife. (He eventually replied to his lawyer, and Abraham Lincoln II's name was engraved on the sarcophagus on February 9, 1984.)

This last of the three great-grandchildren of the six-foot-four Lincoln was joltingly short—not much over five feet. His head seemed to be held down stiffly, so he had to raise up his steady blue eyes beneath shaggy, gray eyebrows. A horseshoe baldness crowned a rather full face that seemed to radiate a patient benignity.

The seventy-nine-year-old spoke with a stutter and in short spurts. He was hard of hearing. According to chatty Elizabeth, his left ear was the better one and his hearing aid needed fixing. The room temperature must have been a muggy 100 degrees, but there was no fan or air conditioner in sight or in use. He said he preferred heat to cold. I saw no Lincoln picture in that room, but there were a few old lithographs on the walls.

We walked out to a nearby porch, where the presence of a table prompted me to ask the old man for his autograph. Having no blank paper, I presented the back of a letter from the army about his uncle's grave in Arlington. He looked at the front side before signing. As he somewhat laboriously inscribed the word "Lincoln," I was moved by the thought that here was the last person on the planet who could use that name as his own and have the great Abraham's blood coursing through his veins. Elizabeth asked to sign her name too.

My host asked whether I'd like to walk down to the river. We passed through some hedges and came upon a drained swimming pool. Nearby were four small stone lions, with their paws above stone shields. "From the House of Parliament," commented Beckwith. I remembered that the grandfather after whom he had been named served as U.S. minister to Britain under Queen Victoria. One lion was cracked and lay sprawled on the grass.

I asked about his only cousin, Lincoln Isham. "He died twelve years ago." I checked the date later and he was correct. There was no question that, despite his age and Parkinson's disease, this man's mind was still sharp. He also said that his sister, Mary, had died and was buried at the Lincoln estate, Hildene, near Manchester, Vermont. Built by his grandfather, Robert Todd Lincoln, in the year of Beckwith's birth, the elegant mansion is featured in the fall issue of the magazine, *Victorian Houses*.

When I said I hoped that I was not tiring him by the walk, little Elizabeth reassured me that he hadn't had his daily walk yet anyway. Before I left, he was easily agreeable to my taking some photographs. As we shook hands goodbye, I noticed that he wore a handsome gold and enamel Masonic ring on his left hand. Mason or no, he allowed me to give him a blessing. (Had not his great-grandfather defended Catholics against the bigots of his day?)

Like his mother, Robert Todd Lincoln Beckwith was thrice married. He wedded Hazel Holland Wilson on March 14, 1937. She died on August 6, 1966, having produced no children of that union.

On November 6, 1967, he married Annamarie Hoffman. A son, Timothy Lincoln Beckwith, was born on October 14, 1968. Beckwith sued for divorce on grounds of adultery. His wife would permit a blood test neither for herself nor her son, nor would she appear in court. A divorce decree was finally granted on August 4, 1976, with the court declaring that on surgical, physiological grounds, the plaintiff could not have begotten the child (who now lives in West Germany). President Lincoln therefore has no great-great grandchildren.

Since Beckwith's only sibling died childless, since his only cousin died likewise without issue, and since his own third marriage proved as fruitless as his previous ones, Robert Todd Lincoln Beckwith has by his death terminated the Lincoln line. Sadly, therefore, the sixteenth president of the United States, as well as all of his descendants, now belong only to the ages.

Postscript

The Lincoln Herald: Winter 1987–88

On the identical day in 1809, two dozen days after the Boston birth of Edgar Allan Poe, Abraham Lincoln and Charles Darwin were born. Hostile cartoonists would later endow the gangling, six-foot-four Kentuckian with simian characteristics. Other observers would come to regard him as one of the best fulfillments ever of the moral potential of that problematic species dubiously dubbed homo sapiens.

The fittest may survive, but not necessarily the finest, nor their bloodline. Lincoln died at fifty-six. And on Christmas Eve 1985, at 6:05 P.M., in a nursing home in Saluda, Virginia, the last Lincoln descendant died of Parkinson's disease and acute coronary insufficiency. At eighty-one Robert Todd Lincoln

Beckwith was a year shy of matching the age of the grandfather after whom he was named.

Born in Riverside, Illinois, on July 19, 1904, Robert Beckwith lived a private, generally undramatic life. During his childhood summers he often resided with his Lincoln grandparents on their Hildene estate near Manchester, Vermont, where his ashes are to be buried. His sister's ashes were already scattered there. They were both Christian Scientists.

President Lincoln's son Robert was a student at Harvard when he first stayed at the famous Equinox Hotel in Manchester, Vermont. He vacationed there with his mother and his brother Tad during the Civil War summers of 1863 and 1864. Supposedly the president himself was booked to stay there in the summer of 1865.

Four decades later, on June 20, 1905, Robert and his family moved to their newly built home, named Hildene, off Route 7 in Manchester. He had bought 412 "hill and valley" acres in 1902, and in 1903 engaged the Boston architectural firm of Shepley, Rutan, and Coolidge to design and build the stately residence. For the next four decades, Robert spent his summers there and died within its walls on July 26, 1926.

His grandson, Robert Todd Lincoln Beckwith, was one year old when Hildene was first occupied and spent many years growing up there under the watchful eye of his grandfather. Beckwith's only sibling, Mary, inherited the property when the builder's widow died in 1937, and she lived there until her own death in 1975.

The estate was left to the Christian Science Church, from whom a group of area citizens, known as Friends of Hildene, bought the property and its twenty-seven buildings in 1978. FOH, Inc. is dedicated to the preservation of property and buildings as an educational and cultural resource and a memorial to Robert Todd Lincoln and his family, now entirely extinct.

Just after the First World War Robert Todd Lincoln's daughter Jessie purchased Woodstock Farm on the Piankatank River near Hartfield in tidewater Virginia, and the elegant antebellum mansion there was her son Robert's main home for the rest of his life. He obtained a law degree in 1935 from the National University in Washington, D.C., but never practiced.

He raised cattle on his farm and enjoyed sailing and studying history.

There are ironies aplenty to be found in the details of the last Lincoln's death. He died in the Confederacy, just off Virginia's Route 17, "Historyland Highway," with its signs pointing to the nearby birthplaces of George Washington and Robert E. Lee. Further on, the road leads to Yorktown and Williamsburg. Within a stone's throw of the site of his wake stands a Confederate memorial emblazoned with the dates 1861–1865 — the years of the Lincoln presidency. He was cremated in Richmond, through whose smoking ruins as the fallen, sniper-ridden capital of the Confederacy President Lincoln audaciously walked, just days before his own death.

The whole Lincoln story is a preternaturally sad one in many ways, justifying retroactively the melancholy in the president's character and often in his visage. But the story of his courage, his humanity, and his astonishing capacity to keep on growing morally and intellectually throughout his life will continue to inspire new members of the species. The good news is that the children of the spirit outlive the children of the flesh.

9. The Heart of St. Valentine's Day

The Baltimore Evening Sun: February 14, 1979

SINCE most of us at some time in our lives are "bewitched, bothered, and bewildered" by the marvelous malady called love, it is fitting that there should be considerable confusion about St. Valentine and the origin of the day that honors his name.

That name comes from the Latin verb *valere*, which means to be strong and healthy, and which has fathered such words as value, validity, valiant, invalid, convalesce, prevail, and avail. The Romans said goodby by telling you to be healthy, and that is what a valedictorian still does in his or her own way.

There are two Saints Valentine whose deaths as martyrs are commemorated on February 14. One was a priest beheaded in his native Rome around A.D. 270 at the order of an emperor named Claudius the Goth. The other was bishop of a town sixty miles from Rome. Both died rather than renounce their faith—or was there only one Valentine, who was first a priest and later a bishop, and whom foggy memories split into two persons?

You needn't be a poet to see how aptly you could substitute the word love for the emperor in the previous paragraph. Does not love produce its own martyrs who refuse to renounce their faith, does it not make us lose our heads at times and split us into several personalities and confuse our identities?

But apparently these considerations have nothing to do with the romantic aspect of St. Valentine's Day. Rather, our ancestors had the impression that birds began to mate on or about February 14 and so, writing his *Parliament of Fowls* about 600 years ago, Geoffrey Chaucer noted: "This was on St. Valentine's Day, when every fowl cometh there to choose his mate."

The record shows that 100 years later, in the England of 1477, one Margery Drews wrote thus to her future husband, John Paston: "If ye could be content with that good [her small dowry] and my poor person, I would be the merriest maiden on ground, a good, true and loving valentine."

Other students of this day think that the French word for beau or wooer, *galantin*, played a role in the romantic connotations of the saint's (saints'?) name.

Still others point out that the pre-Christian Romans held a major celebration in honor of the fertility god Lupercus on February 15, and that the early Christians may have taken over some romantic custom linked with that celebration and tied it to the saint's proximate feast day. This celebration (Lupercalia) went by another name, the Februa, a word that had to do with a cleansing rite and gave us the name of the current month.

Just fifty years ago, the St. Valentine's Day Massacre occurred in Chicago when members of Al Capone's gang are thought to have been trying to cleanse the illegal liquor business of competitors by liquidating seven members of Bugs Moran's gang.

Three years earlier, a famous Hollywood lover named D'Antonguolla died, and massacred thereby many a maiden heart. He was better known as Rudolph Valentino, and one suspects that the romantic overtones of his movie name were no accident.

The heart, broken or otherwise, is of course the symbol of St. Valentine's Day. Though threadbare as a symbol, the "heart" still works its magic in celebrated sentences such as: The heart is a lonely hunter; Sorrow is born of the hasty heart; The heart has reasons unknown to reason.

Not only the moonstruck favor the word: Cardinal Newman's motto, *Cor ad cor loquitur*, means "Heart speaks to heart." One of St. Augustine's most memorable lines comes from a prayer found in his *Confessions*: "Thou has made us for thyself, O Lord, and our hearts are restless till they rest in thee."

Psychotherapist Otto Rank thought that the tragedy of modern romantic love is that lovers try to find in another creature those divine qualities that earlier lovers expected to find only in the creator. (Think of all the love songs and poems that employ words like "divine," "heavenly," "paradise.") Asking divinity of the human beloved often becomes an intolerable burden for the one partner and the cause of bitter disillusionment for the other.

In his story, *The Little Prince*, Antoine de Saint-Exupéry states that what is essential is invisible, and that the roots of the eyes must therefore be in the heart. A modern philosopher develops this line of thought by defining love as a way of seeing.

Saints like Francis of Assisi saw the divine in the lowliest creature, without expecting the fullness of divinity to be found there. He had discovered the loftiest love secret of all when he prayed that he might be more interested in loving than in being loved, "for it is in giving that we receive."

The philosopher Nietzsche was never wiser than when he said we must come to love even our wounds—to say yes to our fates, however unlovely they may seem. The poet Hölderlin spoke the last word, or at least one of the loveliest of words about the link between love and suffering. His thought would make a valentine worth keeping for a lifetime:

"Heart's wave would not curl nor beautifully break into the foam of spirit did not the ageless, silent rock of destiny stand in its path."

10. St. Patrick's Day: A Witty Wake

The Baltimore Evening Sun: March 17, 1981

THE IRISH celebrate a kind of wake each year on St. Patrick's Day. According to tradition, the Apostle of Ireland died on March 17, more than fifteen centuries ago. A lovely legend claims that the sun itself kept a nine-day wake when the great saint died. It took the sun that long to persuade itself to rise on a world no longer brightened by the saint's living eyes.

Like any wake, St. Patrick's Day is a mixture of joy and sorrow — appropriately so for a golden feast that is always surrounded by the grayness of Lent. We are all aware of the troubles that have been afflicting Ireland, especially Northern Ireland, where St. Patrick is buried and where he probably started his missionary labors.

Such sorrows, of course, are nothing new. As historian Roger Chauvire has written: "The history of Ireland is a sad tale, as if she were the victim of an evil spell, moving through the centuries from misfortune to misfortune."

The poet Lionel Johnson expressed this view in another way:

> The wail of Irish winds,
> The cry of Irish seas:
> Eternal sorrow finds
> Eternal voice in these.

The joyful side of the occasion is the evergreen memory of Patrick himself, a man as noble as the patrician meaning of his name. And then there's the memory of all the Irish saints and heroes and poets, and the mistier memory of all the everyday

Irish who knew this secret: that the next best thing to being a saint or a hero or a poet is being able to appreciate them.

Seasoning and illuminating this joyful aspect of Irish history, and of the Irish character, is what we may call the Irish sense of humor. A sense of humor, to be sure, is not an Irish monopoly, though there is a special twist and fragrance to it. But, as with Jewish humor, I think it can be compellingly argued that the very vigor and persistence of it are linked with sorrow. It is as though comedy and tragedy were Siamese twins that cannot be successfully separated.

Consider some of the harsh aspects of Irish reality. No place in Ireland is more than seventy miles from the sea—the mysterious and often cruel sea. That's what surrounded the Irish. What lay beneath their feet was moody soil, one-fifth bog, which too often was the mother of malnutrition or outright famine.

Over their heads was and is perhaps the cloudiest, dampest sky in Europe. More significantly, over their heads politically and for laborious centuries was a foreign and repressive government.

Such daily realities as these made the Irish keenly aware that this world was not paradise, that it could be and often was for them a valley of tears. For many centuries, your typical Irishman had little wealth, little power, and meager opportunity for book learning.

But what he did have natively and what he did develop as the pearl within the oyster of his adversity was a lively appreciation for the spoken word—the wealth of it, the power of it, and the opportunities it brought to his spirit. Deprived in so many commercial and political ways, he compensated by amassing treasures of stories and poems and songs and witty sayings. He hadn't much future in a worldly sense, so he made the best of the present moment, celebrating the pleasures of zesty conversation.

Such conversation was an art form. It was its own excuse for being, and was to be easefully savored like a choice wine. More than one visitor to Ireland through the years has noticed that conversation there is not inhibited by any lack of information about the subject under discussion.

Verbal dexterity and the art of playing dumb were also ideal and idealized weapons for dealing with unfriendly government officials. Even today, an Irishman is likely to answer your question with one of his own. "Could you tell me where the Post Office is?" "Would you be wanting to mail a letter?"

Humor, in particular, feeds on a sense of the absurd and often helps a person outwit absurdity or at least endure absurdity less hurtfully. The Irish needed humor for its survival value. Humor delights in playfulness for its own sake, in the unexpected, in the joy of puncturing the balloons of pomposity and worldly self-importance.

Thus an Irish mother can say that she has a husband and three other children. An Irish tour guide can insist that he never tells a lie except where the truth wouldn't fit. A Dubliner can tell you that the smell of the River Liffey is one of the sights of Dublin. A freeloader will be described as coming for the wedding and staying for the christening.

I myself heard an Irish bus driver, who was actually a teetotaler, speak of wanting "one for the road and two for the ditch." And at a religious rally in Ireland, there was a sign that fervently proclaimed: "God bless the Holy Trinity!"

My own mother's mother, who was born in Ireland on St. Patrick's Day, used to say, when you asked her how she was, that outside of being no good, she was fine. She knew that there are situations others would call serious but not hopeless, while an Irishman would call them hopeless but not serious. And though I never asked her, she might well have said of leprechauns what another Irish woman is reported to have said: namely, that of course she didn't believe in them—but they're there.

And between you, me, and the gatepost, she would have appreciated the Irishman who reassured a bewildered foreigner that he was indeed on the road to Dublin, but who added, after a thoughtful pause, "I think I'd better tell you, though, you're going in the wrong direction." Asked how to get to Dublin, another Irishman responded, "Well, in the first place, if I were wanting to go to Dublin, I'd never start from here."

One of the wrong directions that Ireland never took was trying to conquer another nation by military might—and on that score, Ireland is a rarity among European nations. But Irish wit and poetry and heroism have conquered many an alien heart, as has Dublin's ability to elect a Jewish mayor, and Catholic Ireland's ability to elect a Protestant president.

The captivating spirit of St. Patrick, who may himself have been a Briton, argues for peace and reconciliation among the Irish. Patrick is credited with these words: "There are three kinds of saints: those who are a glory on the mountain tops; those who are gleams on the hillsides; and those who are just a few faint lights in the valleys."

Northern Ireland has been in its own valley of conflict for too many years now. But more and more lights, and even brighter ones, have been glowing there of late in the name of peace and for the end of terrorism.

Yes, St. Patrick's Day always falls in Lent. But it falls as well on the threshold of spring, whose color is hope's and Ireland's too. Not to be missed, the poetry there.

11. Thank God It's (Good) Friday

The Baltimore Evening Sun: March 24, 1978

IN HIS movie, *Annie Hall*, Woody Allen takes his sweetheart to a bookshop and points out several books, all having to do with death. This melancholy merryman's preoccupation with that topic is well known. Consider his earlier movie, *Love and Death*, and his celebrated quip to the effect that he isn't afraid of dying—he just doesn't want to be there when it happens.

One of the books he showed Annie Hall was the 1974 Pulitzer Prize-winning *The Denial of Death* by Ernest Becker. I'm in the process of rereading this spellbinding volume. And I keep running into other people who have purchased the book on the recommendation of still other readers.

An unusual aspect of this volume is that the author, a cultural anthropologist, died in his fiftieth year, not long after the book appeared. In his *Voices and Visions*, Sam Keen published an interview he conducted with Becker while the latter was hospitalized with an illness he knew to be terminal. In his own book, Becker is not very self-revealing. Given the thesis of that book, it is an enthralling experience to hear him talk about his life's work and his deepest convictions as he faced death.

What is the book's thesis? Simply stated, it is that human beings can be best understood by their "denial of death," their need to cope with their awareness of their own vulnerability, their own mortality. ("I, a stranger and afraid, in a world I never made.") Becker tries to present the deepest and richest view of the human condition available to the human mind now that the work of Freud has been better absorbed and the errors of his genius better accounted for.

The author deals with human "heroics"—the ways we try to transcend our mortality—and with neurosis seen as failed heroics. He deals with the inherent limitations of psychotherapy and the consequent relevance of the religious quest.

With respect to this quest, he finds the Danish philosopher Sören Kierkegaard to be astonishingly post-Freudian in his on-target analysis of the way things truly are with this glorious and terrible phenomenon called humankind. Becker was Jewish by birth, as was the man whose "acceptance of death" gave today the arresting name of Good Friday. Woody Allen is explicitly Jewish, of course; as was Freud, who postulated the death instinct. Given the tragic history of the Jews, even before the Holocaust, their almost ethnic sensitivity to vulnerability and their remarkable efforts to transcend it can hardly be regarded as puzzling.

The early Christian philosopher Boethius defined the purpose of philosophy as teaching a man how to die. In his *Divine Comedy*, Dante is called blessed by Purgatorian spirits because he is willing to undergo his journey "in order to die better." And the modern poet, Kenneth Patchen, summed up the whole issue marvelously: "There are so many little dyings that it doesn't matter which of them is death."

So what is good about this Friday? Well, it celebrates a secret many of us learn excruciatingly, if at all: that there are vital and vitalizing ways of "letting go," of not holding on to the past, to other people, to grandiose views and expectations of ourselves—ways that are the necessary prelude to a better and safer kind of richness and freedom.

If it is true that the real gods come when the half-gods go, the terror is that usually we have to dismiss the half-gods first and face again, at least for awhile, the threat of nothingness that produced the half-gods in the first place.

For many people around the world, this process and its promise are symbolized by a dead young man stretched upon a cross—a cross that is composed of an "I" that has been crossed out. The laws of human maturity prove that dying is the price of living. The core of Easter faith is that the same law pertains to that special dying we call death.

What other kind of faith could look upon this Friday, give thanks for it, and dare to call it Good?

12. Easter Says: Choose Life

The Baltimore Evening Sun: April 13, 1979

A YEAR has passed since Easter 1978 and its celebration of life's triumph over death. That feast focuses on Jerusalem, the city over which Christ wept as he saw the sorrows that were to befall it.

In the meantime, another feast of Christmas has come and gone, with its focus on the little town of Bethlehem, and the slaughter there of innocent children.

During this same twelve-month period, two towns have been transmuted from unknown to unforgettable as a horrified nation and a horrified world looked on:

Jonestown, with its mass suicide-massacre, its flight from life, its slaughter of the innocents; and

Middletown, with its flight from death, and its pregnant women and small children fleeing from the radiation of Three Mile Island across the water. ("But woe to those who are with child, or have infants at the breast in those days," said Jesus in Matthew 24:19.) This accident occurred when the ink was scarcely dry on the pages of Pope John Paul II's first world-letter: "Man lives increasingly in fear. He is afraid of what he produces . . . afraid that it can become the means and instrument for an unimaginable self-destruction."

Jonestown and Middletown are dramatic instances of the life-and-death struggle that goes on all over the world, usually in more ignorable ways.

Study the clock. Every time two seconds pass, another human being has died of starvation. Meantime, almost as quietly, the nations of the world lavish their wealth (or their poverty) on the armament business. Last year that business cost an estimated $400 billion. [Make that $930 billion for 1987.]

46

Try to grasp how much money that is. If Jesus had spent four hundred thousand dollars per day on some charity from the moment of his birth until today, he would still not have equaled what the world spent last year alone on the instruments of death and destruction.

I have been focusing on physical death and destruction. Yet, the meaning of Christ's bodily death is precisely this: the death of the body and its sufferings are not the greatest evils in the world. Indeed, in the moral struggle for justice, truth, honor, and efficacious compassion, one's own body, worn-out or shattered, is a worthy gift.

It may be a demanded gift. Simone Weil felt that in the modern world, you must choose between being a victim or an executioner. The crucifixion indicates which choice is better.

But a paradox is at work: a world-view that is "larger than life" can result in a world that is safer for physical life itself. "He who saves his life will lose it; he who loses his life for the sake of the good news will save it."

Heroism is never easy. Christ's handpicked apostles generally failed him at the crucial moment. Through the centuries, Christians have not generally improved on that record at their crucial moments.

Still, as Judge Learned Hand remarked, the "impossible ethics" of Christianity have proven an immense boon to civilization—those ethics that "we can neither wholly accept nor wholly forget."

It is customary to speak of the failure of Christianity in Nazi Germany, as though the record were monochromatic. In tribute to the enduring power of "The Good Friday Spell," the words of Albert Einstein may provide a corrective in this, the centennial year of his birth.

Episcopal bishop Edward R. Welles recently made public a 1945 letter from the great Jewish scientist in which he confirmed that this quotation from him is correct:

"Being a lover of freedom . . . I looked to the universities to defend it, knowing that they had always boasted of their devotion to the cause of truth; but, no, the universities immediately were silenced.

"Then I looked to the great editors of the newspapers whose flaming editorials in days gone by had proclaimed their love of freedom; but they, like the universities, were silenced in a few short weeks.

"Only the church stood squarely across the path of Hitler's campaign for suppressing the truth. I never had any special interest in the church before, but now I feel a great affection and admiration because the church alone has had the courage and persistence to stand for intellectual truth and moral freedom. I am forced to confess that what I once despised I now praise unreservedly."

In his volume, *The German Churches under Hitler* (1979) U.S. historian Ernst Helmreich offers detailed documentation of Einstein's impression. In his opening sentence the scholar asserts that the German churches during the Nazi period were "the only institutions which did not succumb to Hitler's policy of regimentation."

What awaits the world and each of us between now and next Easter? The basic choice was unforgettably formulated in one of the earliest books of the Jewish Bible: "I have set before you life and death, the blessing and the curse. Choose life." (Deuteronomy 30:19.)

13. Of Easter and Atheists

The Baltimore Evening Sun: April 5, 1985

RECENTLY a young friend wrote to me: "Does it still make sense to talk about God? My wife tells me that no intelligent person in the twentieth century who has really examined the evidence could possibly still believe in God."

Some serious thought about atheism seems timely at Eastertide. Let me attempt a definition: atheism is the belief that behind this cosmos that our senses purposefully perceive and our minds intelligently decipher, there is no ultimate reality that is intelligent and purposeful. Therefore the beauties and varieties and patterns of the inner and outer world are the result of blind chance and have no meaning outside themselves.

In this view, human beings create all the "meaning" there is and are responsible only to themselves. Ultimately, though, the history of each human being as well as of the whole race is an absurdity, more or less tragic. This does not mean, however, that an atheist cannot devote himself or herself to the heroic pursuit of human values "just for themselves."

According to statisticians, atheism is professed by a small minority of human beings, though that minority grows every year. Larger is the group that defines itself as agnostic, that is, unable to decide between the claims of theism or atheism. To me agnosticism is more defensible than atheism because it is not so dogmatic and doctrinaire in the direction of darkness.

Among theists there are those who say they believe in God, but on whose daily lives that belief has little, if any impact. By contrast, a practical theist is one whose life wouldn't make sense if God didn't exist. Though some theists may see themselves as "knuckling under" to a jealous and intimidating god, others prefer to think of themselves rather as inviting the Divine Energy to invade their finite, fragmented selves so that they may be knitted into wholeness (holiness) and be used as tools for further divinizing the world, especially by loving it creatively. "Man is born broken," wrote Eugene O'Neill; "God's grace is glue."

The most obvious argument for atheism is that God cannot be seen or heard, at least not by most normal people. The theist might reply that even at the physical level scientific ultimates cannot be directly experienced. So it is at the moral and spiritual level, at least as a probability.

God is deduced as the ultimate ground for such realities as purposeful pattern, the ecstatic experience of beauty, the heroic pursuit of truth, the insistence of conscience, the hunger for holiness, the sense of the sacred as well as of sin, the instinctive repugnance of the notion of ultimate absurdity, and the moral and psychological devastation that can result from the acceptance of such a notion. (In the words of one of Dostoyevski's characters: "If there is no God, then everything is permitted.")

Here's a vital difference, though: scientific arguments can be assessed by the impersonal intellect alone. But the claims of morality and religion must be evaluated by the whole person, including his or her heart, and with an honest sense of one's own biases, weaknesses, and blind spots. More and more humanist thinkers are pointing out the disastrous consequences of the bias in Western civilization that supposes that truth can be grasped only by the analytic, rationalistic, scientific, quantitative mind. Through this bias the mind tries to negate the soul. (See Rollo May's *The Discovery of Being*.)

Since the Holocaust of World War II, a kind of devout atheism has attracted some followers. In this view, it is more religious to decide that God does not exist than to affirm that He does exist and could have prevented the Holocaust but did not do so. I respect this view and its claim to be reasonable. But I also see that it presumes that to be God, God must be able and willing to intervene directly and detectibly in human affairs. It also presumes that human concepts of reasonableness are the ultimate standards of what is or can be true. Yet how often the mysteries of life and of history call those standards into radical question.

As for God's intervention in human affairs: I must confess that the older I get, the less my reason can see that prayer changes things directly. Perhaps Samuel Johnson was right in saying that reason is a poor instrument for grasping the meaning of prayer. Still I would argue thus: a child prays that God may change things; an adult prays that God may change him. Magic tries to control the sacred; religion invites the sacred to control the believer.

In facing the scandal of something as evil as the Holocaust, a person can worsen his theological dilemma by imagining "all that suffering"—as though any one person suffered "all of it." But no one person suffers a Holocaust; one suffers only one's own maximum. Yet in terms of the scandal of innocent or outrageous suffering, the problem with respect to God's existence would be the same if only one person in history had ever unjustly suffered the maximum—though, of course, no suffering scandalizes many of us as much as our own. A further point: if our moral sense of outrage is ultimately based on absurdity or pure subjectivity, then that very outrage loses its objective authority. Or so it seems to me.

The theist may point out that there is a problem of good as well as a problem of evil. What is the ultimate explanation of the goodness we encounter in life? And which experience is the more ultimate: good or evil? I think that either "problem" can be so viewed and so felt as to seem the more overwhelming and convincingly ultimate.

In either case, a leap of faith or a leap of disbelief seems to be required, and sheer reasonableness is left behind. Something inside the questioner that is not pure logic tips the scales mysteriously in the direction of faith or of doubt and denial. "Now I know what is meant by grace," says the narrator in Camus' *The Plague* after he heard a theist say that he can still believe in God despite "the slaughter of the innocent."

It is remarkable how extremes touch each other. There is a kind of reverence and piety that sounds like atheism. (By refusing to worship the popular divinities, were not Jews and early Christians accused of being atheists?) Persons who have had what is called a mystical experience sometimes say that God is so far beyond our mind's grasp, and that His way of existing is so different from what we could imagine, that it might be truer to say He does not "exist." Such is the God beyond God, the God-in-Himself beyond the God-as-we-conceive-Him.

Such mystics will agree: God's only excuse is that He does not "exist"—certainly not according to the tailoring of our finite minds. But let's not be too hard on our minds. If we are in some sense made in God's image, then the God whom we project in our purest thoughts might not be entirely off the mark. Besides, is it not reassuring that a mind at its purest is wise enough to recognize its own limitations when it indulges in God-talk?

The theologian Thomas Aquinas, though sometimes presented as a know-it-all, insisted that all God-talk is analogical, *i.e.*, metaphorical, *i.e.*, poetic, *i.e.*, not literal. He stated flatly that nothing has the same meaning when it is applied to God as it does when it is applied to a creature—including existence, goodness, and fatherliness. At best there is some similarity of relationship, as when (on the creaturely level) both a tree and a book are said to have leaves. The point is, however, that when the subject matter is higher than heads and deeper than hearts, a mythic, poetic, metaphorical way of speaking may be more illuminating and practical than the speech of literal prose.

Take the idea of God as Father. Aquinas would say that since God is not literally our father, it would be wrong to deny Him positive qualities (such as motherliness) normally excluded by fatherliness as we experience it on earth. When Jesus invited us to regard God as Father, he summoned us to relate to Him "as if" He were Father. In so doing, we do better than if we thought of Him as supreme "Itness." For, from the practical point of view, it makes an important human difference whether we relate to God as to a father or as to an It, no matter how far above and beyond such descriptions God in Himself may be.

Those who undergo what they feel is a direct, personal experience of the Absolute, the Ultimate, the Holy, the Wholly Other, the Divine, Pure Reality, the Numinous, usually insist that the experience is ineffable, unspeakable. If you think you can verbalize it adequately, you show only that you haven't truly felt it. "Those who know don't say. Those who say don't know."

Trappist monk Thomas Merton thought that the future of religion lay between those that try to say (preeminently Christianity) and religions that do not try to say (preeminently Buddhism). Though I myself incline toward the wisdom of not trying to say, I have to admit that a major part of Christian theology deals with what should not be said, and therefore such theologizing is not to be totally despised by those who incline toward the "apophatic" (unsaying) tradition that can be found even in Christianity.

Incidentally, those who think that psychiatry is hostile to religion may be intrigued by M. Scott Peck's book, *The Road Less Traveled*. This practicing therapist has a whole section on grace, which he defines as "a powerful force originating outside of human consciousness which nurtures the spiritual growth of human beings." He sees this growth in terms of the ability and desire to reach out to others in loving, giving ways. As such it is an upward, evolutionary thrust struggling against the downward drag of entropy. Viewed in this perspective, St. Paul's words about the war between the flesh and the spirit take on strikingly "scientific" overtones.

Since the suffering of the innocent is the supreme scandal confronting many theists, it is remarkable that the crucifixion of a good man is at the heart of Christianity. It is also remarkable that the Gospel writers were willing to record, as almost the final words of Jesus, his agonized cry: "My God, My God, why hast Thou forsaken me?" Almost the final words. But the worst words were not the last ones.

Acquainted with grief as it is, the Easter story will always speak to the human heart in the heart of its darkness—a story that intrigues, arrests, invites, promises, a story that struggles to prevent the massive doors of despairful meaninglessness from slamming tight forever. That is the tomb that most needs to have the stone rolled away from it.

14. St. Stanislaus: Poland's Thomas à Becket (Feast: April 11)

The Baltimore Evening Sun: May 7, 1979

I N A.D. 1066, William the Conqueror earned his title by conquering England. In A.D. 1076, Holy Roman Emperor Henry IV tried to conquer the reforming pope, Gregory VII, by pushing for his deposition. In return, for the first time in history, a king was excommunicated by a pope. Henry thereupon journeyed to Canossa in northern Italy to seek absolution.

Meanwhile, Henry's troubles with Gregory prompted the Polish King Boleslaus II to break away from the Holy Roman Empire. Though most of this king's subjects were paralyzed by fear of him, the bishop of Cracow was not. When, as the climax of a number of outrages, Boleslaus the Bold kidnapped the wife of a nobleman, Bishop Stanislaus threatened excommunication. When the king persisted, Stanislaus made good his threat.

So, when the king tried to attend mass in Cracow's cathedral, services were suspended by order of the bishop. In a regal fury, Boleslaus tracked down the bishop, who was saying mass in a small chapel on the outskirts of the city. In mid-mass, the forty-nine-year-old bishop was put to the sword by the thirty-nine-year-old king. Three years after Canossa, Pope Gregory placed the whole of Poland under interdict. The king fled to Hungary and died that year of 1079.

In 1253, Stanislaus became the first Pole to be canonized, and has long been revered as one of the chief patron saints of Poland. He is not to be confused with another Polish saint, Stanislaus Kostka, a Jesuit who died in 1568.

As is well known, John Paul II, the current successor to Gregory VII, was the successor to St. Stanislaus in the see of Cracow. This week Polish Catholics are observing the 900th anniversary of the martydom of their patron. Since the struggle of Stanislaus against Boleslaus was a struggle between spiritual power and political power, Polish communists are understandably touchy about this celebration.

Pope John Paul II wanted to attend the celebration by making at this time his first visit home since his election last October. A compromise was worked out, so that the papal visit will occur in early June instead.

Ever since the biblical prophet Nathan accused King David of sin, the clash of right versus might has produced high historical drama—as when St. Ambrose forbade the slaughterous Emperor Theodosius to enter his church until he did penance. Professor William F. Albright deemed the action of the prophet Nathan to be one of the turning points in the history of human conscience. Here was a defenseless mortal telling the supreme power in the land that a higher law than the king's wishes bound them both.

In the tenth decade after the death of Stanislaus, Thomas à Becket was murdered in his cathedral by the henchmen of another king, Henry II. It was almost a rerun of the Cracow event. When in the sixteenth century, another chancellor named Thomas clashed in conscience with another Henry, another martyr was produced. Understandably, Henry VIII then ordered the earlier Thomas's shrine at Canterbury to be plundered and his king-defying name removed from the English church calendar.

The church and churchmen have committed their share of sins and sacrileges. But for long and turbulent centuries, the church has helped produce citizens who render to Caesar what is his, but who know that not everything is his. When the church succeeds, the success is often heroic and memorable, as proved the man who died nine centuries ago on the eleventh of last month.

15. Assisi Thoughts: Do We Live Too Well? (Feast: October 4)

The Baltimore Evening Sun: November 9, 1976

ADMIRERS of Francis of Assisi are celebrating this fall the 750th anniversary of the saint's death—or rather, the astonishing way in which his spirit has survived that death. As celebrants of our own national anniversary, we Americans might better appreciate the longevity of that spirit by noting that six years from now the birthday of St. Francis will be enjoying not a first but a fourth bicentennial.

The spirit of this gentle and joyful *poverello*—"poor little man"—lives on in various ways: in the world's largest religious order, the Franciscans, which he founded in A.D. 1209; in the Christmas crib custom, which he popularized; in countless birdbath and garden statues of the nature-loving saint; in the contemporary movie, *Brother Sun, Sister Moon*; and in the growingly familiar prayer of his, "Lord, make me an instrument of Thy peace."

It strikes me that the spirit of the man who was christened Giovanni Francesco Bernardone, and who was canonized two years after his death, persists into a fresh timeliness for us Americans as we face a growing national concern: the end of affluence.

Especially since the gasoline shortage of a few years ago, we have been hearing warnings about an end to "the age of affluence." For many years, a great many Americans have operated on the assumption that the material wealth of the earth and our right to appropriate it are virtually inexhaustible, and that any man or nation with enough money is entitled to more things, better things, fancier things, more convenient things, more throw-away things, world without end. Amen. (Robert Coles, in a recent study of upper-class American youths, noted their amazing sense of "entitlement.")

The warnings multiply that not only is this assumption false, but that we are going to discover sooner than we think how false it is, and that many of us who have been "under-deprived" are going to have our miseducation rectified. People whose sense of value, success, and happiness has been excessively thing-oriented are in for trouble.

According to the historian Sir Herbert Butterfield, these people are not exclusively the upper class or the would-be upper class. A few years ago he voiced his conviction that the true villain causing some of our worst national and international crises is "the moderate cupidity of Everyman—his ordinary longing to advance a little further than his father, or simply increase his sales—even just his dread of a decline in his standard of living. This, when multiplied by millions, can build up into a tremendous pressure on government."

For his part, St. Francis had this crazy idea about being married to Lady Poverty. Inspired by the biblical warning (or reassurance) that "a man's life does not consist in the abundance of his possessions," he ardently believed that there was a secret happiness in having fewer possessions rather than more. He found a secret too in reckless sharing, and even in letting himself need others to share their goods with him.

It wasn't that "things" are bad in themselves; only that there is something sick in the human eye that blinds it to better kinds of wealth when it gets fixed on lesser, more external kinds of wealth.

Poets often make the same point: "Getting and spending, we lay waste our powers;/Little we see in nature that is ours." Thus, William Wordsworth in his day. In our own, St.-John Perse warned of our waste of what we already have: "We have so little time to be born to this moment." A poet of Francis' own century knew how hard and scary it is *not* to store up your treasure where moths consume and thieves break in. In his *Divine Comedy*, through the mouth of Thomas Aquinas, Dante tells how Francis, "while still a youth, opposed his father for the sake of a lady to whom, as to death, no one unlocks the door." For most of us, Lady Poverty is no lady at all.

But put aside the question of "voluntary poverty." Could it be that even our "reasonable and modest" demands about our standard of living add up to an unreasonable and immoderate total? (Consider what our little spray cans may be doing to earth's ozone blanket.) Could it be that the only cure to many of our social ills will require the average American to make considerable sacrifices of comfort, convenience, and buying power?

Of such questions, worldly wisdom will undoubtedly say: "That way lies madness." Still, in the words of a perceptive recluse from Amherst, Massachusetts: "Much Madness is divinest Sense –/To a discerning Eye –."

Lenin the atheist said that he could have revolutionized the world if he had had the help of a dozen Francises of Assisi. If the United States is the "extraordinarily religious" nation that the latest Gallup poll indicates it to be, the spirit of one Francis of Assisi, "multiplied by millions," could mightily promote a "revolution of lowered expectations" at the material level and reveal to many of us the secret of better kinds of wealth.

For, as this marvelous madman said in his famous prayer: "It is in giving that we receive; it is in dying that we are born." As other doors begin to shut, history may well be inviting us as a nation to unlock the door of these paradoxes.

16. The Dying and Waking of a President

The Baltimore Catholic Review: November 29, 1963; November 20, 1964

A quarter of a century will have passed this year since the fourth presidential assassination in U.S. history. Millions of Americans cannot remember that day; millions of others cannot forget it. These are one citizen's recollections of that somber weekend, recorded when the trauma was still fresh.

I

SINCE Baltimore's *Catholic Review* went to press on Thursdays at the time, Friday, November 22, 1963 would ordinarily have been a relaxed day for the editorial staff, of which I was then a member. But we were just a week away from the fiftieth anniversary of our first issue under that name, and were intensely busy preparing for our special ninety-six-page anniversary edition. We were due to complete work that day on one of three special sections.

I recall listening to the 7 A.M. news that morning and feeling queasy about the announcement that President Kennedy was going to visit Dallas that day. I don't regard my malaise as a premonition. Memories of recent and ugly political episodes in that city merely reinforced my customary apprehension about the vulnerability of public officials. Seeing the movie, *The Manchurian Candidate*, hadn't eased my pessimism on the subject.

Later that morning I glanced at the Associated Press teletype machine in the *Review* office, and noted an advance story about the speech President Kennedy was due to deliver at the Dallas Trade Mart that afternoon.

Time slipped by, and I didn't go out for lunch until the presidential limousine was threading its way through downtown Dallas. I had a 2:00 P.M. appointment, so I made a point of eyeing the clock as I headed for the Cove Restaurant across the street at Park and Franklin.

Managing Editor Dave Maguire joined me for a meatless Friday lunch. We talked about the anniversary issue and were just finishing dessert when our waitress, Mrs. Leona McDonald, came to the table and asked whether we had heard the report that President Kennedy had been shot. We didn't want to believe that the report was serious, or at least that the wound was serious, so we asked for the check with a kind of forced calm, and then headed back to the office.

As we approached the entrance, we sped up our pace. Once inside, we bounded up the stairs to the second floor, where the teletype stood. Grimly subdued, many of the personnel, even from other departments, were clustered around the machine reading the bulletins. The first one had read: "Dallas, (AP)— President Kennedy was shot today as his motorcade left downtown Dallas. Mrs. Kennedy jumped up and grabbed Mr. Kennedy. She cried, 'Oh, no!' The motorcade sped on." It was timed at 1:42 Eastern time.

"Where was he hit?"

"In the head."

That was bad news.

The radio was on, and time and again we would read a report from the AP and then hear it over the radio a few seconds later. As details grew more dismal, we all knelt and said a prayer. Somebody went to the magazine rack and reversed the current issue of *Look* magazine, which had a cover photo of young President Kennedy playing with his little son.

I knew the news sources would soon be after a statement from Bishop Austin Murphy, who was governing the diocese during Archbishop Shehan's absence in Rome at the Vatican Council. I phoned the nearby old cathedral to offer the *Review*'s help in transmitting a statement to the news media. The bishop hadn't yet returned from the installation of Bishop Harry Lee Doll at the Episcopal Church of the Redeemer, where he had been an ecumenical guest, so I left a message.

Not long afterward, the dreaded news came from the lips of a priest. There was an irony here. John Kennedy might well have lost the presidency because of his Catholicism; now, precisely because of his priesthood, Father Huber was able to give the nation its first raw certainty that it had lost a president.

Almost spontaneously, everybody knelt for a second prayer, this time of stunned resignation. What would become of the country? If the assassin was a political fanatic, would the nation be split in two? The president should never have gone to Texas. Somebody turned off the teletype machine. "Eternal rest, grant unto him. . ."

The bishop was on the phone now, and invited me to come around immediately. He was sitting in the archbishop's large study on the second floor, just opposite the giant elm overhanging Mulberry Street. His eyes glistened. "It's terrible, isn't it?" (No doubt he was remembering the murderous bullet which had killed his own youthful brother in the line of duty as an F.B.I. agent.)

We worked over a statement. Since the assassin was still unknown, he decided to warn against the dangers of bitter partisan reaction. He cited one quotation from the president. The choice seemed inevitable, and in the following days it cropped up in speeches and comments again and again as though by a kind of national spontaneity. "Ask not. . ."

The phone rang. Bill Weyse, Director of Public Affairs at WJZ-TV, wanted to know if there was going to be a special service at the old cathedral. A daily 5:30 P.M. mass was already scheduled, and after checking with Monsignor Hopkins, the rector of the old cathedral, the bishop decided to make it a requiem mass and to offer it himself. Why not have the choir and students come over from the nearby St. Mary's Seminary?

Within minutes, the decision was made to have a Solemn Pontifical Mass. The priests on the old cathedral staff were soon busy on several phones inviting prominent civil officials. Many of them, including Governor Millard Tawes, Mayor Theodore McKeldin and U.S. Attorney Joseph Tydings, were seated in the front pews less than three hours later. It was most likely the first such mass offered in the United States for the slain president, whose body was still airborne from Texas.

Father Joseph Connolly, who had charge of television for the archdiocese, phoned to see whether I'd be able to serve as narrator for the mass. Returning to the *Review* office, I located a missal with the proper texts. I knew there would be blank spots to be filled, and it seemed natural to have the president's inaugural address at hand for quoting. It was now less than two hours before the mass would begin—where could I find a copy?

I tried to phone a book store, but our operator couldn't get an outside line. A member of our staff hurried to Pratt Library and then to Remington's Book Store, but a copy couldn't be found on such short notice. Finally someone located in our own files the text which had been sent out by the U.S. Catholic Press Service shortly after the inauguration.

Meantime WJZ-TV was rushing equipment and engineers to the old cathedral, making arrangements with the telephone company for clearing video and audio cables and offering the other Baltimore TV channels the opportunity to pick up the broadcast. Ultimately the mass, beautifully sung by the seminarians and attended by a packed congregation, was carried on all of Baltimore's channels and by radio. Many in Washington viewed it also, and later that night, a tape of it was broadcast at least once in the Baltimore-Washington area.

I later learned that just as I was translating the *Agnus Dei* and offering the three-fold prayer, "Lamb of God . . . have mercy on him . . . grant him peace," the video switched to Andrews Air Force Base where the president's coffin was being taken from the plane. The audio continued, however, and those ancient and poignant words of the mass served as a background to the president's final return home.

It was drizzling lightly after the mass. The downtown streets were dark and growing deserted. Walking back to the *Review* office, I recalled the warm, bright evening three years earlier when I had seen a sun-tanned, vital senator ride up Howard Street a block away, in an open car, on his way to a campaign speech in Pikesville.

I thought of the letter he had sent to the *Review* on January 22, 1960—just a year before his inauguration—after the paper had tried to see the humorous side of some of the reasons being given as to why no Catholic could ever be trusted to be president.

"I just want to say," he had written, "that it was a welcome relief . . . You can be sure that your editorial had a heavy readership in my office. With every good wish, I am, sincerely, Jack Kennedy."

"I am, sincerely." Now, he was no more—at least to human eyes. The sincerity was gone too, and the youthful, enthusiastic vision of a better world. Somebody had said JFK was an idealist without any illusions. There aren't enough of those on the world scene. Now there was one less, one exceedingly less.

The way he tackled problems and met adversity showed how right it is to be an idealist. The way that evil had revenged itself showed how right it is to live without illusions. November 22, 1963, had much to say about the meaning of life. At least, it showed what the important questions really are.

But these were thoughts that came later. At the moment it was scarcely 7:00 P.M. The thought that came spontaneously was how much a measure it was of human genius and of human misery that less than six hours earlier, President Kennedy had been alive in Texas. Now the wax was cold on candles which had burned at his thronged and televised requiem several thousand miles away.

II

During the nineteen hours when it was possible to do so, more than one out of every one thousand Americans paid their respects to a fallen president beneath the Capitol dome. Drawn by the magnetic power of that flag-draped casket, I left Baltimore with Father Joseph Gossman of the old cathedral about 9:00 P.M. on Sunday night.

Driving along the Baltimore-Washington Parkway, we heard a news announcer report that citizens from the states of New York, Pennsylvania, and New Jersey were already swelling the traffic that converged on the Capital.

Looking ahead on the parkway, we could see lengthening rows of red lights on the rear of automobiles, with access roads feeding additional cars into the mainstream. As cars passed us or we them, license plates confirmed the news we had just heard.

By 10:30, after some delays on New York Avenue, we arrived at St. Matthew's Cathedral. Stopping briefly at the rectory, we talked with Father Bernard Gerhardt, who would be assisting Secret Service men in checking the identity of clergymen who came for the presidential funeral.

We also talked with Father Frank Ruppert, who had the unexpected privilege earlier that day of saying mass for the Kennedy family in the White House room where the president lay. At 9:30 that morning, the White House had phoned his pastor, Monsignor John Cartwright, and requested that a priest be sent to offer mass.

Young Father Ruppert was sent to the scene and began the service about 10:30. Since early Saturday morning, he and other priests had been taking turns attending the casket with prayers.

Leaving the rectory we paid a short visit to the cathedral, where preparations for the funeral were still underway. Television technicians were at work in the impressive sanctuary. In the pews, a number of persons knelt at prayer. Several dozen people stood in the back of the church conversing with one another. I couldn't tell whether anyone was keeping an eye on our actions.

Outside, small groups of military men talked quietly. There were No Parking signs along the sidewalks, but several cars were there with slips of paper beneath their windshield wipers. Some said, "Military Ceremonial Detail." One said, "I leave for work at 6:30 A.M. If you want me to move before then, my address is . . ."

Before parking on Constitution Avenue near the back of the Capitol, we drove by the White House shortly before midnight. It was not hard to sense the sad, dramatic events taking place under the lights that blazed against the darkness from many of its rooms.

That we were able to find a parking place so near the Capitol was due to the despair of one driver who decided to pull away when he discovered that it was taking seven hours of waiting to reach the Capitol rotunda. Thinking that such a long waiting period and the growing lateness of the hour would soon cause many to leave the long line, Father Gossman and I tried to find the end of it. We attached ourselves to it on Constitution Avenue and First Street, north of the brightly illuminated Capitol.

Here the line moved down First Street, around the Supreme Court Building, then down "A" Street, going away from the Capitol. We knew that the front of the line was moving in the opposite direction on East Capitol Street, one block to our right. When we crossed intersections we could see that line, but we had no way of knowing how many blocks we would have to walk before we reversed our direction. There were even jokes about where our particular line might really be going.

As it turned out, we had to continue to Thirteenth Street, going, appropriately enough, around Lincoln Park. The pace of the crowd was fairly brisk at times—we saw one man stumble and hurt himself.

The temperature was now going down into the thirties and neared the freezing point before we reached the Capitol at 7:00 A.M. In Lincoln Park and at intersections, the open space gave the wind greater force and caused the crowd, at times fifteen or so persons wide, to huddle even more closely together.

Especially when the line halted for periods of ten or more minutes, "cheaters" from behind would walk along the outside of the line and try to push into advanced positions. At times, a loud protest greeted such tactics.

"This is neither the time nor the place for pushing ahead," said one policeman sternly and repeatedly as he moved past the line. Towards the end of the procession, ropes along the streetside of the crowd helped to maintain order.

Long pauses gave you plenty of time to note the bright half moon, the steely stars, the overhead trees with their last few withered leaves. From time to time, trucks stopped nearby to deliver bundles of newspapers to stores, and vendors passed by selling cigarettes and coffee.

Transistor radios brought heartening news that several persons at a time were now passing through the rotunda. Various radio stations signed off with *The Star-Spangled Banner*. A few hours later, the same music recurred on stations which were beginning their broadcast day.

As the cold, slow minutes wore on, the crowd grew increasingly silent. During long delays, some would sit on curbs or lean sleepily against fences. Young children, holding a parental hand, or perched on their fathers' backs, bore up with military patience.

At intersections there were sudden bursts of energy as people tried to run across the street before policemen interposed their authority again. At one crossing, about 4:00 A.M., the sole policeman seemed to despair of keeping the intersection clear. He boarded a bus and rode off as its solitary passenger.

Occasionally a flashing police car sped by, or the siren of an ambulance broke the frigid silence. Near us, a teenage girl from Winchester, Virginia, fainted away. Like Civil War General Philip Henry Sheridan, she was indeed "up from Winchester at the break of day."

The crowd, of course, was as diverse as could be. It seemed timely to remember Edmund Burke's remark that public calamity is a mighty leveler. The young and the old were there, the wealthy and the poor, whites and Negroes, civilians and servicemen. Groups of servicemen had been passing us on the street for some time when a person in the crowd shouted to a soldier in our midst, "Servicemen are permitted to go directly to the Capitol." "That's all right," he answered, "I'll wait in line."

About 6:00 A.M., we reached the Supreme Court Building again. A few lights went on in the Folger Shakespeare Library across the street. "Cheer up," a passerby announced in a friendly voice. "You're in the homestretch. You've only an hour to go." He was just about right.

Behind us, the eastern sky began to brighten slowly. The gleaming white of the Capitol stood out vividly against the western dark. Television crewmen began to take their places again on its steps. We watched with quiet envy as policemen entered "emergency units" to get a cup of steaming coffee.

It was exactly 7:00 in the morning as we passed banks of flowers and filed by the casket in the rotunda, the warm rotunda. The scene was just as incredible as it had been on television. In little more than a minute, we were leaving the Capitol on its opposite side. There wasn't much to say. But neither of us regretted having stood all night in the cold to see a single coffin for a single minute beneath the Stars and Stripes.

17. Thanksdoing Day, the Romans Would Have Called It

The Baltimore Evening Sun: November 23, 1978

I HAVE a friend who sends Thanksgiving cards instead of Christmas cards. Each year around this time, he thinks back over the past year, picks out the people who have been especially good to him and mails them a thank-you note.

He does his thinking and then he does his thanking. In so doing, he relives the fact that in our language the word "thank" comes from the word "think." Experience verifies that the thankful person is the thoughtful person.

Experience also verifies that from the moment of conception we are all on the receiving end of countless gifts. Gratitude, then, should be as natural as breathing; ingratitude should strike us as a monstrosity. Hence the point of an old saying: Gratitude is the least of the virtues; the lack of it is the worst of the vices.

Actually, saying "I thank you" is so natural that in our language we have worn down the three word phrase to two words: "Thank you." We drop out the "I"—as though the generosity of our benefactor has shriveled up our own egotism, for the moment at least.

Often we express our gratitude by a single word: "Thanks." In this case, we reduce the message to its core. Notice, though, we use the plural noun, "thanks." We don't merely give a thank; we give thanks.

The plural suggests abundance, as though in imitation of the abundance we have received. "Thanks" as a plural also suggests that we keep on expressing gratitude, especially to the most generous persons in our lives.

The ancient Romans didn't "give" thanks. They "did" their thanks—*Gratias agimus.* They would have called our American holiday Thanksdoing Day.

There is good psychology here. Genuine emotions tend to embody themselves in practical deeds. Gratitude is contagious, too, making givers out of receivers. When a stranger holds open a door for you, don't you find yourself inclined to do the same for the person behind you?

Although atheists and agnostics are certainly capable of deep gratitude for the gifts of life, there is something primevally religious about this whole business of gratitude. One of the most notable rituals of Christianity, the Eucharist, derives its name from the Greek word for thanksgiving. On the Thursday of the Last Supper, even in the face of death, Jesus is described as "having given thanks." Even today, when Greeks say thanks, they say *eucharisto*, though they now pronounce it "ef-har-east-TOE."

Generally religious, too, is the saying of grace before meals. (Charles Lamb charmingly expanded this notion to include grace before Shakespeare.) This word "grace" harks back to the *gratias* which the Romans did when they did their thanking. Connected with gracious, grateful, and gratis, *gratia* meant a favor, something pleasing done to you for which you showed yourself pleasantly thankful in return.

Faced with a good meal, especially when surrounded by loved ones, we can be grateful that life brings us delightful things as well as sad and painful ones. We can also be grateful that the gifts we receive help us to help those in need.

Whether we are religious or not, Thanksgiving is most filling and fulfilling when it becomes Thanksdoing. And for that, we are happily not restricted to the last Thursday in November.

Nor is our gratitude necessarily restricted to the delightful things. Recalling a difficult time in his life, U.N. Secretary General Dag Hammarskjöld wrote: "Cry. Cry if you must. But do not complain. The path chose you. And in the end, you shall say thank you."

18. Despair and Hope: A Christmas Collage

The Baltimore Evening Sun: December 24, 1975

OVERSEAS: Catholics fighting Protestants; Muslims fighting Jews; Christians fighting Muslims. At home: whites fighting blacks; Indians fighting whites; you name it.

"Peace on earth, goodwill to men"? Or, "Bah! Humbug!"?

• You are flying south to address a youth convention. The woman sitting next to you is a retired teacher. "After all your years as a teacher, what would you say to these young people?"

"Tell them: there are times when the bravest and most important thing a human being can do is to put one foot in front of the other."

• A family sits wordlessly at the dinner table. Finally the teenaged daughter throws down her spoon: "How can you all go on as though nothing has happened?" The rest of the family stares, but the mother speaks, a mother who has just buried her son. "Dear child, we don't go on as though nothing has happened. We just go on."

• The words of a wise man haunt you: "Nothing dies but something's born." For him, this is an absolute law of the human spirit. Go ahead—feel the pain of loss; let it shudder through you. Then you will be free to see what compensating gift is trying to give itself. Was Marcel Proust on to this secret when he wrote: "We are healed of a suffering only by experiencing it to the full"?

• But are we healed alone? A psychiatrist finally confesses to his depressed patient: "I feel hopeless about helping you. I have tried everything, but I see I am getting nowhere."

Suddenly the patient starts to improve. For months all the world had seemed hopeful—except his guilty, hopeless self.

Now he is no longer alone, but begins to accept his despair as a human experience that need not be permanent, that need not alienate a person from the human race. We are all kin in our woundedness.

• The poet Rainer Maria Rilke wrestled with his demons and survived to write: "Those ancient myths about dragons which at the last minute turn into princesses, perhaps they are saying something true. Perhaps all the dragons of our lives are princesses who are only waiting to see us once beautiful and brave. Perhaps everything terrible is, in its deepest being, something helpless that needs help from us."

What if crime and hatred and prejudice and violence are not really powerful demons, but helpless things that are only waiting?

• The Christmas story urges its welcome warning: you can never be sure when hope will be born, or where. My task for hope is the work at hand. A courageous Anglican bishop had blunt enough advice for even our local confusions: "Do the next right thing. We generally know what that is, even when the big picture is obscure."

That hillside cave in Bethlehem: It could have seemed a dead end. Who could have guessed that so many would find it a tunnel?

19. A Feast for the Bent-out-of-Shape

The Baltimore Evening Sun: December 24, 1976

I MET her about a year ago. She was a retired nurse, now in her eighties. Since Christmas was near, she began reminiscing about the ghosts of Christmases past.

She recalled the year when she was working at a home for crippled children. By some oversight, nobody went out to buy a tree for the children until late on Christmas Eve. By then, only a few scrawny, misshapen ones were left.

Embarrassed, the nurses decorated the woebegone tree as best they could. Morning came and the children were led into the room with the tree and the gifts. The adults waited nervously while the youngsters surveyed the scene.

Finally, one youngster spoke up: "That tree's just right. It's all crooked, just like us."

Surely, one of the most winning aspects of the Christmas story, indeed of the Christ story, is that it is all twisted—just like us and our thwarted, distorted lives: an expectant woman making her way on dark and dangerous roads; no room in the inn; an animal manger for a cradle; a king, jealous and murderous; life in an obscure town and in an occupied nation; a group of rag-tag disciples who miss the point, quarrel, betray, deny, desert; a shameful, contorted death; burial in another man's grave.

And yet: "Even now, in sordid particulars, the eternal design may appear." Perhaps T. S. Eliot, who knew well enough of life's contortions, would permit his words to be amended: "Especially now, in sordid particulars . . ." Love and loyalty and courage and every such beauty all shine most luminously, most revealingly in the grimmest settings. ("Glory be to the darkness for what it has taught me about the light.")

Part of that eternal design urges the aptness of forgiveness. No one ever argued for that aptness more aptly than W. H. Auden: "Love your crooked neighbor with your crooked heart." Our hearts are not necessarily crooked in the criminal sense; but they are battered and bruised and wrenched — or likely to become so without much warning. They need compassion, even from themselves, for themselves.

The twist of being human weaves the human comedy into the human tragedy. Last Christmastide, I visited a mental hospital with a kindly, elderly woman. She saw a patient sitting in a wheelchair with a can of beer on his knee. She thought he was taking contributions, so she took a quarter from her purse and dropped it into his beer. "You didn't have to do that!" the startled man said with a smile, half thankful, half forgiving.

All the wonderful, crazy, sorrowful strands of humanness are woven into the story of Christ, "a man like us who liked us," a man who took people as they were before he tried to show them what they were and could become.

He would, I'm sure, have appreciated my ten-year-old nephew Jimmy, who attends a parochial school. When I asked him what he liked best about religion, he thought a minute and then answered: "It comes just before lunch."

Christ's kind of religion comes right before lunch, during lunch, just after supper, in the messy midst of life and death, of failures and fresh starts. "The critical moment," said the same Eliot, "is always now, and here."

Through the convulsed ages of nearly a score of centuries, men and women have seen or sensed in the person of the Child of Bethlehem this conviction of the poet John W. Lynch: "God's way with men has been to take men's way/And that's the glory and the scandal both." For, in Christ, the divine revealed itself:

> With all our old simplicities unmarred,
> With no rejection of the flesh we bear,
> The hearts we love with, and the pain we know.
> He slept our sleep, and with us dreamed our dreams.

20. Christmas Joy is Joy Despite

The Baltimore Evening Sun: December 24, 1981

"In the midst of the wasteland, Joyce found life, and life abundantly. That inheritance may well be the distinctive vocation of the modern novelist: to locate, in the heart of a terrible and potentially suicidal century, causes for rejoicing." Critic Frank McConnell, on James Joyce's upcoming centenary, February 2, 1982.

THE FIRST official comment on the meaning of Christmas mentions joy, that most pursued, most elusive of experiences. "I bring you tidings of great joy." Thus the angel of Christmas night.

Months earlier there had been a foreshadowing, or better, a forebrightening of this meaning. When the expectant Mary visited the expectant mother of John the Baptist, the unborn latter "jumped for joy."

Faithfully, Christmas carols have echoed this meaning. Handel tumbled down the scale deliriously backwards as he proclaimed: "Joy to the world, the Lord is come." Gentlemen (and ladies, too, surely) are entitled to rest merry because of these tidings of comfort and joy, comfort and joy.

When the deaf Beethoven was searching for a climactic way to crown his titanic Ninth Symphony, he chose to orchestrate the words of Friedrich von Schiller's "Ode to Joy." The resulting marriage of words and music is undoubtedly one of the supreme artistic expressions of *Freude,* that beautiful God-spark, heaven's own daughter.

At the heart of that "Ode," as set to music, we are told repeatedly: *Alle Menschen werden Brüder wo dein sanfter Flügel weilt*—"All men become brothers where your gentle wing reposes."

The angel of Christmas imparted a similar universality to the joy he announced when he said that joy "shall be to all the people." Such joy is not the same thing as pleasure, its most popular fake. Nor need it be annulled by pain, not even by tragedy. (Life, says a modern novelist, is a tragedy filled with joy.)

An instance of these truths occurred some months ago in a room on the eighth floor of Baltimore's University Hospital. Twelve-year-old Francis is the one with leukemia, but he's not the one in bed. Francis is visiting his ten-year-old brother, Michael, lying there worried in the bed by the door. Michael had been acting strangely for the past year—ever since his older brother's leukemia had been diagnosed. Michael had even been seeing a psychiatrist.

Finally, the doctors discovered the truth. He had a brain tumor.

So the surgeons performed the delicate surgery, and Michael's head became a turban of bandages. But the surgery paralyzed his swallowing reflex, so a tracheotomy was next. A tube projected from Michael's throat.

In the meantime, Francis had been mysteriously stricken with a high fever. Was it the result of a recent spinal tap? In any case, he had to be hospitalized for tests. He was put in the room with Michael. The parents shared the vigil between the two beds.

Francis grew delirious and began to moan. The sound of this fraternal distress filtered through Michael's bandages. Since Michael couldn't speak, he pointed to the corner of the room. What did he want? The wheelchair? He nodded his head, yes. Perhaps he wanted to be taken away from the sound of his brother, or maybe he just needed a change of position.

So they lifted Michael into the wheelchair.

"Do you want to move out into the hall?"

He shook his head, no.

"Where then?"

He pointed to his brother's bed. Puzzled, they wheeled him to the side of Francis.

That's when Michael, head all bound and tube jutting from his neck, reached out from his self-centering sufferings, and sitting there long and wordlessly, held his older brother's hand.

In the midst of pain, or perhaps with pain as the needed foil, one young boy gave a jolt of joy to those who saw and those who heard and possibly to him who felt a brother's hand.

Yes, men become brothers where the wings of joy repose. But isn't the reality more powerful the other way round? Do not the wings of joy beat most ecstatically where men become brothers by becoming brotherly?

Thank you, Michael. Your truth is stronger and more joy-giving than any novelist's fiction.

Note (1987): Michael told his older brother he was not afraid to die, so he would smooth the way by dying first. He succumbed on Monday, February 1, 1982 in Westernport, Maryland. Francis died on Friday of that week. Joseph, a healthy two-year-old brother, now bears their brave names between his first and his last.

21. The Point of the Poinsettia

The Baltimore Sun: December 24, 1986

IT WAS the day after Thanksgiving, quite a few years ago now. Wearing my black suit and clerical collar, I walked into a Baltimore drug store and found it fairly drooping with Christmas decorations. A man who was probably the manager caught sight of me and said with an apologetic smile: "We certainly make a mess of your friend's birthday!"

It took me some seconds to figure out what this stranger meant. To this day, I annually recall that touching remark.

For all its typically human messiness, Christmas does celebrate the birth of Jesus. In despair, many a person has asked: "Why was I ever born?" In the Gospels, Jesus speaks twice of why he was born: "I have come that men may have life," and "The Son of Man has come to give his life." To give life and to give his life: a twofold project, intriguingly interwoven.

Probably because of the poinsettia, red and green seem to have taken over as the Christmas colors. They aptly symbolize the program of Jesus. Red is the color of blood; green is the color of life. (The words "grass," "grow" and "green" are from the same ancient word root, and bespeak vitality. Our word "bless" comes from our word "blood.")

The point: it is through the literal or metaphorical shedding of blood in loving sacrifice (by one human being) that vitality is produced, assured, enhanced (for another). The prize is life. The price is blood. Remarkably, in the Christ story, Jesus is not only the Good Shepherd who feeds his flock in green pastures. He is also the Lamb of God who stands as though slain.

The power of the Christ story and its universal, persistent appeal surely relate to a fact of life that wise human beings everywhere have discovered and variously formulated: (your and my) human potential is growingly green to the extent that

it has been nourished by (someone else's) red blood of generous self-giving. (Watch parents watch children on Christmas
morn.)

When things go spectacularly wrong in our blessed country,
the deepest explanations are usually moral or spiritual. Speaking of the current Iran-contra scandal, one commentator saw
behind it "an American social phenomenon: an obstinate
indifference to anything except immediate issues and immediate results, and a conviction that any problem can be fixed: that
there is nothing that money, or guns, cannot buy."

The Christ story is not about such self-centered immediacies.
Nor is the human project. Viktor E. Frankl, concentration-camp
survivor and author of the classic *Man's Search for Meaning,*
wrote these pertinent words: "To be human is always to be directed toward and pointing toward something or someone
other than oneself—toward a meaning to be fulfilled, another
human being to be encountered, a cause to be served, a person
to be loved.

"Only to the extent that someone is living out this self-transcendence is he truly human or does she become her true self.
One becomes a true self not by concerning oneself with self-
actualization, but by forgetting oneself, overlooking oneself
and focusing outward.

"What is called self-actualization is, and must remain, the
unintended effect of self-transcendence. It is ruinous and self-
defeating to make it the target of intention. And what is true of
self-actualization also holds for identity and happiness. It is the
very 'pursuit of happiness' that obviates happiness."

I am at my greenest best, then, when forgivingly and self-
forgivingly I strive to be my most generous red for somebody
or something else. And so, on this holyday, may God rest us
merry—by helping us see that, for all its messiness, Christmas
celebrates the birthday of a friend of humankind . . . and a
friend of that self-transcendence that gives rest to the hectic
heart in the evergreen pastures of true joy, true peace, true
happiness.

22. *Cantique de No Oil:* Carol for a Season of Shortages

This 1973 Oil Embargo acrostic remains timely, I feel, because—as Mother Teresa says—there are many ways to be poor . . . just as there are many ways to be rich.

L et nothing you dismay, abundant friend,
Y elp though headlines may of shortages,
I nclement months ahead and rationing—
N ever did a crisis lacks its grace:
G ood folks grow more warm by sharing warmth.

I nheritors of music, books, and brains
N ow we're spurred to travel more within,

A nd take more heedful trips to where we are.

M ay these startling luxuries be yours:
A mple wassails of water, banquets of bread,
N oticed feast of breathed-in air, of friends,
G ratitude for gratitude itself,
E cstasies of painlessness, and clues from
R egal treasures nesting in our straw.

23. The Song You Sing on New Year's Eve

The Baltimore Evening Sun: December 31, 1980

> Should auld acquaintance be forgot
> And never brought to mind?
> Should auld acquaintance be forgot,
> And days of auld lang syne?
>
> For auld lang syne, my dear,
> For auld lang syne,
> We'll take a cup of kindness yet,
> For auld lang syne.

OLD acquaintance shouldn't be forgot, nor should the story of that most favored of New Year's songs. The song, of course, is "Auld Lang Syne," which was an antique Scottish way of saying Old Long Since, *i.e.* Old Long Ago.

When Robert Burns was born in the Scotland of 1759, there already existed two collections of Scots songs that included an "Auld Lang Syne." The older volume (1711) began its version this way:

> Should old Acquaintance be forgot
> And never thought upon,
> The Flames of Love extinguished,
> And freely past and gone?

The younger collection (1724) began thus:

> Should auld acquaintance be forgot
> Tho' they return with scars?
> These are the noble hero's lot,
> Obtained in glorious wars.

By the time Bobbie Burns was twenty-nine, he himself was busily engaged in collecting old Scottish songs for James Johnson's multivolumed *Scots Musical Museum.* On December 7 of that year (1788) he wrote to a friend and praised the "exceedingly expressive" phrase "auld lang syne." He included a five-verse poem, with chorus, which used that phrase repeatedly. "Light be the turf," he added, "on the breast of the heaven-inspired Poet who composed this glorious fragment." Was he playfully referring to himself?

Nearly five years later, with some slight changes, he sent the same song to editor Johnson with this remark: "The following song, the old song of the olden times, which has never been in print, nor even in manuscript, until I took it down from an old man's singing, is enough to recommend any air." Burns admitted that the melody that he sent along with the words was but mediocre.

Burns had already warned his readers about "the best-laid schemes o' mice and men," and he himself died at thirty-seven, several months before the *Museum* volume containing "Auld Lang Syne" was published. Sadder still, his last child was born on the day of his burial in 1796.

Burns had also been helping George Thomson with his work, *Select Collection of Original Scottish Airs.* When the 1799 volume of this collection appeared, it contained Burns's version of "Auld Lang Syne" basically as it had appeared three years earlier in the *Museum.* But the words were now accompanied for the first time in print with the melody now commonly used.

This traditional melody itself first appeared in print in 1759 (the year of Burns's birth) in a volume entitled *Reels,* by Robert Bremner. William Shield later used this melody in the overture to his opera *Rosina,* which premiered in London in 1783. Remarkably, that same melody (which closely resembled "Comin' Through the Rye") was used to accompany another song in that 1796 volume of *Museum,* which first printed Burns's version of "Auld Lang Syne," at that time set to another tune!

Burns never claimed to have written the words, but modern scholarship inclines to suspect that the words are almost certainly his, though the chorus and probably the first stanza predate the ploughboy poet who was a contemporary of Mozart and lived almost as briefly. So Bobbie should be remembered whenever people around the globe lock arms, and sway, and sing the most famous song of Britain's greatest lyricist and one of history's supreme love poets—though he probably never heard his song sung as the world now sings it.

Part Two

Around the World

24. The Vietnam Memorial: The Graffiti of Grief

The Baltimore Sunday Sun: January 13, 1983

EN YEARS ago today the agreement for a cease-fire and the withdrawal of American troops from Vietnam was initialed in Paris by Henry A. Kissinger for the United States and by Le Duc Tho for North Vietnam. Thus the longest war in American history limped toward its exhausted end.

Now a Vietnam Veterans Memorial has been finally and freshly dedicated in our nation's capital. It stands in Constitution Gardens between the Washington Monument and the Lincoln Memorial, though closer to the latter.

Across the nearby Potomac at Arlington National Cemetery, there are thousands of graves with names on their white markers. But at the heart of that cemetery lie some nameless graves at the Tomb of the Unknown Soldier. Washington's West Potomac Park will now have at its heart this giant black marker with its graveless names.

Even tracking down the site is a symbolic venture. Depending on your approach, it can be obvious, or it can be hard to find, out of sight, almost underground—as was the war and its meaning for many at home in America, and for many of its soldiers "over there." The same has been true of the war's glory, both during it and since.

There's an appropriate ambiguity also in the multiple V shape of the monument. Horizontally two walls of polished black India granite meet at an angle of approximately 125 degrees. Each wall is 264 feet, 8 inches long, so that both the wall and its adjacent pathway describe a great V when they are viewed above, from the north. Viewed from the south, east or west, however, the wall makes an inverted V on the vertical.

That V nags at the mind: Vietnam . . . Veterans . . . Victims . . . Villages . . . Violence . . . Vengeance . . . Vanity . . . Victories . . . Vanquished . . . the V sign that symbolized peace.

The meaning of Vietnam was hard to find and is still so. Hard to find, too, is the name of any specific victim honored by this Wailing Wall. The 57,939 grit-blasted names are not listed alphabetically but in sequence of death. This arrangement means that many a soldier's name is surrounded by the names of buddies who died at the same time, in the same place. You wonder: Is there any other monument in the world with so many human names inscribed? Would the war have ended sooner if these names had been carved on a monument, one by mournful one, as the deaths were actually occurring?

(*Life* magazine did that, in a sense, in its edition of the week of June 23, 1969. It devoted eleven pages to photographs of all the Americans who died in Vietnam during the previous week.)

But even thus arranged, the names on the monument do not flow in one unbroken direction. They begin in the middle óf the monument, where the panels are more than 10 feet high and carry 137 lines of names—5 to a line, as on all 140 panels. The names then progress to the right—or east—in the direction of the Washington Monument. The casualties on this wall date from July 1959 to May 1968. (The 70 panels on each wall gradually decrease in height as they move from the center. The outermost ones are about an inch high.)

To continue chronologically the viewer must walk to the far west end of the monument—toward the Lincoln Memorial—then continue back toward the center, where the names at the bottom of the tallest left panel date from the Mayaguez incident of May 15, 1975. Thus it happens that the earliest and the latest deaths are listed on the two highest panels, which are side by side. The "circle" is closed and the dying done for those who fell in Southeast Asia.

There are directories on hand that list the dead alphabetically and give their dates of birth and death, their hometown, and the panel and line on which each name appears. The bottom of each panel tells you the number of the panel, but each number is used twice—once for the east wall panels and once for the west. Panels 1E and 1W are side by side, but 70E is farthest from 70W. On the margins of the larger panels every tenth line bears a mark to help you count down to a sought-after line.

Every name is accompanied by a diamond-shaped mark if his or her death has been confirmed. Those 1,300 or so who are still missing are marked with a cross. If a death is later confirmed, a diamond mark will be superimposed. Should a missing person turn up alive, a circle will be engraved around the cross. So it may turn out that a living person's name is among the dead and will eventually be designated as living.

Among the names, I found my own full name, a young man from my father's native Philadelphia. Was he an unknown kin? In any case, he stands for all the servicemen who ever died in my name.

More surely I sought and found the name of Joseph F. Keeney, a youngster from a troubled home whom I grew close to when I was chaplain at the Children's Village run by the Baltimore Archdiocese. When he became too old to remain at the village, he lived in my charge elsewhere the summer before he went to Boys Town in Nebraska. He sent me his picture from Vietnam, where he was killed on the eve of his twenty-second birthday. I conducted his funeral and presided at his burial in Baltimore's National Cemetery. Little did Joe imagine that someday his name would be carved in stone between two of the nation's most famous monuments. The price was dear.

Like so many visitors, I felt the need to touch the name of a loved one, to personalize these graffiti of grief. How Joe used to delight in the fact that his initials were JFK! But this cascade of names is too much. Did this name next to Joe's name belong to a black or a white? Was he a husband, a father, a fiancé, or just a sweetheart? Were most of the lost in their twenties?

And what of the South Vietnamese, whom we were officially befriending? If they were to build a similar monument to their dead, it would have to be at least ten times the size of the American one.

The words of General William Sherman stir in the memory: "I am sick and tired of war. Its glory is all moonshine. It is only those who have never fired a shot nor heard the shrieks and groans of the wounded who cry aloud for blood, more vengeance, more desolation. War is hell."

What an apt coincidence that, out of the 1,421 entries submitted, the design chosen for this memorial to one particular hell came from a student in her twenties with an Oriental name. Maya Ying Lin is a native of Athens, Ohio. Sophocles was a citizen of the original Athens, and some of its most magnificent monuments were built during his ninety years of life in the golden fifth century B.C.

But his words have turned out to be monuments more lasting than stone. He put words into the mouth of Electra that might well have graced our newest national monument. This was that ancient Electra to whom mourning was becoming, as it becomes all who visit the memorial, this vertical Reflecting Pool of national tears: "How," she asked, "when the dead are in question, can it ever be honorable to forget?"

Upon our honor may we never forget these youthful dead nor the bitter lessons we required them to teach us. For, as a poet said of another wall of sadness, in Jerusalem: "There are men with hearts of stone, and stones with the hearts of men."

25. *My* Vietnam Problems

The Baltimore Catholic Review: September 23, 1966

As movies, books and TV dramas increasingly reexamine the Vietnam War, U.S. veterans gain more of the understanding and help they deserve. The anti-war movement requires empathetic remembrance too. Mid-way through that longest of U.S. wars, this swan song editorial summarized many of the aspects of that conflict which were troubling a growing number of patriotic American citizens, though ninety-percent of U.S. fatalities had not yet occurred.

IN ONE way or another, every American is "bothered" about Vietnam. For what they're worth, I'd like to list some of the things that are bothering me.

I do so with Pope Paul's latest encyclical ringing in my ears. In particular, I hear phrases like: "disastrous calamity threatening the human family . . . the greatest possible tragedy . . . monstrous catastrophe . . . before it is too late . . .strive with every means available to prevent the further spread of the conflagration . . . with piercing cry and with tears . . . We cry to them in God's name to stop."

Some of my Vietnam problems stem from basic philosophical, ethical and theological beliefs. I put absolute trust in no mere man: whether he is in the White House, in the Pentagon, in Congress, or anywhere else. My concept of "original sin" means that every person making decisions in our government is liable to mistaken judgments, weakness of the will, blinding passions, unconscious motivations.

I do not put absolute trust in "experts." The experts predicted that Red China would not enter the Korean War if our troops invaded North Korea. The Chinese did enter, at a terrible cost in lives. When a truce came, we ended up where we were before we invaded the North.

President Kennedy came to rue the trust he placed in "experts" before the invasion of Cuba. He said the Cuban fiasco might have been prevented if a leading American newspaper had printed what it knew about the approaching invasion.

Time and again, U.S. experts in South Vietnam have been surprised by various political upheavals in that piteous country. At times, nonexpert newsmen got closer to the truth than the experts did. (It is fatally easy to hear what you want to hear, and to say what you think your superiors want to hear.)

I believe in the corrupting influence of power. America is the richest and most militarily powerful nation in the world. History shows that extraordinary physical power exerts irrational influences on those who possess it. General Eisenhower's farewell words as president were a famous warning against the perilous influence of the military-industrial complex on our national policy. National defense is big business. Military men are trained to think like military men and to see problems chiefly in military terms.

Politicians, too, have as a major temptation the desire to stay in power. They are often in a position to control knowledge of the facts, to create overpowering propaganda, and even to come to believe their own propaganda.

I believe that blind nationalism, my-country-right-or-wrong-ism, is immoral and un-Christian. My Christian loyalties are more sacred than my national loyalties. My duties to the whole human family are higher than my duties to one geographical family. They are certainly higher than my loyalties to the relatively few fallible human beings who happen to be making the decisions within a given political administration.

Although I love my country, am grateful to it, admire its many heroes on the battlefield and off, and sympathize with the monumental problems of its leaders, I am not convinced that the America of 1966 is God's pure sword of righteousness summoned to save a sinful, non-American world. This America is a nation growingly plagued with moral and spiritual problems.

It is a nation in which five little children were bombed in church, where youngsters on their way to school are beaten by racists, where millions of citizens live unnoticed on the edge of destitution. We are the only nation that ever dropped atom bombs on noncombatant civilians.

Now, all of these considerations do not in themselves determine my personal views on the Vietnam dilemma. As a matter of fact, I happen to believe that the basic administration intention is to defend the majority of the South Vietnamese from a takeover by minority internal forces or by oppressive external forces. I believe that this intention is honorable and defensible—even though it could be factually in error.

What bothers me particularly in this September of 1966 are some of the military means the U.S. government has been adopting, and more important, some of the steps it may take in the future; for example, further intensification of the destructive aspects of the war through bombings or through an invasion of North Vietnam.

At this crucial juncture in history, I'm bothered by the massive lack of world support for the drift of American policy. The Declaration of Independence was written out of "a Decent Respect to the Opinions of Mankind." Yet even the friendly president of the Philippines could say last week that the United States is not winning the minds and hearts of Asia. (Why not?) He claims we do not sufficiently understand the Asian mind and the Asian's need "not to lose face." (What does this say about the way we ask Hanoi for negotiations?)

I am disturbed when U.N. Secretary General U Thant, an Asian and a spokesman for mankind, can say of Vietnam: "I see nothing but danger in the idea . . . that the conflict is a kind of holy war between two powerful political ideologies. The survival of the people of Vietnam must be seen as the real issue." If the Vietnam struggle were truly and clearly a "holy war," would Pope Paul be speaking the way he has?

I am disturbed when a former adviser and speechwriter for Presidents Kennedy and Johnson can say of this administration: "We are buried in statements and speeches about negotiations and peace, the defense of freedom and the dangers of communism . . . Much of it is important and sincere and well-meaning. Some is intended to deceive. Some is deliberate lie and distortion." Thus spoke Richard N. Goodwin, who added, "The bombing of North Vietnam has been a failure and may turn out to be a disaster."

In last Sunday's *New York Times*, another adviser to the two presidents, Arthur Schlesinger, Jr., made a similar, disturbing evaluation of our policy of escalation. Like many another, he laments the fact that the Vietnamese war is becoming more and more an American war against Asians, instead of a war between Asians, with limited American involvement.

Reread the various statements and predictions made by administration spokesmen as they tried to explain each new escalation of the war. It is a sorry record. Each time, they justify "one more step" to lessen American casualties. Then they announce a harsher step because the previous one didn't work. And more Americans die—not to mention others.

Is it better for 10,000 escalated Americans to die in an intensified war than for 1,000 unescalated Americans to die in a severely limited war?

Read too what U.S. napalm (explosive jellied gasoline) is doing: "It burns people to death in the most excruciating way . . . burns through the skin, eats away the tissue, muscle and bone." (And an Ecumenical Council of the Church once condemned the crossbow as inhuman!) How many Vietnamese civilians are being turned by their saviors into "blackened, screaming shards"?

North Vietnam is the size of Georgia. We have been bombing it almost daily for two years. Presently, we drop on it more tonnage per month than we did on all of Europe and Africa at the peak of World War II, more than on the enemy at the peak of the Korean War. Yet General Westmoreland recently admitted: "There is no indication that the resolve of the leadership in Hanoi has been reduced." Haven't we proved that military escalation isn't the answer?

Our escalation is often justified as ultimately an indirect fight against Red China. I'm not convinced of this argument. The Vietnamese are ancient enemies of China. Vietnamese communists are not necessarily going to be pro-Chinese, any more than Russian communists or North Korean communists are. Of course, there are ways of forcing the Red Chinese (and the Russians) into the war. (How would we Americans feel, for instance, if Chinese planes violated our borders, as the United States admits its planes might recently have done to China?)

I think Pope Paul's encyclical calls for the United States to de-escalate the war, perhaps in terms of U Thant's repeated plea: end the bombing of the north, begin to limit military action on both sides, see that all interested parties in Vietnam are represented at negotiations. I believe the Holy Father is expecting American Catholics to let their government realize that they will support decisions against escalation of the war.

The Vicar of Christ affirms that "A settlement should be reached now, even at the expense of some inconvenience or loss." American Catholics should be willing to support some lesser inconvenience, some lesser loss on America's part, rather than risk even greater slaughter and greater loss in the future.

Perhaps we will be asked to risk only some loss of face, some loss of impatience and righteousness, some loss of absolute goals and absolute rhetoric. It will be a small price to pay in the name of humanity, and in the name of those many, many Americans who are otherwise likely to die.

26. Grief or God's Peace? Saint-Gaudens' Adams Memorial

The New York Times: December 1, 1985

". . . the most beautiful thing ever fashioned by the hand of man on this continent." Alexander Woollcott

ACENTURY ago today, across the square from the White House, a Washington celebrity died by her own hand, and a masterpiece of sculpture found its occasion. The forty-two-year-old suicide was Marian Hooper Adams, who thirteen years earlier had married Henry Brooks Adams. His grandfather and great-grandfather had been occupants of the famous house across from his residence at 1607 H Street.

Though Henry and "Clover" were natives of Boston, they had first met in England just after the Civil War. Adams was serving in London as private secretary for his father, Charles, whom Lincoln had appointed minister to England in 1861.

Depressed by the death of her own father, the childless Marian Adams swallowed potassium cyanide while Henry was paying an emergency Sunday visit to his dentist. She was one of the first U.S. women to take a serious interest in photography, and the chemical was available in her dark room. Washington papers like *The Post*, *The Evening Star*, and *The Critic* first reported her death as due merely to paralysis of the heart, but the truth soon leaked out.

The capital was stunned. Mrs. Adams was widely regarded as the leading Washington hostess of her day. Her salon on Lafayette Square was *the* place to be invited. Busy as a journalist, novelist, and historian, Henry was content to sit back at

94

parties and let his wife shine. Years earlier in Boston, William and Henry James had noted the intellectual grace of this witty and sharp-tongued woman whom Henry judged "a perfect Voltaire in petticoats."

Her death devastated her forty-seven-year-old husband, who never remarried. To create a memorial for her grave in Washington's Rock Creek Cemetery (near the 5000 block of North Capitol Street), Adams turned in 1888 to his Irish-born friend, Augustus Saint-Gaudens (1848–1907), who is generally reckoned the preeminent U.S. sculptor of the late nineteenth century. Other noteworthy works of his are the standing Lincoln in Lincoln Park, Chicago, and the mounted General William Sherman in New York City.

Working in his New York studio on West 36th Street, Saint-Gaudens had by early 1891 completed what many consider his masterpiece: a somewhat larger-than-life bronze statue of a draped and cowled figure seated on rock and leaning against a highly polished backdrop. The setting, which includes a semi-circular granite seat (an exedra) opposite the statue, was designed by another celebrated friend, Stanford White.

There is about the memorial an air of mystery, emphasized by the cowled face. To begin with, the memorial is hidden within a circle of shrubs and holly trees. But most remarkably, the memorial is wordless: no name, no date, no epitaph—not even the sculptor's identity. Thus there is no indication that Henry Adams himself is buried there (1918), apart from the two intersecting wreaths carved on the far side of the backdrop.

His classic autobiography, *The Education of Henry Adams*, was published shortly after his death and won a Pulitzer prize. Even though he originally wrote it for private circulation, he is so reticent about his wife and her desolating death that he talks about the statue without even mentioning whom it memorializes. "The interest of the figure was not in its meaning," he writes, "but in the response of the observer."

That assertion can be disputed, but the reactions and questions of viewers are undeniably intriguing: Is the figure modeled on Marian Adams? (No.) Is the figure female or male? (It is deliberately indeterminate.) Are the eyes open or shut or half open? What is its message: grief? despair? brave dignity? noble resignation? numbness? serene contemplation?

Adams had very definite ideas about what he wanted the statue to represent, but not at first. The year after his wife's death, while still mulling over the matter of a monument, Adams paid an extended visit to Japan in the company of another artist friend, John LaFarge. They spent long hours studying Buddhist statues, especially at the Shrine of Nikko north of Tokyo. (There is a Japanese proverb: "Do not use the word magnificent until you have seen Nikko.")

Gazing at the great Buddha of Kamakura and at Kikko's Goddess of Compassion (Kwannon, shrouded in flowing drapery), Adams grew convinced that art should pursue beauty the way that the Buddha sought Nirvana—by letting the self be absorbed into the universal and the infinite, by anonymity, by the extinction of the ego and its ceaseless spasms. In Sanskrit, Nirvana means "blown out." It bespeaks the serenity that comes when the flame of compulsive self-seeking has been extinguished.

Back in the United States, Adams began to speak and write of his "Buddha statue." He gave it a motto from the medieval poet Petrarch: *Eterna vita e veder Dio*—eternal life consists in seeing God, in timeless contemplation of the ultimate. That's why he could state in a letter of 1896: "The whole meaning and feeling of the figure is in its universality and anonymity. My own name for it is 'The Peace of God.' LaFarge would call it Kwannon."

Though churchless, Adams was an ardent admirer of high medieval Christianity and its cathedrals, and he saw a parallel between the Goddess of Compassion Kwannon and the Virgin Mary. After his death, a prayer he had composed in 1901 to the Virgin of Chartres was found in his wallet. He had long preferred the Virgin to the Dynamo, that deity of technology. "All the steam in the world," he wrote, "could not, like the Virgin, build Chartres."

To help Saint-Gaudens in his work, Adams sent him photos of various Buddhas, asking the artist to fuse in the statue the art and thought of both East and West. In his own notes the sculptor wrote: "Buddha. Mental repose. Calm reflection in contrast with violence of nature." Wanting the whole effect to be universal and architecturally sexless, Adams instructed Stanford White that the setting should have "nothing to say." White, however, resisted and was permitted a small classical cornice above the backdrop.

For all his words about peace and surrender, Henry Adams remained a grieving man, and the message of the statue remained for him personally only an ideal and a hope. This was the man who said: "I have always expected the worst, but it was always worse than I expected." He also said: "I lack nothing but what I want. I have no complaints except the universe."

So perhaps the popular name for the statue, "Grief," is not entirely off the mark. The memorial is wordless—do not the Buddhists say, "Those who know do not say; those who say do not know"? But during the first year of Marian Adam's life (1844), Elizabeth Barrett Browning published a sonnet entitled "Grief." Written after the death by drowning of the poet's brother Edward, the poem begins: "I tell you, hopeless grief is passionless." The final words, especially, seem to match the statue marvelously:

> ". . . Deep-hearted man, express
> Grief for thy dead in silence like to death—
> Most like a monumental statue set
> In everlasting watch and moveless woe
> Till itself crumble to the dust beneath.
> Touch it! the marble eyelids are not wet:
> If it could weep, it could arise and go."

27. Circling the States, Name-wise

The Baltimore Evening Sun: August 22, 1972

WITH THEIR long and repeated rollcalls, the political conventions in Miami are once again making household names out of the nation's fifty States. There is a hidden wealth of history and poetry packed into these names.

For instance: Spain, France, and England were the three chief colonizers of what is now the United States. That fact resonates in the Spanish names of California, Colorado, Florida, Montana, and Nevada; in the French names of Louisiana, Maine, and Vermont; and in the English or by-way-of English names of Georgia, Maryland, New Hampshire, New Jersey, New York, the Carolinas, Pennsylvania, Virginia, West Virginia, and Washington.

It is to the American Indians, however, that about half the States fittingly owe their names. Indiana, for its part, goes back through the Latin, Greek, Persian, and Sanskrit to refer to the Indus River, which gave its name to that India toward which the first European settlers of the New World were journeying, and whose inhabitants they thought the American natives were.

To round out the picture: the Greeks gave us the Rhode of Rhode Island, the Aztecs the Mexico of New Mexico, the Marquesan Polynesians gave us Hawaii, and the Aleut Eskimos gave us Alaska.

More colorful is the meaning of all these names. Specific people are memorialized in these States: Delaware of the East, named after Thomas West, the English baron with the French name De La Warr. He was Virginia's first governor. Though the Delaware Bay and eventually the State were named after him, he had no significant personal connection with either. Georgia honors England's King George II; Louisiana, France's Louis XIV; Maryland, England's Henrietta Maria, French-born daughter of a king, mother of kings and wife of England's King Charles I.

This Charles, bisected by decapitation, scored the only double by having both North and South Carolina named after him. He and Henrietta are also the only husband-and-wife team preserved in State names, while she is the only woman to have provided her personal name to a State—and it's the only State that's called a land.

Charles's younger son, Duke of York and future James II of England, had New York named for him. Like his father, he lost his throne—but kept his head. Sir William Penn was ordered by Charles II to honor his father with Pennsylvania and its woods. England's unmarried Queen Elizabeth had her official virginal state honored by Virginia (and eventually West Virginia). Only later did Virginia become a personal name, as in Virginia Dare. Washington became the only State to honor an American, though the area was first named after another George—his enemy, George III! It's the only personal State name not belonging to a king, queen, duke, baron, or sir.

New Mexico alone honors a divinity, the Aztec god Mexitli, though some scholars think Mexico means "at the heart of the moonlake." (Be warned: some of these name explanations are controversial.) Florida provides the only other religious connotation by recalling the Easter "Flower Feast" being celebrated at discovery time by Ponce de Leon and his crew.

Some State names honor groups of people: Texas may come from an Indian word for friends, as does Dakota. Alabama means thicket clearers; Arkansas, downstream people; Idaho, salmon eaters; Illinois, (true) men (or warriors); Kansas, south wind people; Missouri, canoe people; Oklahoma, red people; Utah, people who live higher up.

Other names honor specific places: New Hampshire recalls the county of Hampshire south of London; New Jersey, the English Channel island of Jersey; New Mexico, old Mexico; New York, the city of York in England's Yorkshire; Rhode Island, the Mediterranean island of Rhodes, famous for its Colossus and about the same size as the colony; Hawaii, recalling Kawaiki, the legendary "homeland" of the Polynesian people; and Tennessee, the ancient Cherokee capital whose meaning remains elusive.

Life-giving water is celebrated in a number of names: Arizona, place of little springs—though the springs in question ended up in Mexico; Connecticut, beside the long tidal river; Michigan, great water (or clearing); Minnesota, clear (or cloudy!) water; Mississippi, big river; Nebraska, flat water; Ohio, beautiful (river); Wisconsin, gathering of waters. Oregon, curiously, may come from the French word for hurricane, *ouragan*; unless, even more curiously, it is a corruption of the French word for Wisconsin (the river). There are aquatic implications too in Arkansas' downstream people and Missouri's canoe people.

Land and its variations appear in Massachusetts, near the great hill; Utah, higher-uppers; Montana, mountainous; and Vermont, green mountain. At opposite ends, Alaska and Maine both mean mainland (as opposed to islands) and are the only two States whose names mean the same thing (unless Oregon means Wisconsin). Kentucky means meadowland; Wyoming, at the big plains; Iowa, beautiful land—unless it means dusty faces, or sleep people (good at hypnosis). Penn's woods have already been mentioned.

The aforementioned Florida and the rose of "Rhode" Island give us our only flower references, and Kansas' south wind people our only wind reference. Nevada's "snowy" provides the only precipitation (along with an implied mountain). If Idaho doesn't mean salmon eaters, it may furnish us with our sole solar link by meaning something like sunup. Colorado (reddish) is the only color word as such and serves up another implied water reference. Oklahoma's red people and Vermont's green mountain round out the only other colorations.

It is noteworthy that the north, south and west appear in State names, but not the east. Also, there are four News but no Olds. (At naming time there wasn't even an Old Virginie to be carried back to.) Neither is there any certain reference to birds or animals. If Idahoans are truly salmon eaters, that would give us our solitary food reference, unless Alabamans are not really thicket clearers, but vegetable gatherers.

While Hawaii is our only real island State, real islands are recalled in two non-islands: Rhode Island and New Jersey (which do however include some islands). California, another non-island, is named after an imaginary island depicted in a popular sixteenth century Spanish novel by Ordonez de Montalvo. In his *Las Sergas de Esplandian*, California is described as the world's most rugged island, abounding in gold and ruled by a Queen Calafia. It is peopled by a swarthy, robust, passionate race of women living manless like the Amazons. No comment—except to say that only the Golden State has an entirely fictional name.

But, of course, all names are ultimately fictional or made up. As we've seen in this swift survey, the mostly nameless, faceless people who composed the rollcall of the fifty States did a laudable job of suggesting the fabulous opulence of American geography and history. May their names be blessed.

28. A Cloak of Mystery at a Mexican Shrine

The Baltimore Evening Sun: January 31, 1979

NOT LONG ago, a mysterious piece of cloth captured the attention of the newly resuscitated *Life* magazine. This was the Holy Shroud of Turin, lately on rare public exhibit. Many believe that this was the very shroud in which Jesus was wrapped after his crucifixion.

Another mysterious cloth and its enchanting story won retelling by novelist John Steinbeck in his latter years. Pope John Paul II's visit to the Shrine of Our Lady of Guadalupe a few days ago focused world attention on this same second cloth of mystery.

Measuring sixty-six by forty-one inches, the cloth is a mantle woven from the fibers of the cactus plant. On it appears the colorful and delicate image of a young woman four feet, eight inches tall.

Cloth of this kind usually lasts about twenty years. Yet there is no reasonable doubt that this cloth is more than four centuries old, as are the still-vivid colors—the golds, the green-blues, the rose—which decorate it. The vigor of the color is all the more remarkable in view of the fact that for 116 years countless thousands of smoky candles burned before it without the glass protection it now enjoys.

The story of this mantle goes back to December 9, 1531, a decade after Cortes conquered Mexico City. A fifty-seven-year-old Aztec Indian, recently converted to Christianity and given the Christian name of Juan Diego (John James), was passing a 130-foot hill twelve miles northwest of Mexico City. Hearing strange music, he climbed the hill and saw there a woman radiant and lovely.

Speaking in his native tongue, she identified herself as the mother of Jesus. "I wish and intensely desire that in this place a sanctuary be erected. Here I will demonstrate, I will exhibit, I will give all my love, my compassion, my help and my protection to the people. I am your merciful mother . . . and the mother of all mankind . . . You must go to the house of the bishop and tell him I sent you."

Returning later that day, Juan saw the woman again, and told her the bishop did not believe him. "I ask you, my son, to go again to the bishop."

Juan returned to the bishop the next day and found him more deeply impressed. But the bishop said he still needed some sign that the vision was genuine. The Indian conveyed this message to the woman when he saw her at sunset that second day. "Tomorrow . . . I will give you the sign which will reassure him."

But an uncle of his grew ill the next day and Juan dared not leave him. The illness became so severe that early on the following morning (December 12), Juan hastened past the hill to summon a priest. To avoid being delayed by the lady, he took the path on the opposite side of the hill. To his chagrin, the lady headed him off. Hearing his excuse for missing their appointment, she asserted that his uncle would recover. "Why be afraid? Are you not in the folds of my mantle? In the crossing of my arms?"

She instructed Juan to gather some of the flowers which, to his astonishment, he found blooming on this cold and barren hill. "This is the sign you are to take to the bishop." When he finally gained admittance to the bishop, he opened the white mantle in which he carried the various Castilian roses. As these cascaded to the floor, the image of the gracious lady was found imprinted on the cloth.

The bishop believed, a little chapel was built on the hill, and two weeks later, in a procession that included Cortes himself, the mantle was taken to its first shrine. In 1709, a basilica was dedicated at the foot of the hill; John Kennedy, while president, visited it. At that time the mantle was exhibited over the high altar, as it is now in the still newer basilica recently dedicated.

In 1921, when the mantle was on view near the altar railing, a bomb hidden in a box of flowers exploded near it, shattered windows throughout the church but did not damage the cloak.

At the time of Juan Diego, millions of Mexicans were swiftly converted by the mantle and its story. In our day, five million pilgrims gaze upon it yearly. The full-length figure is crowned with a brown face of touching innocence. Some experts find this face to be Middle Eastern rather than Indian.

The symbols on the cloak clearly told the Mexican Indians that the mother of Jesus, though herself a reverential servant of God, was greater than the sun, the moon, and stars that they once worshipped, sometimes with human sacrifices.

Why is she called Our Lady of Guadalupe? In 1531, there was a well-known shrine to the Madonna in Guadalupe, Spain. The bishop with whom Juan Diego dealt came from Spain and may have misunderstood the Aztec words used by him. Some students of the story believe these words meant, "I will crush the stone serpent" once venerated by the Mexicans.

In any case, the charm of the story and the loveliness of the image have, through the intervening years, managed to touch many a stony heart, to intrigue many a skeptical mind.

29. Grenada: The Invasion of Paradise

The Baltimore Evening Sun: October 26, 1983

ESTERDAY, United States forces invaded Grenada after a coup that resulted in the violent death of the only head of state I almost interviewed (for *The Baltimore Evening Sun*, I had hoped). He was Maurice Bishop, the youthful revolutionary prime minister of that tiny Caribbean island. His wife is a Catholic, and though she was separated from him at that time, she headed the island's tourist bureau.

I was a tourist there in 1981, and my influential host at Ross's Point Inn persuaded her to seek an interview for me. The prime minister's office was a five-minute walk away, in a white, oblong, hilltop building that had once been a hotel. Alas, the time for my visit expired before arrangements could be worked out.

Grenada is the smallest independent nation in the Western Hemisphere. It is also the first English-speaking nation in the world to adopt a Marxist-Socialist government. As an island, Grenada measures 12 by 21 miles and lies about 100 miles north of Venezuela. (Technically, it is the southernmost of the Windward Islands of the Lesser Antilles.) As a nation that gained its independence from Great Britain in 1974, it consists of the main island and a scattering of even smaller nearby islands called the Grenadines.

Columbus sighted the main island on his third voyage (1498) and named it Concepcion. Apparently he never went ashore. That was an irony, for he was searching for spice islands, and here was the only Caribbean island where spices grow naturally. Often called "The Spice Island of the West," this tropical paradise produces nutmeg, cocoa, mace, cloves, allspice, cinnamon, and ginger.

The island soon acquired the name Grenada, possibly because its hilly terrain reminded Spanish sailors of Granada (home of the Alhambra) in their native land. The modern spelling is probably due to French influence, dating from a century of French control. Finally, from 1783 until 1974, Grenada was under British control.

Although it maintains an association with England and still has a governor-general, during the first five years of its independence the island of 100,000 people was under the rather despotic and quixotic sway of the native black prime minister, Sir Eric Gairy.

Four years ago this past March 13, while Gairy was in New York, a small group of revolutionaries under Maurice Bishop seized the country. Bishop, a native son and a London-trained lawyer, promised free elections—which, however, never took place. According to an interview in a 1981 *National Geographic*, Bishop tried to get economic assistance from the United States, but was rebuffed with a maximum offer of $5,000.

So he turned to Cuba and remained closely allied with Fidel Castro until last week. One of the first sights that greeted me at the Grenada airport in 1981 was a poster in Spanish depicting a Russian and a Cuban cosmonaut. At that time, soldiers in the charming capital city of St. George's could be seen carrying Russian-made machine guns. For more than a year, Cuban soldiers had been busily building a giant airport in the south of the island. (No one tried to stop me when I took photos of it under construction.) Rumors told of a Russian nuclear submarine base being built on a nearby island.

The native population is about 50 percent black and 40 percent mixed, and predominantly Roman Catholic. In the past, race relations have been ideal. I found little evidence of religious repression. Caribbean radicals, even Marxist ones, tend to be quite religious. One Marxist rally I heard of began with a reading from the Book of Psalms.

Though once populated by the fierce Carib Indians, Grenada was generally free from violence until the last decade, when Eric Gairy and his "mongoose squad" terrorized his opponents. (I saw one sign in which "Gairy is the best" had been altered to "Gairy is the pest.") Rupert Bishop, the father of the slain prime minister, was killed by Gairy's men and has been revered as a martyr.

In June 1980, a bomb presumably meant for Maurice Bishop killed several bystanders. Later that year, there were five more murders, probably political in origin, though four were said to have been cases of mistaken identity—tourists, mistaken for terrorists. Since the island's only radio station and newspaper are controlled by the People's Revolutionary Government, it is hard to be sure about the true nature of these episodes.

These developments and Bishop's anti-American rhetoric frightened away many Yankee tourists, and others as well. In recent years the lovely beaches have been quite sparsely occupied and a Holiday Inn closed down after a suspicious fire. ("Without the Americans we die," one disconsolate waiter told me.) Cruise ships come less frequently to St. George's, said to be the most picturesque harbor town in the Caribbean. Deep and ubiquitous potholes provide an instant comment on the sad shape of the economy.

Now, U.S. military forces have landed on the island, supposedly out of concern for the one thousand or so Americans living there, largely medical students at an American-run school. Under normal circumstances, no tourists or resident foreigners would have anything to fear from the gentle and amicable natives.

But affairs are now quite uncertain in this captivating island, which is justly called the Caribbean in miniature, and where Haiti's slave-born emperor, Henri Christophe, came into the world, as did Jennifer Hosten, Miss World of 1970. Two years ago I was told that the island was so troubled that many natives would have preferred the return of the repressive Gairy. It remains to be seen what the future will hold for an island where peace has become a stranger in paradise.

30. A Baltimorean Visits *Baile-tig-mor*

The Baltimore Evening Sun: April 11, 1980

I T WAS the first day of spring, midway between St. Patrick's Day and Maryland Day, and an apt time for a Baltimorean of Irish ancestry to visit the other, older Baltimore. It's a small fishing and boating village facing the Atlantic on the southwest coast of Ireland. Visible from some distance away, the Baltimore beacon rises in the form of a whitewashed, missile-shaped tower crowning a hill that marks the entrance to Baltimore Harbour, spelled with a "u."

Located in County Cork, Ireland's largest, this village of perhaps three hundred souls just misses being the southernmost point of the Irish mainland. That honor belongs to the cliffs of Mizen Head, at the tip of another peninsula some twenty miles to the west. The famous Fastnet Rock, however, is *the* southernmost bit of Ireland and it juts out of the ocean about fifteen miles below Baltimore.

Survivors of the recent Fastnet Yacht Race disaster (the yachts were caught in a sudden, furious storm) were brought to Baltimore and lodged in the cozy Baltimore Hotel house at the edge of Baltimore Harbour and Baltimore Bay. There I myself found a friendly staff, an ample bar, a blazing fire, four dogs, and two cats.

Like the American city, Irish Baltimore lies on a river, the Ilen. Like Maryland's this Baltimore is "protected"—Sherkin Island flanks it from a mile off. (Seven miles farther off, Cape Clear Island is the home of Irishmen who still speak the ancient Gaelic tongue.)

Also like the Yankee Baltimore, this village suffered a famous attack from the sea. That was in 1632, when pirates from two Algerian ships massacred a number of the inhabitants and carried away the rest to Africa as slaves. Maryland's

Lord Baltimore, whose estate was in central Ireland, may well have heard of this raid, which antedated by two years the founding of the first and only Catholic colony.

In any case, there is a ballad called "The Sack of Baltimore," written by the Irish poet, Thomas Davis. Its concluding lines are these:

> The yell of 'Allah' breaks above
> The prayer and shriek and roar—
> O blessed God! the Algerine
> Is Lord of Baltimore.

This African connection is rather forgivingly preserved in the Algiers Inn, one of the four pubs brightening this lonely, hilly town.

No genial landmark perpetuates the memory of another sacking endured by Baltimore nearly a century earlier. At that time (1537), the town was ruled by Fineen O'Driscoll, himself celebrated as a sea rover in another ballad by R. W. Joyce.

O'Driscoll at first befriended four Portuguese wine ships that fell into distress as they headed for Waterford. But after he had tasted the wine the sailors offered in gratitude, O'Driscoll decided to seize it all and enslave the Portuguese. The outraged merchants of Waterford thereupon attacked and pillaged the town, and left O'Driscoll's castle in still-visible ruins.

This castle presumably gave Baltimore its name, which seems to mean, in Gaelic, "The Town of the Big House" (*Baile-tig-mor*). The town had an even earlier, more romantic name, "The Fortress of the Jewels" (*Dun na Sead*). I couldn't discover why.

In the War of 1812, the British called the Yankee Baltimore "A nest of pirates." The Irish Baltimore had a similar reputation, and it was by way of weakening the power of the piratical O'Driscoll clan that Englishmen were eventually planted in the town.

These, alas, were the ones who suffered most from the Algerian incursion. Mrs. Hazel O'Kell, the English woman who owns the Hotel Baltimore, believes that was the last time Great Britain was ever invaded.

As I understand it, scholars are still not sure why that other Englishman, George Calvert, chose the name Baltimore for his lordship. His Irish holdings certainly did not include this small

Atlantic port. But the last article I read on the subject claimed that an English lord in those days was free to call himself after any place name he chose.

So maybe there is more than an accidental verbal link between the two Baltimores after all. I surely wanted to think so after I puffingly climbed the wind-whipped hill on which the Baltimore beacon stands and gazed at sunset across the wide Atlantic toward the Baltimore Harbor spelled without the "u," which has always spelled home to me.

31. The Various Wales of Dylan Thomas

The Baltimore Sunday Sun: November 6, 1977

THE BUS driver taking our group of five from Oxford westward to Wales seemed genuinely puzzled. "Why would you want to go to Swansea?"

"Well, we're students of poetry, and that's the birthplace of Dylan Thomas."

"Oh," he replied, "that's the chap your President Carter wants to see buried in Westminster Abbey, isn't it? I hear he was a bit of a bastard. And Swansea isn't the loveliest part of Wales."

And it wasn't. That we learned five hours later, after driving through the hill country of the legendary Cotswolds, reaching Chepstow ("Welcome to Wales") and stopping awhile at the capital city: smoky, industrial Cardiff. By night, however, we could understand why the wide and wheeling beach of the port of Swansea had reminded earlier visitors of the Bay of Naples.

Dylan Marlais Thomas had a rare first name that means sea. From his 1914 Swansea birthplace at 5 Cwndonkin Drive, he could look downhill to where the Atlantic Ocean is called Bristol Channel. Nearby is the Cwndonkin Park, which he celebrated in his writings and where a plaque now quotes him: "Time held me green and dying/Though I sang in my chains like the sea." Thomas spent the first half of his brief life in this Rome of Wales, built on seven hills.

After a late supper at the Bay View Restaurant and some sleep in the Sea Haven Hotel on Oystermouth Road—there was no doubt we were near water!—we headed westward again the next morning. An hour by train brought us to Carmarthen, the supposed birthplace of King Arthur's Merlin, alias Marthen. There's an old tree in town with a sign that warns: "When Merlin's tree shall tumble down/Then shall fall Carmarthen town."

A few miles away was the farm of Thomas's aunt, Annie Jones, the farm now immortalized in what is probably his most famous poem, "Fern Hill." The place is actually called Fernhill, but the poet invoked poetic license to spell it his own way. A final forty-five minutes by bus from Carmarthen put us in Laugharne (pronounced, roughly, "larn"). This was another Wales altogether.

Dylan said he loved small towns by the sea, and small Welsh towns by the sea best of all. Though he had his negative moments about everything, Laugharne was apparently his best of the best, for he spent his last years here and now lies buried in the cemetery of its old Norman church. His Aunt Annie was once a resident of Laugharne. He first lived here himself from 1938 to 1940, then from 1949 until his fatal trip to America in 1953.

On one trip he had left Laugharne to visit—among other U.S. cities—Baltimore, where he read at Johns Hopkins University on March 4, 1952. Now, a quarter of a century later, a grateful Baltimorean and Hopkins alumnus was repaying the visit.

As Thomas saw it, "this timeless, mild, beguiling island of a town" was known for "its seven public-houses, one chapel in action, the church, one factory, two billiard tables, one St. Bernard (without brandy), one policeman, three rivers and a visiting sea." Apparently it wasn't always mild, for the poet's latest biographer, Paul Ferris, says that when there was street fighting or a Saturday night brawl, the family who operated the town generators would throw the switches and plunge Laugharne into darkness. In any case, natives still tell you which pubs and other local sites were in the poet's mind when he composed his "play for voices," "Under Milk Wood."

In a house on stilts overlooking an estuary with green hills behind, Dylan lived with his wife Caitlin and their three children, Llewelyn, Aeron, and Colm. The last was born in Laugharne. I visited this so-called Boat House, now kept as a museum by an educational trust. It was purchased from his widow in 1974, though during the poet's lifetime the Thomases rented it from his most consistent benefactor, a Mrs. Margaret

Taylor. Here he was bedeviled by poor health, back income taxes and other endless debts, too much drinking, an understandably jealous wife, self doubts, and paralysis of the pen.

Farther up the hill, on a path that has been renamed Dylan's Walk, I peered through a window into the one-room shack to which the poet escaped to wrestle with his muse. It had been a bicycle shed before it became his workshop.

Somewhat romantically, a sign over the locked door reads: "In this building Dylan Thomas wrote many of his famous works, seeking inspiration from the panoramic view of the estuary." Actually, the poems written in Laugharne were only six: "Over Sir John's Hill," "In the White Giant's Thigh," "Lament," "Do Not Go Gentle into that Good Night," "Prologue" and "Poem on his Birthday." An earlier (1944) birthday poem, "Poem in October" was "a Laugharne poem: the first place poem I've written," though the pudgy poet with the melodious baritone didn't write it there.

A muscle-testing walk brought me to Dylan's grave alongside the eleventh century Norman church of St. Martin near the opposite edge of town. Reflecting the poverty of his family at the time of his burial twenty-four years ago this month, a plain wooden cross marks the spot in a cemetery that features mostly stone markers. His widow once sought to have his body removed to the garden of the boathouse; though provisional approval was obtained, the project was not pursued.

Doubting my way en route to the cemetery, I had questioned a friendly Welshman, who added the further information that an Irishman is a Welshman who could swim. All the Welsh we met were friendly, verifying the words we found on a greeting card: "Hail Guest, we know not who thou art. If Friend, we greet thee, hand and heart. If Stranger, such no longer be. If Foe, our love will conquer thee." "Welsh" means "stranger," and they seem to know how to treat one.

We found Laugharne still quite unspoiled and the poet keenly alive in many personal memories of the townspeople. One close friend of Dylan named Dai Thomas (no kin) recalled how he was setting off firecrackers outside the poet's mother's house in Laugharne on Guy Fawkes Day (November 5) when the telegram came from America summoning Thomas's wife to his death bed in St. Vincent's Hospital in New York City (1953).

The poet died there four days later of pneumonia, complicated by alcoholism and (possibly) by improper drug injections by a private physician. This tragedy climaxed a devastating year for the poet's mother, Florence. Her husband, "D.J." had died on December 16; her only other grown child, Nancy, on April 16.

The day we left Laugharne we attended services at the church near his grave. By poetic coincidence, the Epistle selection read that day contained the words "death shall have no dominion." Dylan used these words as the title of the first poem of his to be published in a literary magazine.

On the sanctuary floor, I noticed a tombstone with this hauntingly beautiful inscription: *Sors tua mortalis est: non mortale quod optas*—"Your lot is mortal, but not what you long for."

Everything was conspiring to be memorable for our journey to the grave of Dylan and to his "timeless, beautiful, barmy town," where he "just came one day, for the day, and never left, got off the bus and forgot to get on again."

We had to get on again, but we were already dreaming of a return visit. And we weren't so sure anymore that after his turbulent and tormented life, Dylan's bones would rest more willingly anywhere else. Not even at Westminster Abbey.

Postscript: The Poet at Hopkins

Dylan Thomas came to Baltimore a quarter of a century ago this year on invitation from a fellow poet, Elliott Coleman, who from 1946 until 1975 headed the Creative Writing Seminars at Johns Hopkins University. Learning that Thomas was planning a U.S. tour, Professor Coleman communicated with Thomas's agent, John Malcolm Brinnin, and arranged for a reading.

Interviewed recently about the event, the retired teacher eagerly recalled that rainy March 4, 1952, when the Welsh poet knocked at his office door on the Homewood campus. Thomas had come from Washington, where, two days earlier, Coleman had first met him and his fiery wife, Caitlin, at a Georgetown reception given by the head of the National Gallery of Art.

"He was short and plumpish. She was also short, but slight, with pale face, golden freckles, and golden hair. During the reception, husband and wife had one of their famous squabbles. As I left, I reminded Thomas that I would be expecting him in Baltimore. I said to Caitlin, 'I hope you can come too.' 'Why should I?' she retorted.

"When he came alone into my office, he was quite sick, and asked if I could get him a certain medicine. I phoned my doctor, Walter Buck, who ordered it through the Greenway Pharmacy. We walked over there to pick it up, and in the process, I was able to persuade him to have a coke instead of a beer.

"We walked around for about an hour in the drizzle, with Thomas telling me he always suffered from a nervous stomach before his readings. He said that during forty years of teaching, his father never entered a classroom without the same sick sensation.

"It was getting near 4 P.M., and time to go to Remsen Hall. This was the chemistry building, but it housed the largest auditorium on campus. Even so, we had to set up a loudspeaker in another room. Glancing in a mirror on his way, Thomas blurted out, 'O God, I am old!'

"It was about at this point that he jolted me by saying, 'I'm not going to read my own poetry. I hate it so.' I pleaded with him, knowing that the large crowd had come mainly to hear his own works.

"I suggested a compromise—'Why don't you read the other poems first, and then go into some of your own?' He didn't say he would, so after I gave him the brief introduction he didn't need, I sat down right in front of him, looking up, hoping he would see the pleading in my eyes.

"And sure enough, after some Yeats and Auden, he began to recite his own poems. As he did, he seemed to come into his own and to shake off his sickness. He was at his best and gave an awfully good reading. I've never heard better. He got a great applause from the audience."

(*The Baltimore Sun* reported that Thomas insisted from the start, "This isn't a lecture;" and begged, "you won't ask questions, will you?" Noting that he had to read a lot of poems he didn't like before finding poems he did like, he observed that the function of poetry is "to make your toes twinkle." The article concluded: "Having finished, he did not expose himself to the possibility of questions. He fled.")

One of Coleman's students that year was Rose Burgunder, who later met novelist William Styron at a Hopkins lecture and eventually married him. Her mother, Mrs. B. Bernei Burgunder, gave a dinner for Thomas that evening in her Lawina Road home. In his fellow poet's view, Thomas proved himself a "delightful" guest on that occasion, despite his reputation for boisterous behavior.

As for the poetry of the visit, the seventy-one-year-old professor emeritus summed it up this way: "It was one of the most memorable readings we ever had at the seminars." His own vivid recollections allowed no doubt of that.

32. A Summer in Jubilee England

The Baltimore Evening Sun: September 8, 1977

EIGHT chilly summer weeks in England during Queen Elizabeth's silver anniversary. Amid an avalanche of impressions, what stands out?

The fact that the Thames, "liquid history," was once a tributary of the Rhine; that greater London measures more than 600 square miles; that its metropolitan population of twelve million comprises about one-fourth of the population of Great Britain.

This capital city features statues of Washington, Lincoln and FDR, and has a Carter lane. [For Baltimoreans there are streets named Lexington, Calvert, Guilford, Monument, Lombard, Park, York, and Pimlico.]

For lovers of quaint place-names, London provides Rotten Row, Spital Square, Houndsditch, Threadneedle Street, Turn Again Lane, and the churches of All-Hallows-by-the-Tower and St. Vedast-Alias-Foster. (Oxford has its Quaking Bridge; Cambridge its St. Bene't Street, and there's the town of Bury St. Edmunds.)

At London's Cora Park, adults are not admitted unless accompanied by a youngster . . . in Westminster Abbey the poet Ben Jonson is buried standing up . . . in the financial district of this city of the House of Lords, the inscription over the Royal Exchange quotes the Bible: "The Earth is the Lord's and the fullness thereof" . . . in the sexy Soho district a shop sign reads: Ready to Wear Clothes (in this weather, not a moment too soon) . . . at the British Museum you can see a Latin letter from Reformer John Calvin that signs off, *vere tuus*, literally "yours truly."

London's underground is the world's oldest and largest. At some stations there are three levels of escalators; the one at

Archway Station has 100 steps. Ads are all over the "tubes," *e.g.*, "*The Times* has an eye for a lie and a tooth for the truth."

The Doughty Street home of Charles Dickens, the novelist of London, exhibits an 1842 letter from Baltimore in which the author complains of the aggressiveness of his American admirers.

One of the saddest sights in England is six words at the end of an 1820 letter exhibited in the London home where the poet John Keats lived before heading for Rome and his imminent death at age twenty-five. He is concluding his last letter to the mother of his former fiancée. Below his signature he suddenly addresses his lost love: "Good bye Fanny! God bless you."

The front pages of newspapers give you the daily "lighting up" time for your headlights . . . the boot, bonnet, and wings of a car are its trunk, hood, and fenders . . . take away means carryout; give way means yield: way out means not chic but exit . . . left luggage is checked luggage . . . people who have been shot or otherwise externally injured are said to be "ill" . . . never bring red and white flowers to a sick person— they are a bad omen (blood on sheets? The War of the Roses?) . . . if you give a knife as a gift, give some money too, to emphasize your friendly intentions.

England, the size of New York state, is full of memorial plaques, often quite wordy. But in the London church where poet John Milton is buried you can read: "Thomas Stagg, vestry clerk of this parish from the 8th day of March 1731 to the 19th day of Feb. 1772, on which day he died in the 76th year of his age. That is all."

(An English boy is said to have asked his father about the names on a church plaque. "They are the parishioners who died in the service." "Which one, the 10:30 or the 12:15?")

The British are fond of naming their homes, and painting or carving the names over their front doors. One doctor calls his place Bedsyde Manor . . . wall scrawls proclaim, "Legalise Cannabis" . . . in an exhibition at Cambridge's Fitzwilliam Museum, a seventeenth century artist is described by a contemporary as "a very friendly good-natured man as could be, but shiftless to the world, and dyed not rich."

Also in Cambridge, these signs happen to stand side by side: Lion's Yard and Short Stay . . . at the Oxford headquarters of the Rhodes scholarships, a Greek inscription near the entrance warns: Let No Smoke-Bearing Person Enter . . . every year on his birthday, a new quill pen is placed in the hand of Shakespeare's bust above his grave . . . an anonymous donor gave 174 rose bushes to honor Winston Churchill's churchyard grave . . . for nostalgic Americans there are numerous Esso (not Exxon) service stations.

After several days of rain and clouds, there was a sudden brightening of the skies. "Don't be alarmed," said our tour guide, "that is probably just the sun."

In Cambridge, I stood gazing at a rough-hewn, unpretty statue of Talos, legendary man of bronze. He looked like a rudimentary Frankenstein-type monster. An elderly lady, passing by, declared dryly: "That's another idea of ours."

A young American girl asked an Oxford taxi driver what the temperature was. He said he knew only hot and cold. Her mother said, "Well, it wouldn't help us anyway; over here they give the temperature in centipedes."

One of England's most famous chain stores is Marks and Spencer. In London's Highgate Cemetery, Karl Marx and Herbert Spencer are buried just across from each other. Poet Christina Rossetti is buried there too, but Marx is the feature attraction. Looking for his grave, I met what I presumed was a caretaker. "Pardon me, sir . . ." "Down there," he pointed, before I finished my question. "And Christina Rossetti?" "I don't know about 'im, but the 'ead one, 'e's down there."

There's a church across the street from the site of Shakespeare's death. I wondered whether he might have attended that church, so I asked a teenager who seemed connected with the place: "Could you tell me how far back this church goes?"

"Only to that wall, sir."

33. A Yank at Oxford

The Baltimore Evening Sun: August 15, 1977

Oxford gray, oxford shoes, oxford shirts, the Oxford Movement, the Oxford English Dictionary, the Oxford University Press: you've heard of Oxford all your life and now, here you are, spending two months of the summer of 1977 teaching at one of the thirty-four colleges comprising "the university" with its 11,000 full-time students.

You come as a Marylander familiar with a namesake Oxford on your own Eastern Shore. You come as a Baltimorean eager to visit Trinity College where the first two Lords Baltimore studied—the father, before Shakespeare's death; the son, just after it. Visiting central Oxford's hospital, you do a double take as you see wards with names like Osler, Halsted, and Blalock—people you always linked with Baltimore's Johns Hopkins Hospital.

But getting back to Shakespeare (a national pastime here), you can visit a room in the heart of Oxford where the Bard himself is said to have knit up the raveled sleeve of care on his way between London (sixty miles to the southeast) and Stratford (forty miles to the northwest).

Oxford shares the Thames with London; in fact, its name refers to a ford in that river where oxen could cross. All over town, on lampposts, bridges, and sweatshirts you can see the city emblem of an ox crossing water. The city's Latin motto, affirming that truth is strong, presumably means as strong as an ox.

Oxford's truth is remarkably strong—it has persisted as a centrally located city ("the golden heart of Britain") for more than a thousand years. It is mind-bogglingly rich and complex. For one thing, the heart of historic Oxford, including the university—which was never "founded" but just started to happen around A.D. 1170, after English students were expelled or recalled from Paris—is packed into an area not more than a half mile square. The official city has a population of only 120,000.

Visiting these ancient and famous colleges with their inevitable dining halls, chapels, libraries, dorms, and grassy quads, and seeing how they cast their shadows one on the other, you get the impression of some magical Merlin fixing a magnet here and summoning into a cluster these heights and depths and widths of genius, charm, and history.

Take the matter of architecture alone. Within the same block, often mixed within the same structure, you find examples of Saxon, Norman, Perpendicular, Tudor, Renaissance, Baroque, Victorian, and contemporary. As for pubs (there are more than 150), the Bear Inn claims to be 737 years old; one or two architecturally quaint others are more vague and merely assert an eleventh century birth.

Or take a brief walk down High Street. (Walks down any Oxford street tend to be brief; they like to change their names every two or three blocks.) Depending on your guidebook, this central street, known locally as "The High," is the loveliest avenue in the kingdom, or in Europe. In any case, you cross westward over the Cherwell River bridge and come to Magdalen ("Maudlin") College with its celebrated tower (currently bescaffolded and despired).

You are now within five minutes of Queen's College, New College (A.D. 1379!), All Souls, Merton (the oldest?), Oriel, Lincoln College (the birthplace of Methodism), and University College. From this last, the poet Percy Bysshe Shelley was expelled as an atheist, but welcomed back later as a gleaming white statue, drowned and nude.

You are also a few minutes from one of the world's most prestigious libraries, the Bodleian, and one of England's most famous churches, the official university church of St. Mary the Virgin. (You climb the 127 steps of its bell tower for one of the best views of Oxford and its horizon, green and golden.) There Archbishop Cranmer was condemned to death; there, John Wesley and Cardinal Newman preached.

Mention of the archbishop recalls a recent example of the way the centuries intertwine here at Oxford. On a summer's day, you shook hands with the 100th archbishop of Canterbury (retired) after feastday services at St. Mary Magdalene's

Church. In the sanctuary behind Archbishop Michael Ramsey was an ancient mural depicting the murder of his predecessor, Thomas à Becket, in A.D. 1170. Just outside the church door was the Martyrs Monument commemorating the death of another predecessor, Thomas Cranmer, in A.D. 1556.

Around the corner on Broad Street—"The Broad"—a flat cross in the middle of the road remembers where Cranmer, Latimer, and Ridley—Cambridge men, all—were burned at the stake. Incidentally, a town-gown clash in A.D. 1209 led some students and teachers to flee seventy miles northeast to Cambridge, where they stayed to start "the other" university.

Guidebooks skip across centuries like flipped pages as they cite other illustrious names linked with Oxford: Roger Bacon, Duns Scotus, Richard the Lion-Hearted (born here), Wolsey, Penn, Raleigh, Wren, Ruskin, Halley, Lewis Carroll, Tolkien, Gerard Manley Hopkins, T. S. Eliot, Graham Greene, Yeats, Santayana, C. S. Lewis.

You have no doubt that any time would be a good time to be in Oxford. But the weather news from scorching Baltimore makes Oxford's highs in the sixties especially enjoyable. (You are surprised to learn that you are north of Newfoundland.) And though the skies often suggest where the idea of Oxford gray came from, July and August are the sunniest months, with the almanac promising an average of 5.9 hours of shine per day.

It is also the summer of the Queen's silver jubilee. And though once-imperial Britain has her share of current problems, Oxford is an ideal reminder of a treasure about which England, the English-speaking world, and all modern civilization can be justifiably jubilant.

34. Poland the Field . . . of Battle

The Baltimore Evening Sun: June 1, 1979

POPE John Paul's visit to Poland, which begins tomorrow, will focus world attention on that buffer state that has been so tormented by history and yet has contributed so much to it.

This Poland, which has so often been a battlefield, derives its name from a Slavic word that means "field." By implication, Poland is a land of field dwellers, like the shepherds of Bethlehem.

Its name has well-known daughters: a polonaise is a Polish dance—Chopin made the world aware of that—but it is also a woman's dress. Though of Bohemian origin, the word polka probably meant a Polish woman before it meant a dance. (This word is no kin of "polka dots," which may well have come from poking dots.)

The world of chemistry honors the native land of Madame Curie (born Maria Sklodowska) in the radioactive element known as polonium (atomic number: 84). She herself was honored by Nobel prizes in 1903 and 1911; her daughter Irene won yet another prize in 1935.

Within Poland itself the most honored woman is Jewish—Our Lady of Czestochowa, at whose shrine town the pope will spend several days. She is the mother of Christ as revered in an ancient icon that has been venerated in the south-central city of Czestochowa since A.D. 1382. Actually, it is a painting on wood of the Madonna and Child. Their figures have turned black, perhaps from the smoke of myriad candles. There are three slashes on the Virgin's right cheek—a desecration dating from 1430.

Tradition attributes the painting to the Gospel writer St. Luke, and the wood itself to the Nazareth carpenter shop of St. Joseph, foster father of Jesus. The icon is said to have come to Constantinople by way of Jerusalem. Then, around 988, it was given to the wife of Vladimir of Kiev, whence it eventually passed into the hands of a Ukrainian prince named Ladislaus Opolszyk. It was he who brought it to Czestochowa, where he built a chapel for it and founded a monastery to guard it.

In 1656, after the monastery withstood a Swedish siege, Our Lady of Czestochowa was proclaimed Queen of Poland. This devotion is a supreme example of the intertwining of Polish Catholicism and nationalism.

Today more than a million pilgrims visit this "Lourdes" of Poland annually. A replica of the icon is featured in the National Shrine on the campus of the Catholic University in Washington, D.C. Modern critical research assigns the icon a ninth century Greek or Greek-Italian origin; but there is no doubt of its impact on Polish history.

Another Polish Nobel prize winner (1905) was that nation's most famous novelist, Henryk Sienkiewicz. The present pope made reference to him in his inaugural sermon when he recalled the legend of St. Peter's flight from Rome. The apostle met the risen Christ on that occasion and asked Him: *Quo Vadis?* ("Where are you going?") Sienkiewicz used these words for the title of his most celebrated novel, which has been translated into more than thirty languages. This 1896 masterpiece dramatizes the life of the early Christians in Rome under the Emperor Nero.

A story dating from about A.D. 200 tells how Peter, Rome's first bishop, was persuaded to flee from Rome as persecution brewed. Taking the Appian Way, he encountered Christ and asked Him where He was going. "To Rome, to be crucified again." A blushing Peter got the point and turned back to face his own martyrdom.

On the Appian Way even today you can find a *Domine, Quo Vadis?* chapel near the Ardentine caves where the Nazis killed 335 Italians in a reprisal execution.

Sienkiewicz, incidentally, lived near Los Angeles for about two years in the 1870s. His fierce anti-Russian sentiments made him and have kept him a hero of Polish nationalists. He died on November 15, 1916, while working for the Polish Red Cross in Switzerland. He is buried in the Cracow cathedral Pope John Paul will visit at the end of his trip. That is the cathedral John Paul exchanged last October for the Basilica that honors St. Peter's grave, the grave in which he was buried after his upside-down crucifixion.

35. At the Party: Israel Reaches Thirty

The Baltimore Evening Sun: June 1, 1978

A CARD in my hotel room advised: In Case of Air Raid Alarm, Go Straight to the Shelter. There was no alarm, but soldiers with M-16 rifles were plentifully in view, even in the hotel lobby. And no wonder. This was Jerusalem, the capital city of a nation celebrating its thirtieth birthday with terrorist attacks freshly in mind. At the end, *The Jerusalem Post* could sigh, "Israel Free of Terror Attempts," and cite a "giant security operation."

Our group of forty-three from the Baltimore area, including several survivors of Auschwitz, were staying at the Jerusalem Hilton, an apt name etymologically for a hill town hotel, twenty-four hundred feet above sea level. In the royal suite, two floors above my room, Egyptian and Israeli peace delegates had met earlier this year.

Looking north from my room, I could see the nearby Romema area where the Allenby Monument recalls that on December 9, 1917 "the Holy City was surrendered to the 60th London Division." Thus began thirty years of turbulent association with England—a link reflected by King George Street in the heart of Jerusalem.

Had I been able to look south I would have seen, at about the same distance, the two main sites of Israel's current celebration: Mt. Herzl, where the father of Zionism is buried; and the Hebrew University Stadium, the gift of a couple from Michigan. (Ubiquitous plaques reveal that this is a gifted nation in that special sense too.)

Our group was lucky enough to get tickets to both places and both events. There could hardly have been a more moving way for an outsider to see and feel what this ancient and astonishing land means to the Jewish people.

At sundown May 10, as the air grew chilly, the speaker of the Knesset, Israel's Congress, arrived at Mt. Herzl to preside at the conclusion of a day of remembrance for the nation's fallen defenders. That day had begun at 8 P.M. the night before with a long wail of sirens. I had been walking to the Old City and had just come into thrilling view of the illuminated Western Wall when all traffic halted and pedestrians stood in silence. This is a young nation built on a dream and out of unspeakable sufferings. Since its birth it has known war on the average of once every seven years.

Now, from a flame at the tomb of its first dreamer, Theodor Herzl, twelve torches were lit by children and grandchildren of various national heroes. While a chorus sang softly, each youngster spoke briefly in Hebrew. Finally, everyone sang what to me is one of the world's most haunting anthems, the majestic *Hatikvah* ("Hope"). Having just visited the city's Holocaust Memorial at Yad Vashem, I felt overwhelmingly the mystique of this tiny nation.

The next morning, with President Yitzak Shamir and Prime Minister Menachem Begin presiding, more than 2,000 soldiers paraded crisply in a score of units at the crowded stadium. The soldiers, men and women, seemed depressingly young but high spirited. Their features were strikingly various and confirmed the fact that the Israelis of today are a United Nations in themselves. One red-haired and freckle-skinned girl with a shy smile seemed straight from that other Holy Land, Ireland.

The weaponry aspect of the celebration seemed underplayed, though jets in formation flew by at the end, flawlessly forming a figure thirty. Mr. Begin, who from illness had cancelled two appearances on the previous day, spoke briefly here. Now he and the president were pelted with roses by a crowd so enthusiastic and pressing that the honor guard had to intervene. This the soldiers did with such finesse that the audience clapped.

A sour note was struck outside the stadium where a small group of American "Jews for Jesus" were trying to address the dispersing crowd. In the midst of some scuffling and pushing, a girl fell to the ground. A melancholy scene, laced with the irony of the Jewishness of Jesus. The best and the worst: that's what you get from religion.

A happier American note was the ecstatic response given to Leontyne Price that evening at an outdoor concert near the Jaffa Gate in Jerusalem. As this stately black woman sang Gershwin's "Summertime," the air seemed to grow warmer with hope—*hatikvah*. Someday soon the living would be easier, because—like the dove to the ark—*shalom* would return for good to this city of peace, this Jeru-shalom.

Here, in this most ancient and sacred of cities, people of all races, colors, and creeds would discover and reveal once again how goodly and pleasant a thing it is when brethren dwell at one.

36. Camp David and David's Camp . . . at Jerusalem

The Baltimore Evening Sun: September 6, 1978

As EGYPT'S President Anwar el Sadat and Israel's Premier Menachem Begin ascend Maryland's Catoctin Mountain to meet this week at Camp David, another "Camp David" on another mountain will be on their minds—namely, the city of Jerusalem on the Judean mountain where the Jewish King David located his capital around 1000 B.C.

One of the oldest and most fought-over cities in the world, Jerusalem has known occupation by Egyptian, Canaanite, Philistine (whence Palestine), Jew, Assyrian, Babylonian, Greek, Roman, Persian, Arab, Crusader, Turk, and Briton. It has been destroyed seventeen times. It is still the subject of dispute, especially between Israelis and Arabs. The resolution of the problem of this city must figure in any lasting Middle East peace arrangement.

To Jews, Jerusalem is sacred because of its association with Abraham, the Jewish kingdom, and the first and second temples. To Christians, because of the ministry, death, burial, and resurrection of Jesus. To Moslems (who also venerate Abraham and Jesus), because of its association with Mohammed—he is said to have paid a visit to heaven from this site—and the presence there of two outstanding Islamic shrines: the Dome of the Rock and the Mosque of El Aqsa.

When in 1947 the United Nations voted (33-13) for the partition of Palestine into a Jewish and an Arab state, the internationalization of Jerusalem was also voted. (After a maximum of ten years, its citizens would then vote on its future.)

As the least of evils, this internationalization was accepted at the time by the Jewish leadership. But, as is well known, the Arab leadership rejected the whole U.N. decision. So, when the British left on May 14, 1948, five Arab armies invaded Palestine and joined the native Arabs in attacking and counter-attacking the Jews.

When the cease-fire went into effect that July, the old walled city of Jerusalem was in Jordanian hands. For the first time in its long history, Jerusalem was a divided city with the newer, western part under Jewish control. Israeli citizens, whether Christian, Moslem, or Jewish, were forbidden access to the sacred sites in the Old City.

During the Six Day War in 1967, however, the Israelis captured all of Jerusalem and all the land eastward to the Jordan River, some fifteen miles away. This territory comprises the famous West Bank of current dispute.

Today there are about 270,000 Jews in greater Jerusalem, some 81,000 Moslems and 11,000 Christians. When you consider all the bad memories on all sides, you must marvel that Jerusalem functions as peaceably as it does. Collins's and Lapierre's book *O Jerusalem* graphically itemizes some of those recent memories.

Although even the United States does not recognize Jerusalem as the capital of Israel (nor do most Arab states honor Jordan's claim to the city), the Israelis no longer accept the internationalization plan. They point out that for no other people but themselves has Jerusalem ever been a political and spiritual capital.

They note, moreover, that the sacred shrines of all faiths are honored and protected under Israeli law, and that even natives of enemy Arab states are entitled to visit them. According to Israeli law: "Whoever desecrates or otherwise violates a Holy Place shall be liable to imprisonment for a term of seven years; whoever does anything that is likely to violate the freedom of access of the members of the various religions to the places sacred to them, or to violate their feelings in regard to those places, shall be liable to imprisonment for a term of five years."

During my two visits to Jerusalem (1968, 1978), I heard no serious criticism of the Israeli treatment of Christian or Moslem shrines or pilgrims. Indeed as late as 1975, the policemen assigned to the chief holy places were under the command of a Moslem officer, and they included Christians and Druses.

To be sure, in 1948 a group of radical Israeli militants (the Stern Gang) had plans to destroy the Dome of the Rock and the El Aqsa Mosque on the site of Solomon's Temple. But this plan was in direct defiance of leader Ben Gurion's directive that no harm be done to any sacred place.

Because the spirit of Ben Gurion triumphed and has persisted, I for one would have no objection if the status quo were made permanent in Jerusalem—no matter what changes were reasonably sought and conceded elsewhere in Israel in the spirit of fairness and in the interests of peace.

37. A Visit to the Patriarch of Constantinople

The Baltimore Evening Sun: July 13, 1972

NEWS of the death of the Greek Orthodox Patriarch Athenagoras of Constantinople brought promptly to my mind cherished memories of a visit I had with him just about four years ago.

I was on a pilgrimage that had taken me through Greece to the Holy Land, where, just a few blocks from our Jerusalem hotel on the Mount of Olives, the patriarch had had an historic meeting with Pope Paul VI in January, 1964. Our group was now spending a few days in Turkey before our final stopping place, Rome.

For many centuries, the leading spiritual centers of Christendom had been just these very cities—Jerusalem, Constantinople, and Rome, along with Antioch (where Christians were first called Christians) and Alexandria in Egypt. These were the focal points of the great patriarchates, whose bishops were "the ruling father," as the word patriarch means.

In Constantinople—the city of Constantine, the first Christian Roman Emperor—we could still see the ruins of the great aqueduct built by Constantine in the early three hundreds. To this strategic site, modern Istanbul, where Europe gazes at Asia across the waters of the Bosporus, Constantine moved his imperial court and established a "new Rome" in the East that was to last a thousand years. Also known as Byzantium, this splendid city was the heart of the Byzantine Empire, and its ruling bishop naturally grew in stature as an influential figure of both church and state.

Through the centuries the patriarch of Constantinople also naturally developed as the chief rival to the bishop of old Rome, the sole patriarch of the West. It is a little-known symbol of happier times that each of the four Eastern patriarchs was once honorary pastor of one of Rome's major basilica churches. That of the patriarch of Constantinople was St. Peter's Basilica!

A better-known but sadder story tells of the series of mis-understandings, church-state intrigues, hurt feelings and poor communications that led to the harmful split between Rome and Constantinople in the 1050s.

As a visitor to modern Turkey, which is 98 percent non-Christian, I found it hard to imagine the former majesty of the patriarchate of Constantinople. The headquarters of this spiritual leader of the Eastern Orthodox Churches not in union with Rome is located in the oldest part of the city, in a rundown section called the Phanar. Behind protective walls, you find a little church scarcely bigger than a chapel, and the humble residence and offices of the patriarch.

Meeting a lone priest, I asked whether there was any chance I might pay my respects to the patriarch. The priest, courteous but unsmiling, answered in English that the patriarch would be at his residence in the early part of the next morning, and I was welcome to come back then.

In the event, there were about seven of us sitting in a little, plainly furnished room for about an hour the next morning. A family of Greeks was there, with what appeared to be kinfolk from France, plus myself, and a seminarian companion. At length we were summoned to a nearby room where a tall, bearded and regal figure embraced each guest warmly and invited all to be seated as he took his chair behind a desk.

He chatted first with the other guests. When we told him we were Americans, his eyes lit up and he instantly sang a line or two from "God Bless America." (He had worked for some years in the United States.) Learning that I was a priest from Baltimore, he said, "How I love your bee-shop, Bee-shop Shehan." It was the archbishop of Baltimore who had been sent to Constantinople by Pope Paul VI at the end of the Second Vatican Council to be his personal representative in a gesture of reconciliation between Catholicism and Orthodoxy. This gesture was meant to annul the mutual excommunications of long ago.

I myself had witnessed the other half of this gesture in St. Peter's Basilica in Rome on December 7, 1965, when the pope embraced a representative of the patriarch. Later that day, the representative placed nine roses on Pope John XXIII's tomb to symbolize the overcoming (at least at one level) of nine centuries of estrangement. Visiting the patriarch almost three years later, I noticed not one, but two pictures of Pope Paul VI on his meagerly decorated walls.

After conversing with each of us briefly and cordially, the patriarch called for a servant, who provided each of us with a cool glass of water and a scoopful of soft white candy. Noticing that I had a camera, the patriarch invited his servant to take my camera and snap a picture of himself standing with the whole group of visitors.

After another embrace from the eighty-year-old churchman, we were on our way out of his spartan residence. Multilingual arrangements had to be made to get names and addresses so that I could mail copies of the precious photograph to the other members of the group. Eventually I did so. Then, some months later, a box of delicious liqueur-filled candies arrived from France. It took me some minutes to figure out who might have sent them to me.

Thinking today of this noble patriarch, of his Gospel simplicity and warm humanity, I find that box of candy from distant strangers a touching symbol of the sweet and spirited brotherhood that radiated from his lofty spirit all his long life.

38. Traveling by Word of Mouth

The Baltimore Evening Sun: June 5, 1984

YOU HAVE perhaps heard of the schoolboy who said that the Crusades were his favorite subject, because he was religious and liked to travel. Most people like to travel, even though (as a teacher of mine used to say) travel was not always the pleasant, comfortable thing that it has not yet become. Indeed, the word "travel" comes from the word "travail," which comes from an instrument of torture composed of three stakes—*tri-pali* in Latin.

One of the most comfortable ways to travel is by a romp through any dictionary that gives you the origin of words. You discover how much word travel can become world travel. Italics will take you to Italy, to Venice in particular, where in A.D. 1501 was published an edition of Virgil which first used italics. Copper will take you to Cyprus, where once upon a time the best copper was mined. Gypsies are so-called because they were thought to have come from Egypt and to be really Egypsies.

Indigo came from India and its blue-dye-producing plant. Peaches came originally from China, but were named after the Persia (Iran) to which they had migrated. The currants in your jelly came from the Greek city-state of Corinth. Ermine came from the weasel of Armenia, a country now shared by Russia, Turkey, and Iran. Damask derived from Damascus, the capital of Syria. Cravats at the neck are tied to Croatia in modern Yugoslavia. Spaniels first barked in Spain.

Lumber seems to be connected with Lombardy; gauze traces itself to the Gaza Strip area, and scallions to the Israeli port of Ascalon.

Magnets attract us back to Magnesia (as in milk of), an ore-rich section of Greece. The word meander wanders back through history to the name of a wandering river in ancient Phrygia. The Phrygians gave us the architectural frieze. Phrygia is now in Turkey, which gave us the gem turquoise and the name of our Thanksgiving bird. Our bird got its name by mistake. It was confused with a guinea fowl, which the Portuguese exported from Africa via Turkey.

The river Volga flows through the word Bulgaria. The word "wander" wanders through the word "vandal"; the Germanic vandals wandered as far as Spain and gave their name to (v)Andalusia. Often oppressed by other wandering tribes, the Slavs became the first slaves.

It's easy to link sardines with Sardinia. In olden days, there was a poisonous plant connected with Sardinia that was supposed to distort the face in death. Such is perhaps the origin of the mocking, twisted smile known as sardonic.

Clothes make the man but places sometimes make the names of clothes. Jeans cover over the word Genoa, where they were first made. Worsted suits started out in Worstead, England. The cloth made at Nimes in southern France was *de Nimes* (from Nimes), or denim, as we would say. Duffel bags were created in the Belgian city of Duffel. Milan was famous especially for women's finery, and hides behind every millinery shop.

It's not hard to guess what kind of car was first manufactured in the French town of Limousin, or what pointed weapon was born in another French town, Bayonne. Bologna was guessably the mother of baloney, Hamburg of hamburgers, Frankfurt of frankfurters, and Wien (Vienna) of wieners.

Moroccan Tangiers puts its stamp on every tangerine. A book on world travel through word travel might well finally drop anchor in the ancient city of Byblos, now in Lebanon. From Byblos, Egyptian papyrus was shipped to Greece. Papyrus gave birth to the word paper. The town of Byblos gave the Greeks their word for book, *biblos*, which gave us our word bible.

Our English word for book comes from the Germanic word for beech tree, whose bark was good for writing on and whose leaves may be imaginatively seen in the leaves of a book. Thus we conclude by arriving back at books, and give praise especially for that treasurable travel book known as the dictionary.

Part Three

Literary Circles

39. The Trojan Horse Was a Grecian Formula

The Baltimore Evening Sun: January 21, 1982

ONE OF the literary events of the year just concluded was David Stockman's resuscitation of the Trojan Horse. According to the national budget director, you will recall, Reaganomics is a Trojan Horse galloping to the aid of the beleaguered rich. Since the Greek and Latin classics are not so well known as once they were, the following hoof-nail sketch is offered in the name of national symbolic clarity.

Current headlines declare that Greece is more afraid of Turkey these days than she is of Russia. It's an old story, since the Troy to which the Greek Helen was abducted stood in what is now northwest Turkey. Outraged that Paris, the son of Troy's king, had run off with the wife of Sparta's king, the Greeks landed near Troy (and Gallipoli) and spent ten years trying to destroy Troy.

Finally, after the death of Achilles (their greatest fighter) the Greeks sailed away in apparent frustration. They left behind on the beach a massive wooden horse. Crouched inside were some of Greece's top fighters.

Some Trojans wanted to dismantle the thing, others to topple it into the sea, and still others to drag it into their city as a war trophy. Many felt it was some sort of religious object and didn't want the bad luck of abusing it.

The Trojan priest Laocoon warned: "Don't trust that horse. Whatever it proves to be, I still fear Greeks, even when they offer gifts." He meant gifts to the gods, but he is often quoted as though he meant the horse was a gift to the Trojans. For his trouble, he and his two sons were attacked and killed by giant sea snakes, which were presumably pro-Greek.

His sister Cassandra backed him up with a dire prophecy, but to the usual effect, which was a noneffect. Apollo had granted her the gift of foresight, but because she had refused his amorous advances he cursed her with a permanent loss of credibility.

Meanwhile the Trojans had captured a Greek named Sinon, who claimed he was a deserter. The Greeks were going to make a human sacrifice out of him in order to get good winds for the trip home, or so he said, lying in his teeth. He also said that the horse was an apology to the goddess Athena, whose Trojan shrine had been violated by two of the Greeks, Odysseus and Diomedes. These had audaciously sneaked into Troy and stolen the sacred statue of Athena known as the Palladium. (Her full name was Pallas Athena and she specialized in wisdom, like the Roman goddess Minerva.)

Sinon (whom Dante later put into the hell of falsifiers) further stated that the Greeks made the horse so big in order to discourage the Trojans from trying to take it into their city—for the horse would bring good luck to whoever possessed it and bad luck to anyone who harmed it.

The Trojans believed Sinon and hauled the horse into their walled citadel. Later that night, when Sinon saw a flare from the returning Greek ships, he opened a bar to the horse's belly and let the Greek warriors loose on the unsuspecting and celebrating Trojans.

You might expect to find this story in Homer's *Iliad*, the saga of the Trojan War. (Ilium was another name for Troy.) But that book ends with the burial of Hector, the Trojan commander-in-chief—an event that preceded the withdrawal of the Greeks. You do find references to the horse in three flashback scenes in Homer's *Odyssey*, that tale of the homecoming of the wily Greek chieftain Odysseus (alias Ulysses), who is credited with hatching the idea of the horse in the first place.

According to rough guesses, the Trojan War occurred between 1250 and 1150 B.C., and Homer's tales were written down about 750 B.C. The most detailed classical account of the Trojan Horse (which was really Grecian) occurs in the second book of Virgil's *Aeneid*, written in Latin in the twenties B.C. In that second book or chapter, the Trojan escapee Aeneas tells the story of Troy's downfall at a banquet given for him by Dido, the friendly queen of Carthage.

It is to this Virgil, dead 2000 years, that we owe Laocoon's warning words and the story of his serpentine death as depicted in the famous statue now in the Vatican Museum. The Romans regarded themselves as descendants of the Trojans through those hearty survivors, Aeneas and his wandering companions. So the Trojan priest, Laocoon, victim of the Trojan Horse, has a fitting home away from home in the diocese of the chief priest of Rome.

40. Two Thousand Years Dead, Virgil Lives on in Your Wallet

The Baltimore Evening Sun: September 21, 1981

H E DIED 2000 years ago today, on the southeast coast of Italy. But his words live on. Where? Among other places, in the wallets and purses of Americans.

I'm referring to the greatest of the Latin poets, Virgil—or more precisely, Publius Vergilius Maro (70–19 B.C.). The first "i" in his middle name is a misspelling that is now so fixed and widespread that even scholars tend to spell Vergil as Virgil.

His fame rests on three books: his *Eclogues*, ten short pastoral poems also called *Bucolics* and amounting to 829 lines; his *Georgics*, a poem singing the praises of Italian farming to the tune of 2,188 lines; and his grand epic about the origin and destiny of Rome, the *Aeneid*, with its twelve "books" and 9,896 lines.

Though it has had its detractors, many critics incline to say that the *Aeneid* is the principal secular book of the Western world. "It has always been easy to argue that it is the best poem" (W. F. Jackson Knight). "For two thousand years, it has been the most widely read and studied and imitated of all the poetry of antiquity" (R. D. Williams).

But what of Virgil's secret life in our purses and wallets? Since 1935, the great seal of the United States in both its obverse and reverse form has appeared on the back of the dollar bill. Two and possibly three of the mottoes on that seal were taken from Virgil.

For six years after the signing of the Declaration of Independence, and through the work of three sequential committees and fourteen individuals, Congress tried to settle on a design for the seal of the new nation. Finally, on June 20, 1782, Charles Thomson, secretary of the Congress for nearly fifteen years, presented a two-sided design, which was accepted that same day.

Born in County Derry, Ireland, Thomson was a fiery patriot known as "the Sam Adams of Philadelphia." For the seal he modified and simplified previous designs and added two Virgilian mottoes to the reverse side—the side with the left eye above a pyramid.

Flanking that eye are the two Latin words, *ANNUIT COEPTIS*. *Annuit* means "he/she/it is favorable" or "has been favorable." In its roots *annuit* depicts a nodding of the head (*nuo*) towards (*ad*) someone or something. In some editions of Virgil, the word is spelled the original way, *adnuit*—except that he used the verb in its imperative form, *adnue*—"do be favorable!"

Coeptis means "to the beginnings." Virgil uses these two words, *annue coeptis*, twice in his writings. In the forty-first line of his *Georgics* the poet invokes his patron Caesar Augustus, and begs him to be favorable to the poet's new beginnings, namely, the *Georgics*.

Later, while composing the *Aeneid*, he describes the son of Aeneas getting ready to go into his first battle. This youthful Ascanius (alias Julus and thus the supposed ancestor of Julius Caesar) raises a prayer to the god Jupiter: *Annue coeptis* (Book IX, line 625): "Do be favorable to (my) beginnings (as a fighter)."

As a U.S. motto, the words are usually taken to mean: "God has favored (our) beginnings." In his "Remarks and Explanation" for Congress, Charles Thomson wrote: "The pyramid signifies Strength and Duration: The Eye over it and the Motto allude to the many signal interpositions of providence in favour of the American cause."

Underneath the pyramid is a scroll containing three more Latin words: *NOVUS ORDO SECLORUM*. In his fourth and most famous *Eclogue*, Virgil is celebrating the birth of a wonder boy. Some Christians later thought the poet was prophetically referring to Christ. In any case, "No short poem in any language has been so much discussed" (E. V. Rieu).

In the fifth line of that *Eclogue*, Virgil cited this as one of the effects of the birth of this boy: "The great order of the ages is born afresh," *i.e.*, a new cycle of history will begin. Thomson took Virgil's two words, *ordo seclorum* ("the order of the ages") but added *novus* ("new") as a substitute for the three Virgilian words *ab integro nascitur* ("is born afresh").

In Thomson's words: "The date underneath is that of the Declaration of Independence and the words under it signify the beginning of the New America Aera, which commences from that date." Though Thomson obviously thought of the two mottoes as separate, some have joined them to mean: "The new order of the ages has favored our beginnings."

Finally, a word about the motto on the main side of the seal: *E PLURIBUS UNUM* ("Out of many, one"). That was the motto of *Gentleman's Magazine*, once published in London and well-known to our founding fathers. No one knows the ultimate source of the phrase, but in addition to the poet Horace and the saint, Augustine of Hippo, Virgil is a possibility.

For there is a poem of 124 lines called *Moretum* ("The Salad"), which is attributed to Virgil, though not with certainty. In line 104 it states: *Color est e pluribus unus* ("Color is one thing out of many").

So goes the story of our national mottoes. That Virgil could have played such a key role in the selection of so few words is an indication of his rank in literary history. To focus on this role is a small but telling salute, on the second millennium of his death, to a man who has been called "The Father of the West."

41. A Fourteenth-Century Landing on Mars

The Baltimore Evening Sun: July 20, 1976

IN FICTION, Martians have been landing on the earth for quite a few decades now. But who was the first earthling to land on Mars—in fiction, at least?

Several years have passed since the Russians established the first factual human contact with our nearest planetary neighbor away from the sun. Now, on a Tuesday, a day of the week that has long been associated with Mars, and which the French still call mardi or Mars-day, the United States has also made human contact with the smaller-than-earth planet currently 210 million miles from us and 141 million miles from the sun.

This planet most likely derived its name from its ruddy color and from the fact that Mars was for the ancient Romans the god of war and bloodshed. That same god, who was the father of Rome's founder, Romulus, gave his name to the month of March and to the names Marcia, Marcus, Mark, and Martin. (A nice touch here, that the project director for the latest landing is James Martin.)

But, back to fiction, which often anticipates fact. To the best of my knowledge, the first earthling to reach Mars in the flesh was none other than Dante Alighieri, in many ways a son of that Rome which Mars grandfathered. He did so on the afternoon of Wednesday, April 13, A.D. 1300, in the company of Beatrice, the beloved and idealized woman who had preceded him to the next world ten years earlier.

Both Dante and Beatrice were natives of Florence, whose original patron had been the same Mars. In Christian times, St. John the Baptist had replaced Mars as the city's patron. For this reason (according to legend), Mars was always plaguing Florence with wars. He would have plagued it even more had not a statue of himself remained near the famous Ponte Vecchio of that turbulent city.

(This was the bridge that the departing Nazis had planned to blow up, but the Florentines outwitted them. This same city, by the bicentennial way, also gave the world Amerigo Vespucci, and gave Baltimore the model for its infamous Bromo-Seltzer tower at Eutaw and Lombard Streets.)

Dante tells of his visit to Mars in the "Paradiso" section of his *Divine Comedy*. In the company of the Roman poet Virgil, he had entered Hell on Good Friday, April 8, 1300. On Easter Sunday, they arrived at the base of the Mount of Purgatory and spent the next three days climbing to the Garden of Eden at the summit.

There Beatrice took over as Dante's guide. According to the cosmic blueprints of the time, the realm of God lay far out in space, past the known planets and the stars. With the speed of lightning, Dante rose through these ten "heavens" until he achieved the very sight of God.

Mars was the fifth heaven through which Dante passed, having transcended the moon, Mercury, Venus, and the sun. Although all the saints are with God in the outermost heaven, they reveal themselves to Dante at various levels of the heavens, in accord with certain aspects of their personalities and deeds on earth.

In Mars are reflected the spirits of human beings who were martial on behalf of spiritual values. These included such fighters as Charlemagne, his heroic nephew Roland, and Duke Godfrey, the first Christian king of Jerusalem.

Most dramatically, in Mars Dante meets his great-great grandfather, Cacciaguida, a crusader who "from martyrdom came into this peace." Addressing his descendant in Cantos XV–XVIII, Cacciaguida foretells Dante's lifelong exile from Florence: "You will leave everything loved most dearly . . . you will learn how salty tastes the bread of another, how hard it is to climb and descend his stairs."

Dante wonders whether he should tell the truth about his journey to the next world and whom he saw where. Yet, "if I am a timid friend of truth, I fear to lose life among those who will call this time 'ancient'."

His ancestor reassures him: "Make your entire vision manifest, and let the scratching be where the itching is. For if at first your words are bitter, when digested, they will leave a vital nourishment."

Thus it is that some of the most memorable and moving of the 14,200 lines of the *Commedia* were spoken on Mars. After Dante had passed beyond Jupiter (named for the father of Mars), and Saturn (named for the father of Jupiter), he glanced back over the path of his rocket-like flight. He smiled at the humble appearance of the earth—"that little threshing floor which makes us so fierce."

What a pleasant twist, if space exploration would prompt us earthlings to smile a bit at our pomposities; if revelation about other worlds such as Mars would gentle us with large-minded awe, and render us less fierce and martial with our fellow passengers on this spaceship called earth.

42. A Letter to Dante About Hell's Hottest Place

The Baltimore Evening Sun: April 10, 1984

DEAR Dante:

Well it happened again. President Kennedy did it in one of his speeches. *New York Times* book reviewers do it. Now a distinguished local newspaper did it in two recent editorials. It's that mistaken reference to how you treat the "morally indifferent" in the "Inferno" section of your *Divine Comedy*.

People keep saying that you put such souls in the hottest part of hell, or in the lowest part. Presumably they are the same part. Yet you actually departed from tradition and made the lowest part of hell the coldest part, with the monstrous Satan frozen in ice up to his waist.

But, in any case, you didn't put the "morally neutral" in the depths of hell. If anything, you put them in the highest part of hell. As described in your third canto, these wretched souls "lived without infamy and without praise." In fact, they "never really lived." You classify them with those angels who were neither "rebellious, nor faithful to God, but for themselves."

So contemptible are these souls that neither heaven nor hell wants them. So you assign them to a kind of vestibule of hell, above the downward spiral that encases other sinners. These uncommitted souls "displeasing both to God and to his enemies," these folk who never took a stand, are forced to race after a constantly shifting banner. Naked, they are stung by wasps and hornets; maggots feed on their blood and tears. Nothing lofty or grand about the fate of these gnatty people. But you mention nothing about fire or heat.

Also, contrary to your usual practice in the *Divine Comedy*, you don't mention any names, so ignominious is this self-centered crowd. (And that's what ignominy literally means: "namelessness".) True, you say that you saw the shade of "him who, through cowardice, made the great refusal." But scholars can only guess that you meant Celestine V, the pope who resigned and whom the church later canonized. His resignation allowed your favorite enemy, Boniface VIII, to become pope.

Scholars give you credit for inventing this idea of a special place in hell for those who "in moments of great moral crisis maintain their neutrality." This idea keeps intriguing people more than six centuries later. The place you allot to the morally neutral may not be the lowest and the hottest in hell, but it is surely the most disgraceful and contemptible place. And that is usually what people mean when they misquote you on this point. So I presume that you regard such well-meant mistakes as venial sins at the worst.

43. A Visit to the Dickinson Homestead

The Baltimore Evening Sun: December 12, 1983

A CENTURY ago at this time, Emily Dickinson was still living as a recluse in her home in western Massachusetts. She had just celebrated her fifty-third birthday on December 10.

She was still dazed by the sudden death, two months earlier, of her beloved eight-year-old nephew Gilbert. Three months after her birthday, her friend and lover, Judge Otis Phillips Lord, would die. Three months after that loss, the poet would suffer the first attack of her final illness—probably the kidney disease nephritis. "The doctor calls it 'revenge of the nerves'," she wrote, "but who but Death had wronged them?" She herself died on May 15, 1886.

For some time now, the Folger Shakespeare Library in Washington, D.C., has been celebrating her birthdays with a special lecture on her life and work. This year Baltimore's own Josephine Jacobsen did the honors.

I myself am still bathing in the afterglow of a visit I made to the poet's home last month. It is still a private house, but parts of it are open to visitors a few hours a week. During an earlier visit to the charming college town of Amherst, I had gazed at the house at 280 Main Street, sorry that I missed the visiting hours.

Last month, on a rainy Saturday, I missed the regular visiting hours again. But it happened to be parents' weekend at Amherst College and special tours had been arranged. I don't know whether I and my young companion looked like father and son, but nobody challenged us when we approached the front door. Most of the parents' name tags were hidden by their raincoats anyway. To consolidate my good luck, I quickly and ostentatiously dropped a five dollar bill in the donation basket just inside the door.

So there I was, sitting in the parlor of this famous house that grandfather Samuel Dickinson had built in 1813 as the first brick house in town. The friendly guide took our small group past the hallway portrait of red-haired Emily with her brother Austin and sister Lavinia ("Vinnie"), up the staircase where Emily used to sit listening to the piano being played downstairs, and into her second-floor bedroom with its two windows facing Main Street.

This room contains the cradle in which she had been rocked. Though born in this house, and possibly in this room, Emily from age nine to twenty-four lived with her family in a house about a mile away. When finances improved, the family moved back to the so-called "Homestead." There Emily spent the rest of her years, scarcely venturing out of its confines during the last fifteen of them. During all those years she visited only once her brother's house next door, "the Evergreens"—on the night that his son Gilbert died. The pathway to that house, said the poet, was wide enough for two who love.

Our guide opened the closet in this room where Emily died and produced one of the famous white dresses she wore exclusively in her later years. It was then that I became aware that in our group was an actress from Argentina who over the past two years and more has played the role of Emily seven hundred times in a Spanish version of *The Belle of Amherst*, the one-person play made famous by Julie Harris.

The South American actress was named China Zorrilla. "My original name was Concepcion," she told me later, "but I grew tired of being called Miss Concepcion by English-speaking people." Noting that the dress would fit the actress, who performs her role in a white dress, the guide invited her to recite some of the lines from the play. By this time Zorrilla was so moved that she couldn't speak. She left the room momentarily, composed herself, and then returned to the door sill. There she recited in Spanish a twelve-line poem about life after death: "Will there really be a 'Morning'?/Is there such a thing as 'Day'?/Could I see it from the mountains/If I were as tall as they? . . ."

Who could miss the power of that scene and what it told of the power of words? A withdrawn, unrecognized poet most likely wrote these words in this very room. Now, more than a century later, comes an actress from the other end of the hemisphere and recites in a foreign language these secret thoughts of a woman who saw only a dozen or so of her 1,775 poems published in her lifetime. Indeed it wasn't until after her death that her sister Vinnie discovered in a bureau in this room dozens of small packets of poems, many stitched together by Emily herself. Now the magic in those packets draws pilgrims of poetry from all over the world to this hideaway house.

In one of the few explicit Civil War poems she wrote in the explosively creative year of 1862, Emily had written about "Scarlet Maryland," probably in reference to the supremely sanguinary Battle of Antietam. A decade earlier her father had attended a Whig convention in Baltimore. (Later that year he was elected to Congress; Emily visited him in Washington in early 1855.) While in Baltimore, Mr. Dickinson called on Susan Gilbert, his future daughter-in-law, who was then teaching school in the Monumental City.

At that time Emily was very fond of Sue, a moody woman who would have an ambivalent impact on the poet. During the school year 1851-52, Emily wrote to her about the current moon: ". . . this 'sweet silver moon' smiles in on me and Vinnie, and then it goes so far before it gets to you—but you never told me if there was any moon in Baltimore . . . I asked her to let me ride a little while ago—and told her I would get out when she got as far as Baltimore, but she only smiled to herself and sailed on."

After leaving her house, I paid a second visit to the poet's grave, not far away. Having shunned in life the streets of Amherst, she asked to be borne out the kitchen door and across the fields to the family plot, which is enclosed by a black metal fence. On her stone appear the words: "Called Back: May 15, 1886." She had read an 1883 novel entitled *Called Back*. In her last letter she wrote only those two words to her Norcross cousins.

I felt called back by this grave and found it covered with wet autumn leaves and a small bunch of violets. Did the donor of the flowers know that the poet's coffin and burial dress were adorned with only field blue violets? Writing in her youth about the death of a friend, Emily had mentioned this West Cemetery, established a century before her nearby birth: "I have walked there sweet summer evenings and read the names on the stones, and wondered who would come and give me the same memorial."

On that rainy afternoon of a New England fall, it seemed right for me to recall one of her early poems:

If I shouldn't be alive
When the Robins come,
Give the one in Red Cravat
A Memorial crumb.

And if I couldn't thank you,
Being fast asleep,
You will know I'm trying
With my Granite lip!

44. To Emily Dickinson: This is Your Letter from the World

The Baltimore Evening Sun: May 15, 1986

DEAR Emily Elizabeth Dickinson:

In 1862, when you were thirty-two and in the fiercest burst of your creativity—you wrote about a poem a day that year—you spoke of your poems as your "letter to the World/That never wrote to Me." When you died one century ago this evening—"just before the whistles sounded six"—only a dozen or so of your poems had been published—all anonymously. In the meantime the world has certainly been writing about you; and I'm presuming to write to you belatedly on behalf of that world of admirers who think of you as an astonishing gift to the planet.

Like many another, I probably first encountered you in high school literature classes when I read such lines as "I'll tell you how the Sun rose;" "I never saw a Moor;" "I'm Nobody! Who are you?" (Odd: they all begin with the "I" you increasingly hid from public view. You said you couldn't bear to live "aloud"—the Racket would shame you so.) Verses such as these could be thought of as merely "quaint" or "cute." Critics even accuse you of being sentimental in such lines as "If I can stop one Heart from breaking/I shall not live in vain."

Luckily I read more of you and ran across poems more tough and terrible, like "I felt a Funeral, in my Brain;" "Apparently with no surprise;" and "My Life had stood—a Loaded Gun." (You rarely gave your poems titles, so they usually get identified by their first lines, and reveal their author by their unique use of dashes, and curious capitalizations.) Your lines have a way of cropping up potently all over the place—in

Sophie's Choice, for instance—the book and the movie ("Ample make this Bed.").

The more I read of your poetry, the more I wanted to know about you. I became a devotee. (Like your English contemporary, the Jesuit Gerard Manley Hopkins, you are a patron saint of every unpublished and underpublished poet and would-be poet.) I have twice visited your native town of Amherst, ninety miles west of Boston. Your home there is open to the public a few hours each week.

In 1983 I devoted five months to reading all 1,775 of your *Complete Poems* as edited by Thomas H. Johnson. I needn't tell you that not all are "completed" or equally powerful. You had the courage to experiment with a new kind of poetic language, and what we often see is rough genius rather than merely polished talent.

Through the years your various editors tried at times to make you sound more respectable, but Johnson's 1955 edition gives us the pure you. For instance, after you say "There's a certain Slant of light/Winter afternoons—" you compare it to the "heft" of cathedral tunes, not to the "weight" of them. As a youngster I didn't know that anybody else was depressed by that heavy light, which I usually noticed on Sunday afternoons. You softened my lonesomeness when you spoke of the "imperial affliction" of that "Heavenly Hurt."

Sometimes it's clear you couldn't decide on the best word. So you left several unchosen choices on your manuscript and an editor has to decide which word to reproduce. (Did that spider in poem 1167 crawl "assiduously" or "deliberately" or "determinately" or "impertinently?") The fascinating story of how, starting in 1890, your poems were published little by little by various feuding and protective editors is well told in Millicent Todd Bingham's *Ancestors' Brocades*.

At the start of this month I gratefully attended a two-day conference on your life and work held at Washington's Folger Shakespeare Library, which is administered by Amherst College. In the shadow of the Supreme Court building and the Library of Congress, the Folger beautifies a neighborhood you probably strolled through in 1855 when you visited your father the congressman.

There was room for only 253 persons at the conference, and the quietly announced event sold out almost instantly. I especially wanted to hear two speakers whose superlative books on you I had recently read: Richard B. Sewall (*The Life of Emily Dickinson*), and John Cody (*After Great Pain*). There were speakers from Japan and Poland as well.

Everyone wonders why, dressed all in bridal white, you almost never left your home during the last fifteen to twenty years of your life, and only once visited the home of your beloved brother Austin, who lived next door with his troubling and troubled wife Sue. This was the Sue for whom you wrote some 270 poems and to whom you wrote letters when she taught school in Baltimore in the early 1850s. She had left Baltimore by the time you probably passed through it twice on the B&O when you made that trip to Washington, the farthest bodily journey of your life and one of the few.

You are known and loved around the world today because, with practically no encouragement, you had the lonesome audacity to follow your special star, because of the magical way you made numb words electrify, because of your clear-eyed, fleshy-hearted staring into the master themes of love and death and nature and poetry and eternity. You fascinate because of your shadows, your web of improbabilities, your "sumptuous Destitution." You amaze by the way you fulgurate into deeps within us that we scarcely knew were there, or for which we had despaired of words or images.

In your fifty-sixth year, after several fainting spells, you died of kidney disease. A wreath of field blue violets was the sole decoration of your coffin; a knot of the same flowers lay at your neck. According to your instructions, six Irishmen (including a Daniel Moynihan) who had worked on the family grounds bore your mortal remains "out the back door, around through the garden, through the opened barn from front to back, and then through the grassy fields to the family plot, always in sight of the house."

As a young girl you had written of this graveyard: "I have walked there sweet summer evenings and read the names on the stones, and wondered who would come and give me the same memorial." (Not true of you your words of poem 1147: "After a hundred years/Nobody knows the place," though strangers do increasingly stroll there and spell at "the lone Orthography/Of the Elder Dead.")

You ended another poem this way: "And if I couldn't thank you,/ Being fast asleep,/ You will know I'm trying/ With my Granite lip!" Today, around the world, many will be giving you that same memorial, at least in spirit. It is rather they who will be saying "thank you" for the news you are still conveying through the living lips of your letter to the world. Your prayer in that poem has been answered. Your "Sweet countrymen" of every nation do indeed "judge tenderly" of you.

45. So Long to Elliott Coleman: Everyman's Poet

The Baltimore Evening Sun: February 27, 1980

SO LONG
should never be said lightly
or loudly
it has too much of an echo
whisper it
so long   —Elliott Coleman

EVERYONE, I suppose, has a mental picture of what a poet is supposed to look like and of how a poet is supposed to behave. Death has now removed from the Baltimore scene the man who, for myself and many other admirers, most nearly matched our imaginings.

Not only did Elliott Coleman feel and respond and produce as a poet, he looked the part. A tall, spare man beset with increasing infirmities as the years mounted, he had a face whose skin never ceased to be fair, whose hair turned silky white as he aged, and whose blue-green eyes possessed an arresting beauty.

One of his final students first saw him the summer before last as he walked erectly but haltingly into a college dining hall at Oxford. "Those eyes," this woman in her twenties said of this man in his seventies—"they were the loveliest I had ever seen in my life."

And then there was his voice. As befits a poet, he respected the sounds of words and spoke them with an easy elegance.

He had to be cajoled into reading his own works, but when he did he revealed how a writer gifted with a melodious and sensitive voice can uniquely vitalize his own words.

A special instance comes to mind: One of his later poems was inspired by a piece of white coral given him by a chambermaid on the island of St. Croix. Reflecting the many tiny openings in the "dear skeleton," the poem was stitched together by a series of "O"s that floated down or across the pages. What his voice did with those near nothings startled me at my first hearing and has haunted me since.

Despite the power of his voice and of his words, Elliott Coleman was a man of many silences and a creator of increasingly laconic poems. He was generally reticent about his own life and achievements and about the many celebrated personalities he had met—authors like T. S. Eliot (on whose eighteenth birthday he was born), André Gide, Robert Frost, W. H. Auden, and Dylan Thomas.

He was the antithesis of the self-promoter. This may be the main reason why David Ray, in *Contemporary Poets of the English Language*, could call him "one of the most neglected poets in America."

Though neglectful of himself he paid plenary attention to the hopes and intentions and talents of his students at Johns Hopkins. Anyone who has ever tried to deal with the sensitivities of aspiring poets knows how draining it can be to read their writings seriously, make delicate criticisms, and speak aptly encouraging words. This Professor Coleman did for thirty years and more.

Students who kept caring to create were the favored sons and daughters of this childless man. To the very end of his life, packages from many far-flung authors sought him out with books sometimes dedicated to him, usually gratefully autographed. As he grew too tired to answer Christmas cards, he would read them, kiss them, and drop them into his wastebasket.

In his sunnier moments this poet could be entertained to the point of riotous mirth. Witnesses were not likely to forget how he would slap his leg and burst into roof-lifting laughter at a bon mot or a relished anecdote. And how he could italicize that characteristic word, "mar . . . velous"!

Yet he was a privately melancholy man. He once warned:

> Never look unless you are ready
> for everything
> or nothing.

He looked unblinkingly and responsively at the sorrows and tragedies of life:

> Cambodia caper
> so painless
> on paper.

In his darkest time though, he came to fear that everything might be nothing. As he wrote in his late poem, "Winter Over Nothing:"

> O that Something so full of Something
> Should turn out to be Nothing . . .
> O that Somebody so full of Somebody
> Should become   Nobody   Nothing.

In one of his classes I submitted a haiku: "This flow of time that/merged us once, forks us now. Should/I curse or bless it?" He returned it with the comment, "I don't know."

But, in the words of a fellow poet, he did know that "there are things of beauty here, and sorrow is our praise."

Once on a blindingly bright day I offered him a pair of sunglasses during an auto trip. "No thanks," he replied: "I have so little time left to look at things, I can't bear to put any darkness over my eyes."

Just a few weeks ago I was telling him of a situation that looked like sweetness and light, but was actually pathetic: "I felt that someone should get up and scream." His comeback was instantaneous: "Someone should always be getting up and screaming."

The poems of Elliott Coleman did not scream, but they were his sacred way of getting up and pointing out what moved him as a man, what shouldn't be missed, or oughtn't be forgotten.

He himself will not soon be forgotten by his numerous friends and students, who were often both, and who learned in their various, perhaps secret ways, of Elliott Coleman's rare

ability to be generous and compassionate. A modern master of
the sonnet, he ended one of them with words that many of his
friends now find truer of himself than he could ever have
guessed:

> . . . only the brave are any good:
> They're dead: and I am dazzled by their blood.

46. Katherine Anne Porter: The End of the Long Story

The Baltimore Evening Sun: September 30, 1980

WHEN I first visited the sickbed of Katherine Anne Porter, we both thought it would be her deathbed. Like Old Nannie in her short story, "The Last Leaf," the eighty-seven-year-old writer was "expecting her own death momentarily."

In person and over the phone she was to speak to me constantly about dying. "I'm going to die, and I'm going to do it as soon as I can." "I need to die." "I'm busy dying; it's the hardest job I ever had."

In 1977 she had suffered a stroke that left her writing hand useless. I met her in January, 1978, when she lived on the fifteenth floor of the Westchester Apartments near College Park, Maryland. She had nurses around the clock, and during my thirty subsequent visits over the next twenty-eight months, she was always in bed, except for the two or three times I found her in a wheelchair.

Last April she was transferred to a new and final bed at a nursing home in Silver Spring, Maryland. I paid her a last visit a few days after her ninetieth birthday in mid-May. (I was afterwards grounded by heart surgery.) A woman friend who had written a dissertation on the role of women in Miss Porter's fiction was her sole companion at the end, which occurred at 4 P.M. on the eighteenth day of this month.

At last she had the peace she had earned. A handwritten note on the door of her Westchester suite had requested that in view of her need for rest and quiet, uninvited callers should consider themselves disinvited. Some autograph hunter had clipped away her signature.

Inside that suite I was allowed to see the simple but gaily colored coffin she kept in a closet. I also saw on her walls several pictures she had taken of the poet Hart Crane when she befriended him in Mexico in the early 1930s. It was on his way back from Mexico to the United States that he leaped or fell to his death from a ship.

In a lighter vein she confirmed for me a legendary story: late one night, at a writers' colony, an overwrought poet banged on Miss Porter's door. "Katherine Anne," she said, "I'm going to commit suicide, and you're the only one I care to tell about it." "Well, thank you, dearie," replied Miss Porter, escorting the lady to the door, "be sure to let me know how it all turns out." (There was no suicide.)

Propped up in bed beneath a gilt-edged painting of the Madonna and Child, she seemed a tiny woman indeed. But hers was a face still marvelously alive, and crowned with elegant silver-white hair. You were struck at once by her engulfing smile, her ingratiating Southern voice, her wit, and her feistiness. When she couldn't find some word she was looking for, she might grow mightily vexed, or she might mock herself playfully with a string of nonsense syllables.

She was no softie, this Texan who claimed kinship with Daniel Boone, Sydney Porter (alias O. Henry), and Cole Porter. During a violent summer storm she once told me how, as a child, she loved to lie on the ground during such storms. "Don't you know that's dangerous?" her wifeless father asked. "Sure I do," replied the youngster.

"And that was that."

On another occasion she spoke about the consolation of having done your best—"Angels can do no more." Then after a slight pause, she added: "Or maybe they can. I'll see them soon and ask them."

I once mentioned W. H. Auden's remark that life is a blessing even when you can't bless it. "Darn him!" she joked: "He *would* say that. That's what I've always tried to say in my stories."

She gave me a copy of her *Collected Stories*, which won for her the Pulitzer prize and the National Book Award in 1966. Of these 26 stories, "Pale Horse, Pale Rider" is the favorite of many, with its theme of war, sickness, and self-sacrificing love. "It really happened to me," she said; "it was my first experience of death, and it changed my whole life. But I don't regret it." More than sixty years after the event, her eyes brimmed with tears as she recalled the Adam of the story (actually Alexander) who died after nursing her through the flu epidemic of the First World War.

Those tears belied somewhat a comment she made after listening to the Prayers for the Dying contained in the Roman Ritual. "This message we have of tenderness and love—it's the only thing that breaks me up." Some time later she phoned to ask me for another visit: "I know you can't say anything new, but I want to hear the old things again."

Katherine Anne also gifted me with a copy of her *Collected Essays* (1973). In it she had asserted: ". . . only the work of saints and artists gives us any reason to believe that the human race is worth belonging to." Educated for a while in a convent school, she told me she once thought of becoming a nun, but the sisters said that her call was to the world. Nevertheless she pursued her writing career as a genuine vocation and endured a built-in asceticism by refusing to sacrifice her integrity to popularity.

This copy of her essays is enriched with her own handwritten comments and footnotes. For example, in the text she lists some of her favorite playwrights, but leaves out George Bernard Shaw. "And Shaw," she scrawled at the bottom of the page, "what about Shaw? I knew and adored his plays before I knew any of these others, and yet to leave him out. Shame on me."

After working on it for twenty years, she published *Ship of Fools* in her seventy-second year. With it she finally achieved popularity and affluence. The latter allowed her at long last to buy some jewelry containing her birthstone, emerald. Sad to say, she was not permitted to wear any of these hard-won and dearly prized trophies in her final years. Her court-appointed guardian felt legally responsible for them and put them under lock and key.

A third book she gave me was the text of a symposium on her writings. In this volume too she added choice comments.

One critic speaks of the story of hers in which a wife "dispassionately" murders her rival. Miss Porter had underlined the adverb and jotted in the margin: "Better take another look at this story."

The same critic asserted that the most noble of her characters are confronted with the obliteration of hope. "The tiny particle of light must always be snuffed out," he wrote. In reaction to which she wrote: "Why, no! The particle of light still lives."

This gallant woman has at last achieved her death, but her artistic vision of the roots of human tragedy lives on in many particles of light embedded in her writings. For myself, a high point of that vision glows in the only passage in *Ship of Fools* that is emphasized by italics:

"What they were saying to each other was only, *Love me, love me in spite of all! whether or not I love you, whether I am fit to love, whether you are able to love, even if there is no such thing as love, love me.*"

Love was italicized in her own life. Someone once remarked to her: "Katherine Anne, wherever you have lived, there have always been people who loved you." She had a memorable explanation: "Well, I always loved them first, and that sort of helped them get used to the idea."

47. Robert Penn Warren: The First U.S. Poet Laureate

February 28, 1986

OVER THE past year, moviegoers have had a chance to see and hear Robert Penn Warren in a documentary on Huey Long that has been screened around the country. (Warren's 1946 Pulitzer prize-winning novel, *All the King's Men*, was based on the career of that power-hungry governor and U.S. senator from Louisiana.) Last June a wider audience probably saw Warren in a Herman Melville documentary aired over public TV.

Now the eighty-year-old native of Kentucky has been named the first U.S. poet laureate by the librarian of Congress. For this is a versatile man of letters who has achieved national recognition for his poetry as well as his prose. For more than fifty years the privately funded position of consultant in poetry at the Library of Congress (to which will now be linked the transient title of laureate) has been looked upon as a kind of unofficial laureateship. Robert Frost, Robert Lowell, and Baltimore's Josephine Jacobsen have held the post for the basic one-year term, which in some cases has been renewed.

The title of poet laureate dates back to seventeenth-century England. Poets Ben Jonson ("Drink to me only with thine eyes"), William Davenant, and John Dryden are variously cited as the first to have been given the role of paid court poet by an English sovereign. Wordsworth, Tennyson, and Masefield were later laureates. Thomas Gray and Sir Walter Scott refused the honor; the current honoree is Ted Hughes, widower of the ill-fated U.S. poet Sylvia Plath.

For many decades England's poets laureate wrote New Year's and birthday verses for their royal patron: these were often set to music and performed for the royal self. Since Queen Victoria's time, however, the honor has brought with it no specific duties. Still, many U.S. poets have opposed the idea of a native poet laureate, since the notion of "official poetry" strikes them as repugnant. But it appears that the U.S. law sponsored by Hawaii's Senator Matsunaga will not require any official poetry from the laureate, though it will presumably taint the consultant's expanded role with some official money. Still, no one expects poet Warren to dilute his independence of thought or expression. Look not to him for any puff of pentameters in praise of the presidential puppy.

The poet is "laureate" because he is judged worthy to be crowned with sweet-smelling laurel leaves, an ancient Greek and Roman symbol of victory and eminence. With the laurel wreath were crowned poets, military heroes, priests, and victors in the Olympic Games. Laurel leaves were considered to be sacred to Apollo (the god of light, music, medicine, prophecy, and poetry) because while he was pursuing the lovely nymph Daphne, she was changed into a laurel tree. At Apollo's shrine at Delphi, the resident prophetess reportedly chewed laurel leaves (alias sweet bay) by way of falling into her prophetic trance. Some scholars believe that the name of this influential leaf is hiding in the words Laurence (Lawrence), baccalaureate, and bachelor.

In the current movie *Out of Africa*, Meryl Streep recites a poem of A. E. Housman in which he says of a victorious athlete who died young: "And early though the laurel grows,/It withers quicker than the rose." Six and a half centuries ago, toward the end of his *Divine Comedy*, Dante (who is often depicted wearing a laurel wreath) voices his greatest earthly hope: "If ever it happens that the sacred poem/to which heaven and earth have set hand/and which has kept me lean for many years/overcomes the cruelty which has barred me [from my native city] . . . I will return a poet . . . and receive the laurel crown." Florence never crowned him, but civilization has.

Great poetry is the flower of a great civilization. But, as Walt Whitman warned, great literature requires great readers. Lovers of art in all its guises can only hope that the choice of such a worthy first poet laureate may prove to be a good omen for the future vigor of the muse in American society.

48. Josephine Jacobsen: *My* Poet Laureate

IN JANUARY, 1961 I was a young priest stationed at the old cathedral rectory in downtown Baltimore. One night at supper the rector asked, "Who had the afternoon mass last Sunday?" A bit nervously, I answered that I did. "Well, here's a letter for you."

It was a brief note from a Josephine Jacobsen expressing her appreciation of something I had said in my sermon about mindless and unChristian kinds of anti-Communism. (She later told me she had sent only one other letter in reaction to a sermon—and that was to lament a priest's uncharitable remarks about non-Catholics, a rather large group that included her husband.)

Her name was familiar to me because I had read and been impressed by her poetry reviews in Baltimore's *Evening Sun*. She seemed to go out of her way to say something positive about any book under discussion. She would doubtless be an exception to W. H. Auden's warning that it is almost impossible to review a bad book without showing off.

I answered her letter, suggested a get-together, and had my first conversation with her at *The Catholic Review* office where I was serving as an editor in the early Sixties. Eventually I interviewed her for the paper, to which she also submitted an occasional poem, story or poetry review.

As time went by I came to know her amiable and book-loving husband Eric, the retired president of the nation's oldest tea-importing company, but still a demon tennis player. In 1982 they celebrated their golden anniversary. ("He is far and away the best thing that ever happened in my life.")

I also met their gifted son Erlend and his six children, all of whom lived out of state, and the eldest of whom, dashing

Ricky, was tragically killed in his early twenties in a motorcycle accident. A graduate of the Creative Writing Seminars at Johns Hopkins, Erlend has taught literature at a number of colleges and published several small books of poetry.

I eventually visited the modest Jacobsen apartment near the Hopkins campus, and their summer home in Whitefield, New Hampshire. A few times I joined them for a vacation at their favorite spot in the Caribbean island of Grenada. A final bonus over the past quarter of a century was coming to know some of their large number of ardent and estimable friends—including poets such as Elliott Coleman and Ann Stanford.

By the time she was a teenager Josephine had already published her first poems in the respected children's magazine *St. Nicholas* and won its gold and silver medals for poetry. Freshly out of her teens she published her first book, *Marble Satyr and Other Poems*. Her second book of poems, *Let Each Man Remember*, was published in 1940, when she was 32. (The founding editor Harriet Monroe took some of these poems for *Poetry* magazine; every succeeding editor has published her too.)

The third, *For the Unlost*, appeared the year after the end of the Second World War, during which her husband served as a volunteer ambulance driver in the American Field Service in Italy. A fifth volume, *The Human Climate*, came out in 1953. Subsequent collections of poetry were: *The Animal Inside* (1966), *The Shade-Seller* (1974)—a National Book Award nominee—*The Chinese Insomniacs* (1981), and *The Sisters* (1987).

It wasn't until the year I met her that her first short story was published, in the magazine *Commonweal*. Although *McCall's* and *Mademoiselle* have featured several of her stories, most of them have graced the pages of quality literary magazines like *Epoch*, *Kenyon Review* and *Prairie Schooner*. Two well-received collections have appeared: *A Walk with Raschid* (1978) and *Adios, Mr. Moxley* (1987). The former won a place on the American Library Association's small, annual list of Notable Books.

One of its stories, "On the Island," has been frequently anthologized and, along with pieces by Hemingway and Faulkner, earned a place in the best of the *O. Henry* winners of the previous half-century. It was the only story to appear in both *The Best American Short Stories of 1966* and *The O. Henry* choices for that same year.

A final area of Jacobsen publication deals with modern playwrights and their plays. (She acted in the Baltimore *Vagabonds* years ago and is an avid movie and stage fan.) In collaboration with Dr. William R. Mueller, formerly literature professor at Goucher College, she published *The Testament of Samuel Beckett* (1964) and *Ionesco and Genet: Playwrights of Silence* (1968). The Beckett book was published in England by the prestigious firm of Faber and Faber, and evoked the praise of Beckett himself, before he won the Nobel Prize.

Busy as a wife, mother and grandmother and lacking the discipleship possibilities of a full-time college teacher, Josephine remained mostly a writer's writer until she was sixty-three. Then, in 1971, she became the twenty-first poet and fourth woman to be named Poetry Consultant to the Library of Congress. Following in the footsteps of poets like Robert Frost, Robert Lowell and Elizabeth Bishop, she gained her first national exposure and was granted a then unusual second term in 1972—the first woman to be so honored. Later she served for four years on the literature panel of the National Endowment for the Arts.

Professional recognition finally began to catch up to her. This mostly self-taught woman who never went to college now holds honorary doctorates from three Baltimore colleges: Notre Dame (where her ailing mother once boarded), Goucher, and Towson State. She was elected vice-president of the Poetry Society of America. In 1982 she was granted a literary award from the American Academy and Institute of Arts and Letters: "To read a work of hers is to be mentally and emotionally refreshed, and to taste as well the rare mint of art." In 1987 the Academy of American Poets named her its fifty-second Annual Fellow. The U.S. Catholic community, literary and academic, has given scant recognition to the poet, though in 1982 her poem "Distance," which appeared in *Commonweal*, won a best poetry award from the Catholic Press Association.

In a keenly competitive field where jealousy is not unknown, her professional peers are not stingy with their praise. William Jay Smith thinks she "is one of the few poets writing today whose stories are every bit as good as her poems, and that is very good indeed . . . she is clearly one of the finest poets now writing in America." Joyce Carol Oates admires her "small, perfect, gemlike stories."

A. R. Ammons declares: "It is to her stature as a central human being that I am willing to entrust my own making." Howard Moss finds nature "wonderfully observed" in her poems. Carolyn Kizer, who regards her a member of that endangered species—"a lady"—sees her as "gentle, tactful and incapable of cruelty, though she understands it well. She is the obverse of innocent and more beautiful."

A doctoral dissertation on the writings of Jacobsen was written in 1984 for the University of Maryland by Evelyn Prettyman. Entitled *Commitment to Wonder*, the study traces the core motifs of the poet to her strong, but seldom explicated religious beliefs. Prettyman finds a tone most typical of her subject's writing: "It is the voice of her intellect which insists on all the truth, mingled with her love of God, which compels her to worship. The result is wonder."

But the wonder is not just a thrill at the delightfully amazing. It is the searing mystery of how all the parts of the real can fit together, especially a good God and a world of loss and overwhelming suffering. Prettyman quotes the poet's religious belief that "our world is a mingling of the spiritual and the physical, and therefore beyond human understanding." This belief results "in a passionate opposition to oversimplification, so that her subjects are presented trailing their contradictions and seeming irrelevancies." As the fiction-writer herself has said: "I don't believe in *endings*, tidy or otherwise. If these are real people . . . they are going to have a future, about which the story should enable you to make some fascinating guesses."

Josephine is an intensely private person, and even close friends have to search elsewhere for the details of her personal life. She was born in Canada on August 19, 1908. Her mother, Octavia Winder Skinner Boylan, came from an aristocratic North Carolina family, a Protestant family that included two Episcopal bishops. Impressed by the Notre Dame sisters in Baltimore, her mother became a Catholic some years before the early and sudden death of her first husband, by whom she had a son named John.

Josephine's father, Joseph Boylan, also had a child by his first wife, who also died young. This daughter too died in young adulthood. Mr. Boylan, who had Ohio roots but was raised in Italy, was a medical doctor. He earned degrees (and fencing scars) in Heidelberg and Bonn. After several years as an invalid, he died of a heart attack when Josephine was five. Widowed again, her mother moved with her daughter from city to city until she settled in Baltimore in 1922, and entered her daughter in Roland Park Country School for four years of the only formal education she ever received. In her adopted city Josephine met Eric Jacobsen and married him when she was twenty-three.

Nurtured by that extraordinarily loving relationship, she has gone from strength to strength as a writer and as a person. In her poetry she has evinced a wide variety of styles, from the most traditional to the most innovative. She has never settled into a predictable mold, though there is a steady signature in the seriousness of her themes, the precision and concreteness of her language, the dignity of her tone.

Her diction comprises almost an encyclopedia of physicality as she itemizes human anatomy, kinds of animals and flowers, geographies, seasons, months, hours of the day and of the sleepless night. Her allusions are Biblical, mythic, historical, Catholic and liturgical, though few of her poems are overtly religious. (One of them, "Bush Christmas Eve" is among her favorites and revealingly deals with the theological problem of evil.) Key words are bright, fierce, savage, secret, shadow, shape, and terrible.

Her chief theme, perhaps, is human communication—the need for it, the difficulty of it. "Almost nothing concerns me but communication," begins one poem. Hers is a relentless hunger for communion with "the other"—God, the beloved, animals, nature, the past, the dead, the forgotten. Out of the tragic quality of "the human climate" rises the need for courage, unblinking objectivity, and care. Everywhere impends the sense of the endangered sacred, the impenetrable, the redeemingly beautiful, the silent, the unexpressed, the inexpressible.

Hers is a poetry of sobriety, toughness and ellipticality. It is compressed, its beauty lean and taut. Unpatronizing, it challenges both head and heart. It is an Augustinian, Pascalian poetry of the short-range pessimist, the long-range optimist. Bad enough, she is fond of saying, the gloom-monger who cries "Beware the Mines" in an innocent field. Worse, the Pollyanna who says "No Danger" where the terrain is treacherous.

One love poem in particular, "We Met in the City," captures

in a series of phrases many of her distinctive motifs: "It was most often night . . . Every so often a dawn . . . once a noon exploded . . . We never failed to find each other . . . those meadows of midnight those moonlight stridencies . . . O it was worthwhile!"

What of the poet as a person and a friend? Physically she is a somewhat diminutive person with lively features and an ingratiating voice. You first notice her courtesy and graciousness. She listens to you, tries to discover your interests, remembers what you said. Thus she has been humorously described as "God's gift to the bore." She is normally slow to discuss herself, her life, her work. (It took me a long while to discover her love for dancing and baseball, and her devotion to the singing of Frank Sinatra and Willie Nelson.) Though her artistic themes incline toward the grim she is a cheerful conversationalist. Cheer is her gift to the world, not her comment on it. Her sorrow is not chiefly for herself, but for others.

You soon become aware of her phenomenal energy. I know of no one who is so intense in so many directions at the same time. For that reason she is often in a rush, behind schedule and somewhat out of breath. Still, she never stints the rituals of friendship. Her not infrequent mishaps flow, I'd guess, from her trying to crowd too much into too small a time capsule. She is a relentless correspondent, dashing off letters in her inimitable and occasionally indecipherable script.

Her mind is an astonishment. She seems to have read everything at least twice, remembered all of it, and fit every part of it into a detailed and consistent scheme of truth, beauty and goodness. Though she seldom does so, you suspect she can recite verse after verse of songs and poems she learned long years ago.

She is a woman of ferocious devotions, especially towards her loved ones, her friends, the needy, her convictions about reality (including our ambiguous grasp of it). If there is a feminine version of a wimp, she is the opposite of it, a veritable tigress of truth. Over her paws, she has mittens, velvet but detachable.

For all her courtesy and charity, she has a highly developed sense of outrage concerning wicked people and their wicked machinations. (No doubt she would argue for their pardon once they renounced their wickedness.)

She also knows that many marginal people are beyond her

reach, perhaps beyond all human reach. Still, "We have to be conscious every day of the human beings who lead these secret, desolate, isolated lives . . . they are not going to be found by society, but they've got to be found in our minds."

She once said that her two consuming earthly passions are literature and politics—not that she engages in politics for their own partisan sake, but because she is vitally concerned about how the rich treat the poor and how the powerful treat the weak. So you will never get the impression that she lives in an ivory tower at a safe remove from the rough-and-tumble of everyday events in the political world and elsewhere. She begins a normal day by devouring the morning paper, whose front page (she says) is usually enough to sour the cream in your coffee.

She is religiously devoted too, though she is most private about this key part of her life. Two aspects of Catholicism which especially nourish her are the Eucharist (and its link to the dying and rising Christ) and its devotion of Mary, the Mother of Christ, through whom the divine became human. In an interview with Ms. Prettyman she said: "The Eucharist in the Catholic church is the center of my whole belief in it, because I believe in the inexplicable tangle of body and spirit."

Discussing these matters, the poet made a statement that sounds very close to the bone: "When I was probably fifteen, sixteen, seventeen, I was tremendously troubled by these things—the benign Lord and suffering. And then suddenly, somehow, as I seemed to understand more about poetry, and as I saw my mother suffer and my brother suffer, the Eucharist became the vital reference point of my life. It seemed ultimately, in some way I didn't understand, to make sense . . . It seems to me that the Christian religion is overwhelmingly right for me, because I cannot conceive of any religion sheltering me that didn't acknowledge in its God a degree of human suffering, and, indeed, failure."

Unable to share the simple faith of those who are sure God is good because He made kittens—she can't forget the hyena and the crocodile—she hesitates to invoke a faith resolution in her writings. "When a person says she believes in a design, in an ultimately great and good God, she is making a statement that can be used to ignore all the suffering and all the horror of which life is so often so largely composed."

She prefers to leave the divine and its working in history truly mysterious, rather than to suppose there are comprehensible answers. With a belief in God she finds human communication difficult enough; without such a belief she would find it impossible. She understands those who say they couldn't get out of bed in the morning without a belief in God. Still, "I think I want never to forget that there is a terrible price you pay for believing; that you have to submit your intellect, and the testimony of your senses, and your experience to faith, to what in a great phrase the mass calls 'the mystery of faith.' " (Prettyman dissertation, cited in *New Letters* and in *Woman Poet, South.*)

Another devotion: Josephine has had an extraordinary, life-long sense of vocation as a writer. She even apologizes for the fact that her husband is the greatest concern of her life. She feels that for a genuine artist the work of art itself is the supreme earthly value. I once recklessly spoke to her about people who seem to make a god out of poetry. "Well," she struck back with unwonted sharpness, "it's better than a lot of other gods."

Perhaps because she feels her work has suffered from her lack of a college education, she is surprisingly regretful about that lack: "At times it just lacerates me to think of, oh, if I'd had that experience, the friendships, the contacts, the launching . . . I have never made up my mind to this day whether it was a good or bad thing that I didn't go to college . . . or have the chance to decide for myself."

Her personal everyday schedule is packed and draining enough. Still, she is incredibly generous with other writers, however amateur, reading their works and promoting their professional efforts in any number of self-giving ways. (One such amateur was so obnoxious that Josephine had to dissuade her preternaturally patient husband from disinviting him out of their apartment.) The frenetic pace of her existence makes you wonder where she finds the solitude, the contemplation, the time and energy to do her rigorous, incessant creating as a writer. She is the antithesis of the isolated, dreamy poet serenely wrapped in her own musings, calmly listening hour after languid hour for the susurration of inspiration.

Oscar Wilde claimed he put his talent into his writing and his genius into his living. This poet puts her considerable genius into both. It is as a human being, however, that her variegated and far-flung friends find her most admirable. If, as an ancient theologian said, the glory of God is a person fully alive, Josephine is truly glorious. Emerson spoke of the authentic hero as being immovably centered, and this personally modest, essentially private person is awesomely centered in what she affirms, what she denies and what she does about the complex and encompassing mystery of human existence.

Her rare combination of stellar gifts of head, heart, empathy, emotional toughness, language, religiousness, practical passion and consuming love for one special human being—this daunting synthesis, thoroughly unlikely, thoroughly undeniable, calls to mind the figure of Dante. Certainly her life and writings pulsate with that terrible love which moves the sun and the other stars.

The famous Baedeker guidebooks used the symbol of stars to mark their recommendations and the intensity of them. Josephine Jacobsen, now in her stunningly youthful eightieth year, merits the praise which Elizabeth Asquith Bibesco once bestowed on a friend: "You are such a wonderful Baedeker to life. All the stars are in the right places."

Part Four

Religious Circles

49. The Bible: The Unread Best Seller

The Baltimore Sunday Sun: December 24, 1978

THIS year, by coincidence, Christians are celebrating Christmas and Jews are celebrating Hanukkah on the same day. Christians are celebrating the birth of Christ, "the light of the world," who was taken to the temple in Jerusalem shortly after his birth. In their Feast of Lights, Jews are celebrating the rededication of an earlier temple on the same spot. This occurred in 165 B.C., after the Jewish rebel Judas Maccabaeus recovered control of the temple in his war against the Syrians.

Both celebrations flow from that history of the Jewish people partially recorded by the Bible. Though it remains a perennial best seller, the Bible is probably the world's least-read one—at least in proportion to the number of copies sold. Surely that status is true in terms of the number of people who read the entire Bible. [A 1986 poll found that 93 percent of Americans own at least one Bible, but 45 percent never read it.]

No doubt many people just like having the Bible around as a kind of good luck charm, or as a sign of general benevolence on their part toward the powers that be. In this category was probably the old gentleman who on his deathbed pointed to a dusty Bible and said, "Them's my sentiments."

One problem is that the Bible is a big book, both in its Jewish and Christian editions. Also, parts of it make very arid reading, not to mention difficult or incomprehensible reading, for modern eyes.

Still, as Robert Bellah asserts in his book, *The Broken Covenant*: "Biblical imagery provided the basic framework for imaginative thought in America up until quite recent times, and unconsciously, its control is still formidable." That imagery recently attained the distinction of a TV miniseries, "The Greatest Heroes of the Bible." It was also in the background of Irving Wallace's miniseries, "The Word."

Many parts of the Bible were recited before they were ever committed to paper. And some influential biblical figures— Jesus himself is one—left no personal writings. As spoken word, the Bible can still attract. Witness actor Alec McCowen, who has been filling theaters this past year with his one-man recital (from memory) of the entire Gospel of St. Mark. A few weeks ago he performed at the White House.

Read or unread, new translations of the Bible have been cropping up regularly over the past few decades. In English alone there is developing a veritable alphabet soup of new versions: the RSV (Revised Standard Version); the NEB (New English Bible); the JB (Jerusalem Bible), and the TEV (Today's English Version, alias The Good News Bible). Most recently the full NIV (New International Version) has been published and will no doubt be many a person's Christmas gift this year.

These versions have spawned problems of their own. For instance, when you want to quote Shakespeare or Dickens you can simply quote Shakespeare or Dickens. But nowadays, more than ever, when you want to quote the Bible, you have to decide which translation you want to use. Less and less is the King James Version the literary standard it once was.

More than with perhaps any other book, people take offense when the biblical citation they learned in childhood is tampered with—even when clarity and accuracy are improved, which is not always the case. In the current Catholic liturgy, for example, one excerpt has Jesus say to his disciples at the Last Supper: "I will no longer call you slaves." The translation used to be "servants." Now the implication is that Jesus used to call Peter and the others his "slaves." Heard by an American ear, this word is naturally repugnant, doubly so coming from the mouth of Christ.

It was the figure of Jesus, of course, that divided the Bible into the Old Testament and the New Testament. Recent biblical studies have been emphasizing the Jewishness of Jesus as well as the anti-Judaism of parts of the New Testament. Anti-Judaism is a more accurate word than anti-Semitism—the early Christians, after all, were Semites—but anti-Semitism has been at least unconsciously fostered among Christians by the anti-Judaism of some of the New Testament.

In St. John's Gospel, for instance, "the Jews" usually means the enemies of Jesus, though most of his friends were Jewish too. (This negative implication is not found at all in St. Mark's Gospel, by way of contrast.) I remember my astonishment when Pope Paul VI offered mass in Yankee Stadium in October, 1965 and the Gospel selection began: "At that time the disciples were gathered together and the doors were shut, out of fear of the Jews." What an insensitive choice for a nationally televised mass coming from New York City (which has the world's largest Jewish population) and celebrated in the name of peace and world brotherhood!

Incidentally, while I can think of many understandable reasons why Jews might not want to read the New Testament, I was saddened to discover earlier this year that even the parable of the Good Samaritan was unfamiliar to some of my Jewish companions on a trip to Israel. In so many ways the teachings of Jesus were the flowering of Old Testament morality and spirituality and should, it seems to me, be regarded as a part of Jewish heritage.

A growing number of Christian voices are suggesting that the traditional division of the Bible into Old Testament and New Testament is a put-down of the Old Testament. Better, they say, would be a distinction between the Hebrew Scriptures and the Christian Scriptures. The Christian Bible would include both sets.

This reference to "Scriptures" in the plural is a reminder that the Bible is not so much a book as a little library of books. Actually, the word "Bible" originally meant just "books." How it came to mean so is an interesting story.

If you drive along the Lebanese coast about twenty miles north of Beirut, you will come upon the ruins of the ancient Phoenician city of Byblos. (They are near the modern city of Jubay.) To this city the ancient Egyptians once shipped papyrus, whence it was then distributed all over the Mediterranean world. Papyrus, of course, gave us our word for paper; the seaport of Byblos gave us our word Bible.

Muslims even today often refer to Christians and Jews as "the people of the book." They too, of course, have their own sacred volume, the Koran, which means "the recitation" or "the reading." Last September when President Carter addressed Congress in the presence of Premier Menachem Begin of Israel and President Anwar el Sadat of Egypt, he quoted from both the Hebrew Scriptures and the Christian Scriptures, but not from the Koran. That struck me as an indelicate slip-up, similar to the Yankee Stadium episode. How much effort it takes to remind ourselves, at least in the name of courtesy, that "our" world is not the only world!

In the effort to remain faithful to its precious insights, biblical religion has often acted as though its world were the only one—and this, despite the lessons of the biblical Book of Jonah itself, where the Jewish Jonah gets a reluctant lesson about God's mercy toward even "sinful gentiles." This heart-harming exclusiveness is reflected in some of the more terrible and ferocious passages of the Bible and is even attributed to God himself. Seeing how "God himself" can behave, many a fanatic has felt himself justified in perpetrating the worst atrocities in the name of pure religion.

An infamous example is Psalm 136/137, where the exiled psalmist sits and weeps by the waters of Babylon and then blesses the man who would crush against the rocks the children of his captors. One of my seminary teachers tried to soften this horror by saying: "You must remember, little Babylonians grew up to be big Babylonians."

Just a few weeks ago, in his syndicated newspaper column, Billy Graham tried to explain one of these "slay them all" passages in the Old Testament by insisting that God is just, as well as merciful, and that these sinners had proven their unworthiness by refusing to believe in God. How consoling it must be to have such easy answers! People who believe that every word in the Bible is divinely inspired and literally true have special need of such answers.

Other readers, dealing with these shocking passages, would rather identify with the poet X. J. Kennedy when he wrote "God one day read the Bible and instantly sued for libel." Such a reaction is, to be sure, overstated, since in its many wise, beautiful, and inspiring passages the Bible seems eminently worthy of whatever divine influence might be ascribed to it.

In all such matters there is no substitute for the reader's own conscientious judgment. For even if we decide to accept someone else's view of how we should accept and understand the Scriptures, we must ultimately base *that* decision on our own personal judgment.

Perhaps the general advice of Walt Whitman is apropos here: "Dismiss whatever insults your own soul." For his part, Whitman's contemporary, Abraham Lincoln, said of the Bible that he took into himself whatever he could properly understand and let the rest go.

It would be regrettable, though, if an increasing number of Americans let the whole thing go unread. They will be depriving themselves of the chance to understand their own religious, cultural, and literary heritage. They will be cheating themselves of the chance to be nourished by words, images, and episodes that have motivated some of the best and brightest of our race for long centuries. For all its darknesses, obscurities, even horrors, the Bible is still a feast of lights.

50. No End to Those End-of-the-World Scares

The Baltimore Evening Sun: September 19, 1978

FOR THEIR own special reasons, a great many Americans were waiting nervously as the Middle East peace treaty meetings proceeded at Camp David. For, according to a recent book, which claims to have 250,000 copies in print, the signing of such a peace treaty between Israel and its enemies "will start the final countdown leading to Armageddon."

Armageddon (which was also the title of Leon Uris's 1964 novel) is one of those words known melodiously and Greekly as a *hapax legomenon*. In plainer English, it is a word that occurs only one time in the records of a given language or in a given body of literature. In this case, the word occurs in the sixteenth verse of the sixteenth chapter of the final book of the Christian Scriptures, known as "Revelation" or "The Apocalypse." There, in vivid imagery, the author is giving the location of the ultimate showdown battle between good and evil in the cosmos.

As with many other aspects of this mystical book, the meaning of the location is disputed by scholars. There still exists in Israel an ancient town of Megiddo not far from Nazareth, which lay in one of the fiercest battleground areas of biblical times. Armageddon may be taken to mean in Hebrew "the mountain of Megiddo"—though the Bible makes no reference elsewhere to such a mountain. So much for the initial obscurity surrounding this word.

Such obscurity doesn't bother John F. Walvoord and his son, John E., the co-authors of a revised 1976 book entitled *Armageddon: Oil and the Middle East Crisis*. The theme of that book is what the Bible says about the future of the Middle East and the end of Western civilization. The father has served as president of the Dallas Theological Seminary; his son is a graduate. Their field is the tricky one of biblical prophecy, and in this volume they have a field day.

The book has been scaring the wits out of many of its readers, for it is a doomsday book. Its two hundred pages are full of information about ancient Israel and the events that have produced modern Israel; about the crucial city of Jerusalem and the oil power of the anti-Israel Arabs. From these facts, the authors proceed to construct an imaginative scenario about the colossal catastrophes that lie ahead for the world. They base this scenario on various prophecies scattered throughout the Bible that deal with the "restoration of Israel," God's wrathful judgment on the enemies of Israel, and the Second Coming of Christ.

No matter that these prophecies may have been conditional, may have referred to previous restorations of Israel, and may in some cases have been written as after-the-event flashbacks. The authors seem sure that they refer to modern Israel.

Highlights to come include: the quick rebuilding of the Jewish temple; the emergence of a Mediterranean Confederacy to be taken over by a satanic leader; a Russian invasion of Israel; millions of Red Chinese marching from the East to fight at Armageddon; millions of true Christians suddenly disappearing from the earth. The authors allow that this last development will deepen the religious confusion of our times. I'll bet! This, by the way, is the "rapture" you've been reading about on bumper stickers.

According to the authors, all this must happen in a relative hurry, since it depends on Arab oil clout, and this clout may dwindle away within the next generation.

Although the book abounds in definite facts and definite prophecies, the authors usually slip in a "may be" or "seemingly" or "it could well be" when biblical push gets down to contemporary shove. Also, though this book by fundamentalist Christians might be regarded as pro-Israel, let it be noted that after Armageddon "unbelieving Jews" will have been divinely judged and killed, along with purged, unbelieving non-Jews.

I know good people who have been impressed and depressed by this book. "What hope is there if all of this has been divinely foreordained? And who knows whether he/she is a salvageable Christian or Jew?"

I advise such people to recall that many such "end-of-the-world" prophecies were made in the past and proven false. I advise them to read, and read about, biblical prophecies *in toto*, to discover how hotly contested their meanings are and how selectively they are cited by the authors of this book. I also ask them whether they think God engages in mind-boggling, blood-chilling guessing games.

I myself like the view of Thomas Aquinas and other moralists that there can be a sin of curiosity connected with the desire to know the future. I also like the implications of these words attributed to Jesus: "It is not for you to know the times or dates which the Father has fixed by His own authority" (Acts 1:7). It is the present moment of possible peace that deserves our chief attention, our courage, and our honor.

51. Tampering with a Sacred Text?

The Baltimore Evening Sun: December 8, 1981

AT THE recent meeting of the Catholic bishops in Washington, D.C., it was announced that Pope John Paul II had granted permission for one word attributed to Christ to be dropped from the text of the mass. That word was "men" and occurred in the sacred words of consecration: "This is the cup of my blood . . . It will be shed for you and for all men."

Catholic feminists and others have been insisting that the word "men" is sexist and creates a jolting effect at the heart of the mass. Yet the question arises: by what right did the pope tamper with a sacred text?

The simple answer is that so far as we know, Jesus never said his blood would be shed "for all men." And by so saying, I am not referring to the obvious fact that Jesus didn't speak English. I mean that in the oldest version of Christ's words that we have—the Greek New Testament—Jesus says his blood will be shed *huper pollon*—"for many."

The Greek word *pollon* can be masculine, feminine, or neuter. It's the same word as *polloi* in the phrase *hoi polloi* (the masses), except that the *oi* ending makes it masculine. Even so, such a masculine form of the word can still mean people in general, of either sex—as can our English word "men."

Language scholars tell us that in Aramaic, the Semitic language Jesus used (and for which the Greek in the Christian Scriptures is a translation), the word "many" can, like *hoi polloi*, mean merely a large number of people, without intending any restriction, or meaning less than all. In English, philosophers have similar meanings in mind when they discuss the problem of "the one and the many." They mean one member of a group as opposed to the whole group.

Now it just so happens that some dissident groups in Christian history have taught that Jesus did not in fact die for everybody. Some would say, for instance, that he died only for those who will actually be saved. Crucifixes were designed that narrowed the spread of Christ's arms on the cross and intended thereby to symbolize this dissident view. Such a view was at times partly based on a literal interpretation of what Jesus said at the Last Supper about shedding his blood "for many."

To help head off what Catholic theology would call a misinterpretation, recent translations of the texts of the mass have been using the phrase "for all men." But as we've seen, this is actually a paraphrase that means to be more accurate than a literal translation.

But so far as we know, on that solemn Holy Thursday occasion Jesus said neither "many men" nor "all men." So, far from tampering with a sacred text, the latest version is closer to the pertinent and fundamental biblical texts. So scholars, sticklers, and feminists can all rejoice.

52. *Imitatio Christi:*
A Freethinker's
Favorite Book

The Baltimore Evening Sun: December 21, 1978

WHEN Pope John Paul I died three months ago, he was reportedly holding a copy of *The Imitation of Christ.* Some weeks later I phoned a religious bookstore and learned that there had been a run on copies of that book after the pope's death.

Some customers had never heard of the book or of its presumed author, Thomas à Kempis. But gossip columnist Liz Smith began one of her columns last month with a quote from the fifteenth century devotional writer.

Granted that "role model" may be a recent phrase, the idea is an ancient one. Christmas celebrates the birth of a man who has long been such a model for millions of human beings. Christ invited this response explicitly by saying such things as "Learn of me" and "As I have done so ought you also to do."

But what is this book that bears the specific title, *The Imitation of Christ* (*Imitatio Christi*, in the original)?

Saints like Ignatius Loyola have rated it first after the Bible. Pope John XXIII used to sing its praises. It has been translated from its original Latin into more than fifty languages and remains among the most widely read volumes in the world. (When I was in the seminary, a portion of it was read aloud to us each night after supper.)

The Imitation is a relatively small book. Actually, like the Gospels, it is really four books, each with a varying number of chapters. Some chapters are less than one page long; the average is about two. Each chapter has a title—the opening chapter is "On Following Christ Our Model."

Book One (twenty-five chapters) offers advice on living a Christian life. Book Two (twelve chapters) provides further considerations on leading such a so-called interior life. Book Three (fifty-nine chapters) deals with the interior conversation known as prayer. The final book (eighteen chapters) treats of the devout reception of Holy Communion.

For centuries there has been controversy about the true author of this book, who ironically advises: "Ask not who said this, but give your attention to what is said."

Current scholarly opinion attributes the book to a German monk, Thomas Hammerken. He was born of peasant stock around 1379, in the northwest German city of Kempen—whence his name à Kempis. After a long and obscure life, he died in 1471—about a decade before the birth of Martin Luther.

As a youth, Thomas studied in the nearby Netherlands under the Brothers of the Common Life, a pious society founded not long before by a reform-minded Dutch deacon, Gerard Groote. Some have claimed that *The Imitation* comes from Groote's diary as edited by à Kempis. Thomas entered the Augustinian religious order (as Luther was to do) and spent most of his life at a monastery named Mount St. Agnes, near the Dutch city of Zwolle.

Thomas practiced a type of piety known in its day as the *devotio moderna*—in contrast to the previously dominant kind of devotion that was highly intellectual and speculative. This new approach stressed the human life of Jesus, as distinguished from attempts to analyze his divine nature. It also stressed Bible reading, self-denial, and perfection as the fulfillment of obligations.

As embodied in *The Imitation*, this devotion has been called a forerunner of Protestant piety; at the same time it imparted its flavor to early Jesuit piety. Though written from a monk's point of view—"The dwelt-in cell causes delight"—many "worldly" souls have drawn nourishment from its pages. Mary Ann Evans, alias George Eliot, would probably be termed a religious freethinker. But in her novel, *The Mill on the Floss*, she wrote this pertinent and ardent passage:

"Maggie's eyes glanced down on the books that lay on the window-shelf . . . Thomas à Kempis?—the name had come across her in her reading . . . She took up the little, old, clumsy book with some curiosity . . . She read on and on in the old book . . . She knew nothing of doctrines and systems . . . but this voice out of the far-off middle ages was the direct communication of a human soul's belief and experience, and came to Maggie as an unquestioned message.

"I suppose that is the reason why the small old-fashioned book . . . works miracles to this day, turning bitter waters into sweetness: while expensive sermons and treatises, newly issued, leave all things as they were before. It was written down by a hand that waited for the heart's prompting; it is the chronicle of a solitary, hidden anguish, struggle, trust and triumph—not written on velvet cushions to teach endurance to those who are treading with bleeding feet on the stones.

"And so it remains to all time a lasting record of human needs and human consolations: the voice of a brother who, ages ago, felt and suffered and renounced—in the cloister, perhaps with serge gown and tonsured head, with much chanting and long fasts, and with a fashion of speech different from ours—but under the same silent far-off heavens, and with the same passionate desires, the same strivings, the same failures, the same weariness."

Granted that some Christians down through the centuries have done harm to themselves and to others in the name of Christ, most people who try to imitate the nonviolent Christ are likely to feel that they are better persons and the world a better place for their having done so.

When the aged St. Polycarp was commanded to revile the name of Christ in A.D. 155, he gave his pagan captors a classic response: "Four-score and six years I have served Christ and he hath done me no harm." That is no small praise in the world of Attilas, Hitlers, and Reverend Jim Joneses, where so much evil has followed from the often lethal game of following the leader.

53. Christ as Woman; God as Mother

The Baltimore Evening Sun: May 9, 1984

RECENTLY a crucifix depicting Jesus as a woman was exhibited in the Episcopal Cathedral of St. John the Divine in New York. (It was sculpted by Edwina Sandys in 1975 for the United Nations Decade for Women.) Before long it was ordered removed by church authorities. The near-nudity of the figure, referred to as Christa, no doubt enhanced its startling effect.

There can be no serious doubt about the masculinity of the historic Jesus. He didn't hesitate, though, to refer to himself in maternal terms—as when he said that he longed to gather the people of Jerusalem to himself the way a hen does her chicks. At a time and in a culture that downgraded women, Jesus showed extraordinary sensitivity toward women. Think of Martha and Mary, the woman taken in adultery, Mary Magdalen, and the Samaritan woman at the well.

In spiritual terms, the crucified Jesus stands for all of history's innocent sufferers. In view of the sexual violence inflicted on women, the various discriminations practiced against them, the multiple sorrows of mothers and wives, womankind is rightly linked with Christ crucified. Indeed, it was mostly women who wept for him beneath the cross.

Some months ago headlines were made by a new edition of Bible readings that tried to remove "sexist" references to God. Now this is a different matter from a Christus presented as a Christa. For though Jesus was a male, God is not—at least not in traditional Christian theology. True, the Bible speaks of God as Father, King, Master, Shepherd, and other masculinities. But it also refers to Him as a rock, as living water, as a whirlwind.

The idea behind such namings is this: God is the creator of all things; therefore He embodies, in His own unimaginable way, the positive perfections and none of the imperfections of things created. For that reason he is authoritative as a father, tender as a mother, caring like a shepherd, strong as a rock. In Biblical times masculinity was more suggestive of superiority than femininity. Jesus found it best to relate to God as a loving father. Under the mantle of his special sonship, the followers of Jesus are invited to relate to God in the same way.

But we must never forget that when we engage in "God-talk" we are speaking about the Unspeakable, the Ineffable. ("The name that can be spoken is not the divine name," say the Buddhists.) But regardless of what God is "in Himself," it does make a human difference how we imagine the unimaginable. That's why we use comparison speech—simile, metaphor, analogy, parable. In that sense all religion is comparative religion: "Jesus said 'The Kingdom of heaven is like unto . . .' "

Happily, though, God can be father-like without lacking the positive advantage of being mother-like. "Even if a mother forget her child, I will not forget you," says God through the Hebrew prophet Isaiah.

Thomas Aquinas and other theologians teach that nothing can be said simultaneously of God and of a creature in a univocal (identical) sense—not even that He "exists." Indeed mystics sometimes say that God's way of existing is so unthinkable that we might be less misleading if we said that He doesn't "exist." (For starters: we have our existence, and rather shakily at that. God *is* His existence.)

Atheists, who may be closer than they think to mystics, provide a needed warning to believers against taking God-talk literally. (Langdon Gilkey's illustrative *Naming the Whirlwind* deals in scholarly detail with the slippery issue of God-talk.)

Back to Aquinas: if the word "father" cannot be applied to the man who begot me and to the universal creator in an identical (univocal) sense, does that mean that the word "father" is being used in an entirely different (equivocal) sense—as when we call both a jail and a writing implement a "pen"?

No, there is a third way with words, called analogical—as when we talk of the bed of a sleeper and the bed of a river. These beds are fundamentally different, but there can be seen between them a similarity of relationship. In this instance, the river bottom relates to a body of water the way that a mattress relates to a sleeping body. (Even here, "body" of water is used analogically, poetically, metaphorically.)

Aquinas says that all God-talk is analogical. In fact, a good bit of all talk is analogical. Language itself has been (metaphorically) called "frozen metaphor." It has been claimed that the "heart" of Shakespeare is metaphor. In his book, *Sense and Nonsense in Religion*, Sten Stenson tells how he began his book as an attack on religion, how he discovered en route the role of metaphor in religion, and how he ended up defending religion. [As for the other end of reality, scientist Niels Bohr argued: "When it comes to atoms, language can be used only as poetry."]

In Jewish tradition, God is at one point represented as saying: "Would that you would forget Me and keep My commandments." Translation: don't worry so much about My proper Name. Rather, work harder at being just, merciful, and humble. Good advice (I dare say), even if we need scholars to think and talk about God-talk, its limited necessity, and its necessary limits.

54. Religion: Is It Mostly Inoculation Shots?

The Baltimore Evening Sun: August 18, 1976

IT WOULD be intriguing to know what the man in the street thinks that the man in the pulpit thinks about the latest Gallup survey on religion in America. Upon learning that the United States is "extraordinarily religious," with 94 percent believing in God, 69 percent expecting life after death, 71 percent belonging to some church or synagogue, and 40 percent attending religious services in a typical week, does the man of the cloth say "Hooray for our side"?

Upon learning that there is little evidence of any large-scale turning away from religion in the past fifteen years, that the percentage who feel that religion is increasing its influence on American society has leaped from 14 percent to 39 percent, and that 86 percent of the population feels that religious beliefs are either "very important" (56 percent), or "fairly important" (30 percent), does the delighted divine declare *Deo gratias*? Well, here is a sampling of one clergyman's thoughts, which may not be altogether untypical.

The novelist Graham Greene once warned that preoccupation with "right and wrong" can distract you from the deeper question of "good and evil." Similarly, concern with the quantity of religiousness can steal attention from the more crucial matter of its quality.

In any case, according to the great religious traditions themselves, the ultimate questions are not about how religious people are, or how religion is faring—especially organized religion. The Jewish tradition contains a startling example of priorities in one of its holy books. There God is portrayed as saying to human beings: "Would that you would forget Me and keep My commandments." In other words, God would prefer, in a showdown, that ritual worship be neglected rather than that His commands about mercy and justice be disobeyed. Not that He needs our worship in the first place.

Nurtured by that same tradition, Jesus himself warned: "Not everyone who says to me, Lord, Lord, will enter the kingdom of heaven, but he who does the will of my Father." Ideally, serious-minded adherence to one of the major religious traditions should help a person to become more ethical and loving. But there is such a thing as getting inoculated against the divine and its claim on practical life, i.e., getting a little case of it by way of preventing a big case of it.

There are aspects of the Gallup report that indicate that some of our national religiousness may be an expression of that "cheap grace" against which the German martyr-theologian Dietrich Bonhoeffer warned.

There's nothing new, to be sure, about all of this. We human beings have always had trouble 1) deciding which is the best way to act and 2) getting ourselves to do what we have decided. To the extent that they are religious in character, the current tragedies in Northern Ireland and in Lebanon are reminders that it is easier to have enough religion to make you hate than enough to make you love. I say this without any assurance as to how I would behave in the midst of such tragedies, especially if I were convinced that my loved ones were in peril.

I say it also without any desire to romanticize the irreligious or the antireligious, as contrasted with the religious and their "religious wars." Neither Hitler nor Stalin was noted for his religiousness or his humanity. A person's ultimate concerns are his religion. But the question is not only what my ultimate concerns are, but how I deal with those who do not share them, or who appear ready to attack them.

From the theological aspect, the question is whether a person who calls himself religious actually has ultimate concerns that are religious. The novelist Samuel Butler wrote of those routine Christians who would be as shocked to see Christianity practiced as they would be to hear it denied. Contrast that situation with Cardinal Suhard's definition of believing in God: "Acting in such a way that if God didn't exist your life wouldn't make sense."

My final thoughts about "religious America" spring from what scholars like Peter Berger point out about the sociology of religion, namely, that acceptable religiousness in a given society can function all too readily to sanctify the status quo and the smooth running of that society. By contrast, as the Hebrew prophets exemplify, the deepest demands of religion may call for the disturbance of the status quo and the condemnation of a given society.

In sum: if America's statistical religiousness is truly an index of our sense of the sacred, our reverence for life, our universal benevolence, our capacity for self-control and self-sacrifice, then hooray indeed. If it isn't, I'm not surprised.

But I'm not cynical either. As I grow older, I have more respect for the great number of everyday people who, all things considered, are doing about the best they can. We grapple with the purest concepts of religion the way high schoolers put on a Shakespearean play: it is so worth doing that it is worth doing even rather badly. In fact, biblical religion assures us that's exactly how we'll do without that Outside Help which goes by another name.

55. What Really Happened at Masada?

The Baltimore Evening Sun: May 11, 1981

MILLIONS of Americans watched the recent TV miniseries, "Masada," filmed on location in the Judean desert west of the Dead Sea. Superb acting by stars like Peter O'Toole and Peter Strauss kept audiences captive to the eight-hour saga of 960 Jews who chose death atop a mountain fortress (*masada*) over surrender to the pagan Romans.

As presented on TV that story was based on a 1970 novel, *The Antagonists*, by Ernest Gann. The novel has now been reissued with the new title, *Masada*, and currently seems to be on every paperback shelf.

Many viewers are wondering just how historical the story is and how accurately it was portrayed on TV. They need to know that there is only one significant source of information about the fortress, and that is the writings of the Jewish historian and general, Flavius Josephus.

Josephus was born in Jerusalem about A.D. 37 and died sometime after the year 100. At the start of the Jewish revolt against Rome in A.D. 66, he commanded the Jewish forces in Galilee. After his surrender, he won favor among the Roman leaders and unsuccessfully tried to persuade his fellow Jews to surrender.

Five years after the fall of Jerusalem and the destruction of the Temple (A.D. 70), he published his history of *The Jewish War*, first in Hebrew and then in Greek. Only the Greek version survives. Divided into seven "books," the English translation runs about 263 double-column pages of small print in the volume that I consulted.

The last two chapters of the final "book," i.e., chapters 8 and 9 of book 7, deal with the siege of Masada in A.D. 72–73.

The whole section, covering less than eight pages, tells the history of the fortification, how Jewish zealots had seized it, and how the Roman commander Silva went about besieging it and finally breaking into it with a giant battering ram.

Josephus is more explicit than TV was about the Jewish death plan: "They then chose 10 men by lot to slay all the rest; every one of whom laid himself down by his wife and children on the ground, and threw his arms about them, and they offered their necks to the stroke of those who by lot executed that melancholy office; and when these 10 had, without fear, slain them all, they made the same rule for casting lots for themselves, that he whose lot it was should first kill the other nine, and after all should kill himself."

What Josephus does interestingly say that the TV version omitted is that there were survivors. "There was an ancient woman, and another who was kin to Eleazar, and superior to most women in prudence and learning, with five children, who had concealed themselves in caverns underground . . . when the rest were intent upon the slaughter of one another. (Later) the women came out of their underground cavern and informed the Romans what had been done . . . and the second of them clearly described all, both what was said and what was done."

It was presumably from the memories of these women that Josephus or his source was able to reconstruct the final speech of Eleazar, which exceeds three pages of small print and double columns.

From other sources we know that the Romans kept a garrison on Masada for at least another forty years, and that Silva returned to Rome and became a consul there. In the fifth and sixth centuries groups of monks occupied the hilltop. Then the site became lost to history. In modern times the first recorded visit to it occurred in 1842 in the persons of an American missionary and an English painter.

How reliable is Josephus? Because he was a Jew, many Romans suspected him. Because he had won imperial favor, many Jews suspected and despised him. The *Encyclopedia Judaica* (Jerusalem, 1971) asserts that his works "must be treated with considerable caution."

Actually, Josephus was no partisan of the zealots who died on Masada. They were called *sicarii*—"stabbers"—because of their method of dealing with anyone who disagreed with them, including fellow Jews. Still, Josephus concludes his work on the Jewish war with this reference to the dead of Masada: "The Romans could not do other than wonder at the courage of their resolution and the immovable contempt for death which so great a number of them had shown."

56. Martin Luther at 500

The Baltimore Sunday Sun: November 6, 1983

THURSDAY is the 500th birthday of the father of the Protestant Reformation, a Catholic priest and theologian named Martin Luther. I had nineteen years of Catholic education, almost exclusively in Baltimore, and to the best of my recollection my teachers and textbooks did not make a supervillain of the scrupulous Augustinian monk who at the age of thirty-five began his public attack on some Catholic doctrines and practices of his day.

There were student jokes about his supposed memoirs: "I Was a Teenage Catholic." We cited what James Joyce said when asked whether he had become a Protestant: "I lost my faith but not my senses." We were reminded often enough that Luther broke his vows and married a nun with the slightly sinister name of Katharina von Bora, that his language could be scatalogical, that he had "anti-Semitic outbursts" and that he turned against the peasants who thought they were being inspired by him when they rebelled against their Germanic masters.

The imposing statue of Luther that once stood at the North Avenue entrance to Baltimore's Druid Hill Park and now faces Lake Montebello suggested a rather ferocious, daunting character to my Catholic eyes. A seminary friend of mine liked to fantasize about erecting a statue of St. Patrick next to Luther and thereby, somehow, putting the latter in his place. (Was he thinking of the quip: St. Patrick converted the Irish and St. Boniface did what he could for the Germans?)

In those polemical, preecumenical days, Luther had to be all wrong if we Catholics were to be all right—though some Catholic sources admitted that in Luther's day, here and there, now and then, there had been certain Catholic excesses, regrettable but understandable, especially in the matter of indulgences.

An indulgence is the cancelling of a spiritual debt still due on forgiven sins, a cancelling that results from the performance of pious deeds (such as alms-giving) to which the church has assigned varying spiritual value. Of course, such indulgences could not be sold (Catholic apologists insist) but some overzealous, insufficiently precise and excessively popularizing preachers might have given their congregation a warped impression.

Granted that in my mind Luther was no supervillain. But he was far from a hero, as we were usually repersuaded to believe annually around Reformation Sunday, which fell near the Catholic Feast of Christ the King. I recall marching to the stadium on this feast several times with other Baltimore Catholics and hearing sermons that directly or indirectly put Brother Martin in his unenviable place.

Now, less than three decades after my ordination, I can read in *Time* magazine that "Ecumenical Catholic theologians have come to rank Luther in importance with Augustine and Aquinas. 'No one who came after Luther could match him,' says Father Peer Mann, a Catholic theologian in Mainz. 'On the question of truth, Luther is a lifesaver for Christians.' "

Father George Tavard, a French Catholic expert on Protestantism, is quoted as saying this about the Reformer's key doctrine of justification by faith alone: "Today many Catholic scholars think Luther was right."

What happened? Catholics have found the courage and the honesty to face the facts about Protestant virtues and Catholic sins, especially at the time of the Reformation. Twenty-two years ago, in the wake of the ecumenism of Pope John XXIII, I was reckoning with these facts as I wrote for Baltimore's *Catholic Review* an editorial entitled "The Ecumenical Catholic."

I could quote an Italian Jesuit theologian who was then teaching in Rome itself: "Common sanctity is fairly widespread in Protestantism." (Protestant saints?)

I could quote a Catholic saint, Clement Hofbauer: "Many became Protestants at the time of the Reformation because they wanted to save their souls."

On the subject of Catholic corruption, I could quote a pope of Luther's time (1523), Adrian VI, the last non-Italian pope before the present pope: "The disease has spread from the head to the members, from popes to prelates of lesser degree." (He didn't last long.)

I don't know whether it was made public in its own time, but I could cite a report given in 1537 to the reform-minded

Pope Paul III by a select group of cardinals and other clerics: "The Church of Christ is almost in ruins and in no place has evil been more active than in the Roman Curia [the papal bureaucracy] . . . through our fault, our fault, we repeat, Holy Father."

By 1517 the Catholic practice of indulgences had become an idolatry, in profound contradiction to the Scriptures and to the essence of Christianity. For all his considerable warts, Luther had the courage to lash out against this colossal perversion. Salvation is a free gift and is not to be purchased by toted-up good works and heavy collection plates—though generous Christians can show by their generosity that they understand Christ's words: "Freely you have received, freely give." It is a happy birthday circumstance that on his fifth centenary Catholics can freely give to Brother Martin the praise that he deserves.

Part Five

Church Circles

57. Pius XII and the Holocaust

America: April 4, 1987

I N 1958, thirteen years after World War II ended and the full horror of the Holocaust was first dawning on mankind, an international figure died. The international Jewish community expressed heartfelt condolences. The World Jewish Congress lauded him as a helper of persecuted Jews.

Rabbi Joachim Prinz, national president of the American Jewish Congress, praised the deceased man's "earnest efforts made in the rescue of thousands of victims of the Nazi persecution, including many Jewish men, women, and children."

Speaking for the Jewish community in Rome, Israel Goldstein, western hemisphere executive of the World Jewish Congress, spoke of its "deep appreciation" for the deceased man's World War II "policy of giving shelter and protection to Jews wherever possible."

A spokesman for the Synagogue Council of America attested to the "profound regard" in which the deceased was held by the Jewish community, "which recalls with gratitude the succor and refuge he gave to refugees of all nations during World War II."

Rabbi Maurice N. Eisendrath, president of the Union of American Hebrew Congregations, prophesied that this "revered" figure "will long be remembered for his rescue of many victims of Nazism."

That revered figure was Pope Pius XII. The quotations are from *The New York Times* of October 1958. Also cited was the New York eulogy of Rabbi William Rosenblum, who recalled that "during the Hitler holocaust Pius XII made it possible for thousands of Jewish victims of Nazism and Fascism to be hidden away in monasteries and convents, and Jewish children to be taken into orphanages."

But a recent article and a nationally televised statement by columnist George Will negated Rabbi Eisendrath's prophecy. Once again at issue is the supposed "silence" of the wartime pope, Pius XII.

True, he did not attack Hitler publicly—any more than he attacked the atheistic mass-murderer Stalin by name, or the Allied leaders whose policy of saturation bombing he judged immoral. But he did endlessly denounce the brutalities of war, weighed the dangers of Nazi reprisals against the defenseless, hoped to mediate an early ending of the war, and kept intensifying Vatican efforts on behalf of prisoners of war and their families, and of Jewish refugees. As Michael Marrus notes in his recent *The Holocaust in History*, Vatican records do not reveal "particular indifference to the fate of the Jews, let alone hostility toward them."

Albrecht von Kessel, a German diplomat at the Vatican and later an anti-Hitler conspirator, has given firsthand witness to the pope's policy of helping Jews and other war victims by behind-the-scenes pressure and negotiations.

Reviewing one of the Vatican's eleven volumes of documentation concerning these efforts, historian J. S. Conway noted in the (London) *Times Literary Supplement* of January 23, 1981: "The Vatican's efforts . . . continued to be made [late in the war], despite the depressing record of failure . . . Its resources were always too few, its motives were suspected, and its interventions were frequently ignored or turned aside . . . Those who argue that a more active policy of protest might have achieved better results can see from these documents how implacable and frustrating were the policies of the warring governments to all arguments based either on the rights of the Church or on humanitarian and charitable grounds."

In the interest of fairness, a few other points merit mention: Whatever the pope decided to say or not to say publicly, he did so at a time when 3,000 Catholic priests died and millions of European Christians, especially Poles, suffered at the hands of the Nazis. Some 2,579 priests, brothers, and religious were herded into Dachau. More than one thousand perished. As Jewish historian Martin Gilbert notes in his definitive study, *The Holocaust*, "As well as the 6 million Jews who were murdered, more than 10 million other noncombatants were killed by the Nazis."

Was Pius XII possibly pro-Nazi? A full-page headline in *The Baltimore Sun* of March 3, 1939 declared: "Election of Pacelli Surprise and Disappointment to Followers of Hitler." That same day the *Berlin Morgenpost* was blunt: "The election of Cardinal Pacelli is not accepted with favor in Germany because he was always opposed to Nazism." Had not the future pope said of the Nazis: "They are in reality only miserable plagiarists who dress up old errors with new tinsel . . . they are possessed by the superstition of a race and blood cult." (Lourdes, France: 1935).

Was the pope then perhaps anti-Semitic? In his very first and closely read encyclical as pope (1939), he branded, as the first of modern pernicious errors, "the forgetfulness of that law of human solidarity and charity which is dictated and imposed by our common origin and by the equality of rational nature in all men, to whatever people they belong."

Can there be any doubt as to how these words sounded in the ear of a Hitler already persecuting Jews in the name of Aryan purity and superiority? Later during the war, the pope declared: "For centuries the Jews have been most unjustly treated and despised. It is time they were treated with justice and humanity. God wills it and the church wills it." Here he was echoing the 1938 radio statement of his predecessor, Pius XI, whom he served as papal secretary of state: "Anti-Semitism is a movement in which we Christians can have no part whatsoever . . . spiritually we are Semites."

In his very first Christmas message (1939), shortly after the outbreak of war, Pius XII openly condemned "atrocities . . . against noncombatants, refugees, old people, women and children . . . acts which cry for the vengeance of God."

Two years later *The New York Times* carried a front-page story about Pius XII's 1941 Christmas message. The headline read: "Pope Condemns Persecutions." That same day it editorialized: "The voice of Pius XII is a lonely voice in the silence [!] and darkness enveloping Europe . . . his words sound bold in the Europe of today . . . he is about the only ruler left on the continent of Europe who dares to raise his voice at all . . . the Pope squarely sets himself against Hitlerism."

In his next Christmas message (1942), Pius XII again publicly lamented that "hundreds of thousands of persons, through no fault of their own, have been condemned to death or to progressive extinction."

How did the Axis leaders react to this mid-war denunciation? Mussolini, who had been furious when the pope refused to praise Hitler's attack on "godless" Russia, said the pope "ought never to have opened his mouth." Nazi Foreign Minister Ribbentrop threatened reprisals. The German ambassador to the Holy See wrote: "Here he is clearly speaking on behalf of the Jews . . . and makes himself the mouthpiece of Jewish war criminals."

How did *The New York Times* react this time? It editorialized: "This Christmas more than ever the Pope is a lonely voice crying out of the silence [!] of a continent . . . because the Pope speaks to and in some sense for all the peoples at war, the clear stand he takes on the fundamental issues of the conflict has greater weight and authority.

"When a leader bound impartially to nations on both sides condemns as 'heresy' the new form of national state which subordinates everything to itself, when he assails the exile and persecution of human beings 'for no other reasons than their race or political opinion' . . . the 'impartial' judgment is like a verdict in a high court of justice. Pope Pius expresses as passionately as any leader on our side the war aims of the struggle for freedom."

Despite such words the same newspaper recently and forgetfully editorialized: "Pope Pius XII was shamelessly silent about Nazi Germany's crimes against Jews and non-Jews."

In 1943 the celebrated Rabbi Morris Lazaron of the Baltimore Hebrew Congregation spoke of the pope as the prisoner of the Vatican and asked for prayers on his behalf. On one subject the rabbi had not found the pope silent: "The Pope has condemned anti-Semitism and all its works." In the same issue of Baltimore's *Catholic Review* that quoted the rabbi (November 5, 1943) this headline appears: "Holy See is Eager to Rescue Hebrews." The story told of the arrest of Roman Jews, the concern of the Vatican, and the pope's offer of gold to ransom Jewish hostages.

New evidence has now become available of Pius XII's support of the plan of German generals in 1940 to overthrow Hitler and end the war through negotiation. (For earlier data see

Harold C. Deutsch's *The Conspiracy Against Hitler in the Twilight War*: U. of Minn. Press, 1968.) Published by Cambridge University Press, the book is called *Britain and the Vatican During the Second World War*. Anglican author Owen Chadwick, professor of history at Cambridge since 1958, affirms: "Never in all history had a pope engaged so delicately in a conspiracy to overthrow a tyrant by force."

The book is heavily based on the wartime diaries and diplomatic reports of d'Arcy Godolphin Osborne, British minister to the Holy See from 1936 to 1947. Osborne tells how, with the complicity of London, he sometimes slanted his diplomatic wartime messages to make the Vatican look pro-Axis because he knew there was a Fascist spy in the mailroom and wanted to keep Mussolini from isolating the Vatican any more than it already was. In a matter of minutes Italy could have seized Vatican City, or cut off its heat, electricity, food and cash flow. Also, there was a Gestapo agent in the papal secretariat of state.

Of this wartime pope, presented as such a cold fish by Murphy/Arlington's recent and popular *La Popessa*, the non-Catholic Osborne wrote in a letter to *The London Times*: "So far from being a cool diplomatist, Pius XII was the most warmly humane, kind, generous, and sympathetic (and incidentally saintly) character that it has been my privilege to know in the course of a long life."

When in 1963 the thirty-two-year-old German Rolf Hochhuth first staged his anti-Pius XII play, *The Deputy*, Harry Greenstein, executive director of Baltimore's Associated Jewish Charities, wrote to several local newspapers: "I cannot permit the implication of lack of sympathy for the plight of the Jews by the late beloved Pope Pius XII to go unanswered." Greenstein recalled a wartime meeting with the chief rabbi of Jerusalem, who attested that the pope had saved hundreds of Jews by providing them refuge in the Vatican. Later Mr. Goldstein conveyed the personal blessing of the rabbi to the pope, who said his only regret was not having been able to save more victims.

At the same time, Dr. Otto Dibelius, Evangelical bishop of Berlin, said of the play: "This is a very cheap and highly naive way of writing history." Here in the United States, the national director of the Jewish B'nai B'rith asserted: "Pius XII was to a large extent personally instrumental in organized efforts to help Jewish victims of Nazism. His efforts to ease the lot of Jews continued throughout the war." Another director of that organization spoke of the "magnificent assistance" Pius XII gave his Jewish brethren.

As has already been documented, nearly two decades after the war began those efforts were not forgotten by the people who actually lived through that cataclysmic war, which caused an estimated thirty-five million deaths. When the pope himself died, Israel's president, Itzhak Ben-Zvi, expressed profound sympathy for the grief of the Catholics of his nation. His foreign minister, Golda Meir, said: "When fearful martyrdom came to our people in the decade of Nazi terror, the voice of the Pope was raised for the victims." In his book, *Three Popes and the Jews*, Israeli scholar Pinchas Lapide estimated that of the nearly two million European Jews who escaped Hitler's final solution, Pius XII and the Catholic Church under his direction saved 860,000 Jewish lives.

One comes to wonder how many Pius XIIs there were. Mr. Will's pontiff seems Hochhuthian. Perhaps he will like better the Pius XII that Professor Chadwick documents. At the end of World War II this pope, who had directed religious orders to shelter fugitive Jews and melted Vatican chalices to ransom Roman Jews, made this revealing public statement: "Every word We addressed to the responsible authorities and every one of Our public declarations had to be seriously weighed and considered in the interest of the persecuted themselves in order not to make their situation unwittingly more difficult and unbearable."

The pope was painfully aware that immediately after the Dutch Catholic bishops made public protest against the Nazi deportation of Jews, the Nazis intensified their persecution to include Christians of Jewish origin such as the Carmelite nun Edith Stein. Austrian historian F. Engel-Janosi calculated that 79 percent of Dutch Jews perished, whereas 90 percent of Roman Jews survived.

On this score Leon Poliskov, Jewish author of *The Jews Under the Italian Occupation* allows: "One cannot say that there may not have been pertinent and valid reasons for this silence." Jesuit historian Robert Graham is convinced that any public papal denunciation of Hitler would have resulted in a Nazi massacre of the tens of thousands of native and foreign Jews who were in Italian camps but not in danger of extermination as long as they were under Italian control.

In 1963 the wartime president of Italy's Jewish communities affirmed: "The Church has given us proof that she saved all the men she was in a position to save." The month Pius XII was elected in 1939 *The Baltimore Evening Sun* declared: "It has become clear to rational men around the world that there is no dealing with Adolf Hitler, no stopping him by words."

Nearly a quarter of a century later (1963) Denmark's chief rabbi said: "I think there is a misunderstanding if anyone believes that Pope Pius XII could have exerted any influence upon the brain of an insane man. If the Pope had opened his mouth, Hitler would probably have murdered even more than six million Jews and perhaps ten times ten million Catholics."

A German Jewish couple, whom the pope helped to escape to Spain, said during the *Deputy* controversy: "None of us wanted the pope to take an open stand. We were all fugitives and fugitives do not wish to be pointed at." Similarly, a Polish cardinal begged the pope not to make an open attack on Hitler for his brutality against the Poles.

Let the last word be given to one such Pole, a Jew who suffered personal tragedy at the hands of the Nazis. He is Joseph Lichten of the Anti-Defamation League of B'nai B'rith. In his 1963 pamphlet, *A Question of Judgment*, Lichten affirms his belief that Pius XII did "everything humanly possible to save lives and alleviate suffering among Jews," and that "the evidence moves against the hypothesis that a formal condemnation from Pius would have curtailed the mass murder of Jews."

Meantime, a book awaits its author: a study of just why the pope praised in 1958 for doing so much for the Jews has subsequently become the pope attacked for doing so little for them. Were the Jewish spokesmen of 1958, who had actually lived through the massive horror which was World War II, closer to the truth than the harsh critics who learned of that cataclysm through the calm and neat pages of a history book?

58. John XXIII:
The Background

The Baltimore Sunday Sun: August 19, 1973

DEAD more than a decade now [actually, a quarter-century as of mid-1988], Pope John XXIII is still remembered with a unique fondness by millions of diverse people. Like Francis of Assisi, he is everyman's saint—even for everymen who don't especially believe in saints.

The almost universal admiration he enjoys is remarkable. He won it as an old man winding up his seventies and winding down into his eighties—in a world where old age is increasingly dreaded as the ultimate curse.

He won it as a man with the most unimpressive social and economic background imaginable—a peasant, a son of peasants, a brother of thirteen peasant brothers and sisters.

He won it as a stoutish man at a time when slim is in. And that homely head, prematurely bald—it could have appeared in *Playgirl* only as a warning.

And he was an intensely devout man, an old-fashioned believer of the most unredeemed stripe, who was "wild aware of light unseen and unheard song along the air."

He spent most of his life doing what he was told. As a bishop he took as his motto, "Obedience and Peace," then went docilely off to work for twenty years in obscurity, at times sending unanswered letters to his superiors in Rome.

In the diary he kept, he noted that his main problems came from his superiors and ecclesiastical associates. And when, at the age of seventy-seven, he became *the* ecclesiastical superior of Roman Catholicism, he wrote of "the joy of being able to say that I did nothing to obtain it, absolutely nothing."

And he was probably talking about his personal merit as

well as his own ambitions, for on the night before his election to the papacy, in as yet unpublished notes, he stated: "I feel as if I were an empty bag that the Holy Spirit unexpectedly fills with strength."

As pope he took the name John for a number of interesting and characteristically flavorsome reasons. John was the papal name most frequently used throughout history—and he said he wanted to hide his unworthiness behind the longest list possible. Perhaps as his own little joke, he also noted that most of the previous Johns had short reigns. (An earlier John XXIII, who died in 1419, was a disgraceful anti-pope.)

Born on November 25, 1881, in the tiny Italian village of Sotto il Monte, Angelo Roncalli could later write: "I do not remember a time when I did not want to be a priest."

At eleven he entered the seminary at nearby Bergamo, winning a scholarship in 1901 to a Roman seminary where the pope whom he would succeed was then a young teacher. That same year he began a year of military service—"a true purgatory," which refined him into a sergeant—and then returned to his studies and to ordination in August 1904.

A year of further studies followed—his intellectual achievements have been generally underestimated—and then he was picked to be the secretary of the new bishop of his home diocese, the socially concerned Radini-Tedeschi, whose biography he was to write and whom he called "the polar star of my priesthood."

During World War I, Roncalli served near the bloody front as a medic and a chaplain. In 1920 he was summoned to Rome to coordinate international missionary activities. He was named a bishop in 1925 and sent to Belgrade for ten lonely years as a Vatican diplomat.

The next decade he spent as a diplomat in Greece and Turkey, where his well-known efforts saved thousands of Jews from the Nazis. In 1944 Pius XII personally picked him for the church's top diplomatic spot—nuncio to Paris. DeGaulle insisted that Roncalli practically race to Paris lest it fall to the number two diplomat—the Soviet ambassador—to address New Year's greetings to him in the name of the diplomatic corps.

One of his first acts as nuncio was to pay a healing courtesy call to the Soviet Embassy. "Whenever I see a wall between

Christians," he once said, "I try to remove a brick." The same obviously held true for other walls too.

Seven years later he was named cardinal and made patriarch of Venice for five happy years. Rumors said he might be the next pope. "Crazy, crazy, the lot of them. I am preparing for death." But then the eleventh ballot was taken in the Sistine Chapel on October 28, 1958 . . . and the rest is better-known history.

59. Seventeen Hundred Pentecostal Days: The Papacy of John XXIII

The Catholic Review: June 3, 1963

AFTER the shortest reign since 1829—less than seventeen hundred days—Pope John XXIII has today ended his days as the Vicar of Jesus Christ and the Successor of St. Peter.

The brevity of his stewardship notwithstanding, his four years and seven months as pope will certainly rank as one of the most decisive pontificates of the more than 260 the Christian era has known.

Pride of place among his acts belongs to his initiation of the Twenty-first Ecumenical Council, announced so unexpectedly less than three months after the election of Angelo Giuseppe Roncalli. Within that council itself his two most consequential contributions were the pitch-key of his opening address and his intervention last November 21—"the day that shook Rome"'—to settle an epochal debate in favor of the more pastoral-minded majority of the fathers.

It is true that his death suspends the council and leaves its future entirely in the hands of his successor. (The Council of Trent, it may be hopefully recalled, survived the death of even four popes.) Yet it is almost unthinkable that the project for which the Holy Father was glad to sacrifice his life will die at his death. Even if the inconceivable should occur, however, the forces of renewal that were so dramatically revealed and released during the first session are now irreversibly active throughout the church. Thanks to Pope John, the Counter-Reformation preceded him to the grave and its defensive posture of polemic and legalism has now been happily abandoned.

Thanks to him also, the Catholic Church has rapidly moved from sympathetic watchfulness toward the world ecumenical movement into its very center. Thus the General Assembly of the United Presbyterian Church of America could speak of him a few days ago as "this great ecumenical Pope to whose influence in such large part are due the new and more Christian relationships that have recently been developing amongst all Christians."

Among the most seminal aspects of his ecumenical activity were his establishment three Pentecosts ago of what will probably be a permanent secretariat for the promotion of Christian unity, his nomination of the ideal Cardinal Augustin Bea as its first president, the resultant presence of non-Catholic delegates at the council, and Pope John's audiences with such Christian leaders as the archbishop of Canterbury.

Not only have John's seventeen hundred days evoked and channelized massive energies of revitalization within Catholicism and fostered bonds of affectionate brotherhood between all men who revere the name of Christ. Through his companion world letters, *Mater et Magistra* and, just seven weeks ago, *Pacem in Terris*, the vicar of the prince of peace has gifted all men of good will with detailed programs for solving the world's social problems and dissipating the cloud of nuclear holocaust from the sky of the future. How well he interpreted the desires of all mankind in his final encyclical, the first in history to address itself to all persons of good will, was indicated by the twenty thousand grateful messages he received in the first four days after the publication of this Easter gift.

So much for the briefest resume of his most influential papal actions. The fascination lies in how he could take so many decisive, long steps in so short a span, capturing all the while an almost universal respect and even love. No doubt he inherited the mounting prestige won for the papacy by the last five pontiffs, especially Pope Pius XII, whose forward-looking policies Pope John conceived of himself as simply furthering. No doubt too the threat of absolute war has impelled the hearts of men everywhere to search almost frantically for sane, persuasive leadership on the world scene.

Onto this scene, not five years past, suddenly appeared a relatively obscure figure, a man almost to be pitied for having to replace such a gigantic predecessor. He was already an old man, one of the very few who have ascended the papal throne after the age of seventy-five. Here was a grandfatherly personage who had spent his teens in another century.

At first there was disappointment that the potential of the papacy had fallen into the antique hands of a caretaker pope, a transitional pope. Yet, as a Roman journalist told a Protestant friend of ours, the Holy Spirit knows His business. For this caretaker pope would indeed take astounding care of the church and interpret his universal fatherhood with consuming care for the world at large. This transitional pope would steer the Barque of Peter into one of its most momentous periods of transition. As *Life* magazine editorialized recently, he has "moved that huge old galleon, the Roman Catholic Church, back into the mainstream of world history."

The initial reaction to Pope John himself was one of surprise at his youthful spontaneity and his unpredictability. Had not the same *Life* magazine spoken at his election of those genial traits of his that would have to be hidden beneath papal protocol? Must not the pope, for instance, eat alone and practically immure himself behind a damask curtain? But the new pope would soon be saying that he searched the Scriptures but could not find any requirement that he must dine by himself. Appearing at hospitals, prisons, orphanages, he out-traveled within two months a century of predecessors.

Yet there was a remarkable consistency to his long life. His ordination souvenir of fifty-eight years ago carried a prayer for world peace and Christian unity. The very day after his election, this pope, who was once a soldier, broadcast a plea for peace. Shortly before his death, he published *Peace on Earth* as his last testament.

At his coronation he broke tradition by giving a sermon, stressing Christ's yearning for unity among His disciples. In his deeply affecting address to the non-Catholic guests of the council he summarized his habitual attitude toward his brother Christians of other communions. "He pats you on the arm while he talks with you," said one of these guests who saw him privately, "and it's all you can do not to pat him back."

As pope he soon began to talk of a new Pentecost for the church. What turned out to be his last days on earth had been set aside for a spiritual retreat in preparation for yesterday's feast of Pentecost. Yet even before his election, he had written these words to a fellow bishop: "Pray for a wise and gentle man who can govern; a saint who will make saints of others. Trust in a new Pentecost."

This marked consistency manifested itself also in his personal loyalties. As a young priest he had been a devoted and admiring secretary to his bishop, the saintly Radini-Tedeschi. The robes he wore on the day of his election were those worn by Radini-Tedeschi when Pope St. Pius X consecrated him a bishop in the Sistine Chapel five decades earlier. In the last days of John's life he reportedly rose from his sickbed to work awhile on the biography he was writing of the bishop.

Another explanatory characteristic of the Holy Father was his childlike, evangelical trust in God, a trust that flowered into immense serenity. When he was nuncio to France, statesman Robert Schumann said of him, "He is the only man in Paris in whose company one feels a physical sensation of peace." On his last birthday, the pope made the classic statement, "Any day is a good day to be born on, a good day to die on." No wonder the turbulent, doubtful world took as warmly as it did to this man so full of quiet certitudes.

Humility and detachment from personal ambition also flowed from his signal reliance on Divine Providence. Not long ago he confided to a Methodist bishop that the secret of his life could be found in four recommendations from *The Imitation of Christ*: seek to do the will of others, choose to have less, look for the last place, desire God's will completely. Revealingly, his episcopal motto was "Obedience and Peace."

His imperturbability did not lessen his zeal for good deeds; rather the combination made of him a kind of energetic quietist and nurtured in him an exquisite tactfulness and a shrewd sense of timing. His fatherly handling of various factions within the council may prove to have been one of the master-strokes of church history. Yet this was no tactic, coldly calculated. It was John being his convinced, kindly self.

The same may be said of his view of the pope as the servant of the servants of God, as the bishop of bishops. It was no theatrical gesture that led him to invite visiting bishops to bless their pilgrim groups with him, and that prompted him to descend from his portable throne at the opening of the council and walk awhile behind the processioning fathers. "I too am a bishop," he affirmed on that glorious occasion.

Such dramatic deeds were spontaneous with him, but were not an everyday affair. More typical of him were a relaxing good humor and endearing sallies of wit. Of his own plain features and stocky build he once joked, "The Lord knew I was going to be a pope; you'd think He would have made me more handsome." To a group of American visitors he apologized for needing a translator, but added, "In heaven we shall all speak American."

On occasion he could speak genius. Thus he said to the son-in-law of Soviet premier Khrushchev: "They tell me, sir, that you are an atheist. But surely you will not forbid an old man to send a blessing to your children."

In the mass offered in the Sistine Chapel during the last conclave, the church trustfully recalled God's words in Sacred Writ: "I shall raise up for Myself a faithful priest who will act as one with My heart and My spirit." It would be ungracious to fear for the good estate of the church after God provided it with Pope John XXIII of truly happy memory.

Such a fear would not have troubled John himself. When government officials came to him as patriarch of Venice to lament the death of Pope Pius XII, the then-cardinal listened awhile to their somewhat extravagant condolences, and then answered with Christian realism: "Come, come, now. When one pope dies, they make another."

Such was his confidence in God. His own example then is the best balm for the church and the world in their pardonable grief at his going. His spirit now is where his heart has always been. There he will surely find that peace he embodied and radiated in a troubled world and sought to deserve forever in a better one.

He has left behind him many blessed remembrances. Perhaps one of the most appropriate at this moment is the memory of his final appearance on the day when his dream of a council came true. A large candlelight procession gathered that night beneath his window in St. Peter's Square.

"Let us continue," he begged, "to love one another, emphasizing what unites us, and avoiding all that can keep us divided. And now when you return home, I want you to embrace your children and to tell them that this is the embrace of the pope."

Then he stepped from view. But the light kept shining through the empty window.

60. Paul VI: Personal Remembrances

The Baltimore Evening Sun: August 8, 1978

JUST about three years before he became Paul VI, when he visited Baltimore's new cathedral as the cardinal archbishop of Milan, I had the privilege of giving Giovanni Battista Montini a brief tour of that church. What struck me at the time was his intense concentration and the air of quietude that he radiated. He seemed marked with "passionate inwardness," the quality praised by the philosopher Kierkegaard. For me that quality found distinctive expression in the delicate use he made of his hands.

In public there was also a quality of reserve about him. Those, however, who dealt with him privately and individually spoke of his warmth and directness. Unlike Pope John, whom he had the courage to succeed, Paul seemed so serious that witticisms and jokes never became associated with his image.

The only humorous remark I ever heard attributed to him occurred when he and Cardinal Beran of Prague celebrated a mass shortly after the cardinal was released from Communist confinement and while liturgical changes were being introduced in Italy. As soon as the cardinal came into view, the congregation broke into applause. Said the pope: "Even if such applause is not part of the new liturgy, it is certainly appropriate."

Gentle humor, yes. But such gentleness was characteristic, even when, in his judgment, firmness and unpopular decisions were called for.

The next time I saw Pope Paul, I was attending the opening of the second session of Vatican II—the first of his pontificate. I was present as a journalist and heard his historic apology for the church's guilt at the time of the Reformation. Excellent seats had been reserved for journalists in St. Peter's Basilica, and it was not overlooked that the new pope's father had been a journalist.

Indeed, a few days later, a special audience was granted to us newspaper people. This time some umbrage was taken because the Holy Father addressed us as "gentlemen of the press"—when there were women journalists present.

A week or so later I attended a small audience for Americans given on the occasion of the beatification of the now-St. John Neumann, of Baltimore and Philadelphia. Seated in the second row, I was afforded a very close glimpse of the new pope and his probing way of looking at the person to whom he spoke. Always evident was the gracious quality of *cortesia*.

In December 1965, on the final working day of the Second Vatican Council, when the last documents were voted on, I was able to station myself on the altar steps of St. Peter's while Pope Paul offered the last indoor mass of the council. Such was the official location of a monsignor of papal chamberlain rank, an honor I held in those days.

Thus I was only a few feet from the pope during the mass and at the dramatic moment when he embraced the representative of the Orthodox patriarch and celebrated the end of mutual excommunication issued by predecessors nine centuries earlier. Baltimore's Cardinal Shehan was in Istanbul that same day, embracing the patriarch as the pope's representative.

Earlier that year I had been in Rome for Archbishop Shehan's elevation to the cardinalate. My older brother and I drove near midnight to St. Peter's Square and saw the light that always seemed to be burning in the papal study on the top floor of the Apostolic Palace. A few hours later, a bomb went off at one of the Vatican City's gates, presumably to protest alleged Vatican efforts to keep the anti-Pius XII play, *The Deputy*, from being staged in Rome. As in the instance of the would-be assassin in Manila, this pope was not sheltered from the violence of his time.

My final sight of this embattled man occurred ten years ago this week. He had just issued *Humanae Vitae*, his encyclical against contraception. An instant storm of protest had erupted around the world, as would probably have been the case too had he decided otherwise. I was one of those priests who felt conscientiously and with keen regret that I had to dissent. One of the reasons why I made that dissent public was to speak in personal praise of the man whom other critics had been demeaning.

For myself and many other Catholics it was a bitter, watershed time. Still my admiration for Pope Paul and my appreciation for the meaning and potential of the papacy led me to the summer residence in which he has just died.

I made my way to the inner courtyard, where a torrid sun beat down. If you fainted, you wouldn't have fallen anywhere, so dense was the crowd. At last the pope appeared on his balcony, after what must have been two of the most tormented weeks of his life.

He stood there, an ascetic figure all in white, a sensitive man of flesh and blood, pinioned at the aching center of the turbulent postconciliar church. He said, "We bless those who accept Our encyclical, and We bless those who do not."

In a world of curses and assassins, of bombs and terrorists, it was an unforgettable last sentence, fatherly and characteristic, to have heard him say and to have known he meant.

61. Vatican II: A Decade After Its End

The Baltimore Sunday Sun: February 29, 1976

ONE DAY in August 1968, during the uproar within Catholicism that followed Pope Paul VI's encyclical against contraception, the late Theodore McKeldin invited me to lunch. Obviously distressed by what he had been reading and hearing, he asked me a simple question: "What's going on in the Catholic Church?"

A man with a vast fund of stories, he was probably aware of what Will Rogers said: "I don't belong to any organized political party; I'm a Democrat." What the former Maryland governor and Baltimore mayor saw happening then, and what has transpired in the intervening eight years, has made an unthinkable paraphrase less unthinkable: "I don't belong to any organized religion; I'm a Roman Catholic."

Slightly more than a decade ago, such a quip would have made no sense. Roman Catholicism at that time seemed like the Marine Corps of world religions: tightly knit, disciplined, notable for its esprit and sense of direction.

There is scant need to rehearse here the details of the internal upheaval that has been under way since the closing of the Second Vatican Council in 1965. A listing of the more dramatic signs that something drastic was happening would include the substantial number of nuns, brothers, priests, and even bishops who have withdrawn from their vocational commitments; the widespread rejection, even among the clergy, of Pope Paul's condemnation of contraception; the sharp decline in mass attendance; the heated disputes within families and parishes and religious communities concerning the true marks of a faithful, post-Vatican II Catholic.

The point is that, ten years after the euphoric end of Vatican II, Mr. McKeldin's question is more understandable than ever, even though many persons are undoubtedly sick of the question, or at least bored with it. Many Catholics have become so disaffected that they could not care less about the question or the answer. They may very well take the world's problems more seriously—as Vatican II had urged. But they take the church less seriously—as Vatican II hardly intended.

Still, if I had to attempt an answer to the question, I would preface my remarks by citing a distinction the late Monsignor Ronald Knox once made: the church in heaven, he said, is all saints; the church in purgatory is all souls; and the church on earth is all sorts.

The earthly church is all sorts in a number of ways: thus, the main features of "what is going on" in American or Dutch Catholicism are not necessarily (yet) those of the church in Spain, in Chile, or in Uganda. Even within American Catholicism, what is going on in an inner-city parish in Baltimore or at a university Newman Club may be startlingly different from what a Catholic community is experiencing in a rural town in Iowa. Finally, within a given parish, the religious thoughts, needs, and anxieties of one parishioner may sharply contrast with those of his or her pew mate.

In a sense, there is nothing new about this diversity. On the contrary, among world religions Catholicism has long been "all sorts," outstandingly skilled at blending polychromatic varieties of people, languages, and cultures into an impressive unity. The variety of religious orders, for instance, bespeaks this tolerance for diversity.

What is special now, I think, is that the post-conciliar diversity seems to be destroying or severely damaging the old unity. The Protestant Reformation, of course, was a landmark instance of just such a development. (Incidentally, the Lutheran historian, Jaroslav Pelikan, said a few years ago that Catholics were trying to make in a few years all the mistakes it took Protestants four hundred years to make.)

One of the keenest ironies of the whole present Catholic picture is precisely this: just as the ecumenical movement was drawing Roman Catholicism closer to Protestantism and to Eastern Orthodoxy, Roman Catholicism is undergoing a second Protestant Reformation (Revolution?) within its own ranks. It is as though the Hatfields finally invited the McCoys to a picnic and then the Hatfields began clubbing one another. Or, to follow through on Pope John XXIII's image of what Vatican II was supposed to do: the bishops finally, gingerly opened up a window to let fresh air in and the whole wall started to collapse.

But, back to the blunt question: what is going on in the Catholic Church? There could be "all sorts" of answers. I would say that more and more Catholics are going on their own. Large numbers of Catholics, even those who wish to be known as Catholics, even those who have dedicated themselves to the religious life, simply no longer feel the old confidence in church leadership, the old respect for the wisdom or even the authority of that leadership—which means, primarily, the pope and the Roman Curia and the bishops.

In the old days, Catholicism was a kind of package deal. No one, of course, focuses on every aspect of a religious tradition. But until the mid-1960s, most practicing Catholics were generally confident about the package as a whole, and were by-and-large satisfied with those aspects of their religion that met their personal questions and needs.

The Second Vatican Council produced both immediate tremors and time-bombs: here were many Catholic spokesmen questioning and criticizing and changing various parts of the package, parts many Catholics had always revered as important, if not essential. Such Catholics in the main were laymen with no training in making the subtle distinctions that theologians and intellectuals can so readily make without stripping any mental or emotional gears.

Meat on Friday was no longer "a sin." Mass was not in Latin. Laymen were distributing Holy Communion. The council had said some highly laudatory things about other Christian religions, even non-Christian ones. Why bother, then, to pay the special price of being a Catholic—confession, strict sexual morality, mass every Sunday and on inconvenient holy days?

Then, almost three years after the council ended, came Pope Paul's refusal to reverse the papal ban on contraception, despite the fact that the majority of his expert, hand-picked advisers said that the church could change and should change on this critical point.

Meantime, incendiary social issues were scarring the nation: racism, poverty, the war in Vietnam. The council had called for courageous social involvement based on radical Gospel principles. But, especially in the United States, the bishops as a group seemed to fail miserably in their follow-through. "Yes in Rome; No at home" was the catch-phrase used to describe those bishops who seemed to many activist Catholics to be violating the spirit and the letter of the council after it was over.

On these matters and on others, many Catholics felt that in conscience they had to go their own way in a manner that was foreign to Catholic tradition as they knew it. Social-minded Catholics, for example, often felt closer to atheists and to non-believers in their antiwar attitudes than they did to most of their fellow Catholics, especially church leaders.

For such activist Catholics, if they still cared enough to keep considering themselves Catholics, there arose a sudden and desperate need for some principle of selective obedience. The question was, which rules to obey, which to disobey, which doctrines to believe, which to disbelieve? It was as though, up until then, they had always been trustingly chauffeured by church teaching, so much so that they had not felt the need to know much about driving or to pay much attention to road signs and maps. Now they had to take over the running of their own car morally and spiritually.

Increasing numbers of Catholics began to care less about church teachings and more about biblical teaching, especially Gospel ideals. In the eyes of many, the institutional church, with its tendency to become part of the establishment and to be overly preoccupied with buildings and finances and rules, seemed an outright negation of Gospel simplicity and Christ's concern for the outcast, the underdog, the socially embarrassing.

There was an ironic complication here, more or less perturbing to the back-to-the-Bible Catholic. At this precise historic juncture, more and more Catholic Scripture scholars were joining their non-Catholic confreres in raising questions about traditional Catholic views concerning the nature and words of Christ, as well as the self-understanding of the early church. So the new question became: back to which Bible, or to which part of the Bible, or to whose views of the Bible?

As I itemize these points, two remarks come to mind. One was made by a conservative Irish cardinal in the midst of the council: "Beware, beware: do you want a revolution?" The other was made by Pope Paul VI toward the beginning of his pontificate: "Everything moves: everything is a problem." How apt, both the warning and the description of the aftermath.

I am also reminded of a point often stressed by sociologists of religion: namely, that a vibrant religion is not merely or even chiefly a question of its leadership. It is more decisively the result of a sense of identity that is nurtured and expressed by a ritual that permits and encourages a sense of the sacred.

But here too there are problems. Catholic popular piety has undergone multiple shocks and dislocations. As Garry Wills once put it, the old customs, the rosary, hymns, novenas, incense, and the like were chucked out overnight by people who did not care a fig about such things—things into which popular piety, for all its flaws, had woven a precious sense of the holy and of the enrichingly traditional.

Whatever can be said in defense of the new liturgy and its music, I for one cannot imagine its being able to trigger an experience of the ecstatically divine and majestically "Other" to the degree that the old Latin mass and Gregorian chant could. It saddens me that my own nieces and nephews and so many other young Catholics may never find a worthy substitute for those enrapturing, unforgettable, and life-altering experiences.

In a recent article in *Commonweal* magazine, a sympathetic Protestant theologian from the Yale Divinity School makes some trenchant comments on the current Catholic crisis. With his special background as a non-Catholic observer at Vatican II, George Lindbeck feels that some Catholic progressives have misused the council for ego-tripping and to justify their own capitulation to *modernitas* as well as their devious and unacknowledged departures from what is essential to Christianity itself.

He likewise believes that at the moment Catholics are without a shepherd, for "Catholic consensus-building mechanisms are in greater disarray than in most other churches." Moreover, church authorities have unwittingly de-legitimized themselves by the ambiguities of the council documents themselves. As a result, most factions within the church, from propapal to anti-papal, can claim support from these documents.

At the same time, he maintains that the major excitement in the Christian church these days is on the Catholic side, and that a half-filled Catholic seminary is often a much more lively (as well as chaotic and frustrating) place than a full Protestant one.

"The future of Christianity as a whole, to the degree that it has a future, is now bursting forth in a thousand often absurdly unexpected forms within the Roman Church."

Thus Dr. Lindbeck concludes, striking a positive note. And, of course, there are positive aspects to all this upheaval. There are still people like Dorothy Day, Mother Teresa of Calcutta, Archbishop Camara of Brazil, antirepressive bishops in Chile and Spain, and countless thousands of Catholic laity and religious who are unpublicized heroes in the daily struggle between selfishness and self-giving.

Perhaps these people are more successful than others in believing *through* the church rather than *in* the church. Perhaps they are more successful at seeing that "the church" is needy brothers and sisters and not just disappointed and disappointing prelates. They are probably more concerned about what they can do for the church than for what the church can do for them. And they still see in the ideal of the papacy, however in need of modification, a unique symbol of the Christian unity that Christ prayed for.

The Catholic Church as a whole may in fact be undergoing its own dark night of the soul. (Pity, in particular, the conscientious Catholic parent who wants to transmit the right religious traditions to disinterested or disaffected children.) But if this world is, as the poet John Keats typified it, "a vale of soul-making," Catholicism is at the moment and for the foreseeable future an only too marvelously apt arena for soul searching, soul purging and soul producing.

What is going on in the Catholic Church? A thousand different things—contradictory, exhilarating, depressing, creative, destructive, puzzling, puzzling, puzzling. I have no confident idea where it will all lead, institutionally, or even where it should lead.

But those members who are blessed/cursed with a tragic sense of life will possibly find some special shelter in the storm if, *mutatis mutandis*, they can remain convinced with the saintly Samuel Johnson:

> How small, of all that human hearts endure,
> That part which laws or kings can cause or cure.

62. Nuclear War: Jesus and the U.S. Catholic Bishops

The Baltimore Evening Sun: December 23, 1982

"PARDON me, are you a priest?"
It was lunchtime in a small Baltimore restaurant six weeks ago. The questioner sat to my left, and when I said "Yes," he told me he was a sincere Catholic, but he was deeply disturbed by the meeting of Catholic bishops then discussing war and peace. He had been in army intelligence and knows how bad the Russians are.

Meantime, the man on my right began talking with my companion. "I'm Jewish," he said, "but I applaud the bishops." Soon the headwaiter came over and swelled the discussion.

Dear Bishops: If you wanted discussion on nuclear morality, you're getting it. A non-Catholic friend phoned me and earnestly joked: "If the bishops keep talking like that, they'll make a convert of me." Two ex-seminarians told me the same story: this is the first time in fifteen years they have paid any attention to what the bishops have to say.

When, at their November 15–18 meeting in Washington, some 275 Catholic bishops discussed the second draft of a pastoral letter on war and peace, there were 350 media representatives on hand. More than twenty-five television cameras bore down on these spiritual leaders of 51 million U.S. Catholics, the nation's largest religious denomination.

They bore down on Richmond's bishop, Walter Sullivan, who told me last week that he has been invited seventy times to give his talk on peace. At some campuses he has found Catholic students challenging him while non-Catholic ones support him. Still, a recent Gallup poll shows 77 percent of Americans favoring a bilateral U.S.-Soviet freeze, with 82 percent of Catholics favoring it.

But what do bishops know about "nuclear" matters—are they not as "unclear" to churchmen as they are to most of us? ". . . the bishops took counsel with a substantial number of well-informed civilian and military leaders, and we suspect that as a result they are better informed technically than most of their critics." Who said so? Among others: William Colby, former CIA director; Herbert Scovill, former deputy director; SALT I negotiator Gerard Smith; SALT II negotiator Paul Warnke.

The bishops are due to vote on a final draft during their May 2–3 Chicago meeting next year. Meanwhile, a few observations:

1. Moral theology applied to complex matters can be as delicate as brain surgery. Read what the bishops themselves said, not just the headlines.

2. The draft specifically rejects unilateral disarmament.

3. The bishops' concern is not new: read Vatican II's 1965 statement on modern armaments (in Chapter V of *The Church in the Modern World*). What is ever newer is the ever expanding buildup of ever more lethal, widespread, and bankrupting weapons.

4. The bishops see themselves as fostering serious discussion rather than as handing down dictates from the mountaintop. "This pastoral is more an invitation, than a final synthesis. To say 'No' to nuclear war is both a necessary and a complex task. We see with much less clarity how we translate a 'No' into the personal and public choices which can move us in new directions."

5. Jesus Christ had clear positions on peace making, nonviolence, the murder of innocents, and responding to evil. Some of these ideals are easier for individuals to embrace than sovereign states. Still, a person who wishes to be considered a Christian has to reckon with the teachings of Christ—as the bishops are personally trying to do and are professionally supposed to do.

6. The claims of conscience are higher than the demands of patriotism—certainly higher than any allegiance to specific government policies.

7. A person who would do "anything" to defeat "the god-less Communists" cannot in that regard be called Christian or moral.

8. Of the 373 living U.S. Catholic bishops, 233 have been named since the Second Vatican Council ended. This new breed is making a difference. They know how much respect the bishops lost in the Sixties by failing to exert moral leadership.

9. The stakes are among the highest possible: survival of the planet and of the race. The Christmas story is about peace on earth, the slaughter of the innocents, and the blessed peace-makers. What better season or better reason for thinking about what the bishops are thinking about in their pastoral?

63. Death Comes for the Archbishop: Lawrence Joseph Shehan

The Baltimore Evening Sun: August 28, 1984

AT THE end of this decade, the Catholic archdiocese of Baltimore will mark its bicentennial as the nation's oldest. In all that time only two archbishops of Baltimore have been native Baltimoreans—and these were the only two who ever became cardinals. When James Cardinal Gibbons died in 1921, he was in the 241st day of his 87th year. At that time Lawrence Joseph Shehan was in Rome completing his seminary education and looking forward to his priestly ordination the following year.

Now death has come for this twelfth archbishop of Baltimore in the 162nd day of his 87th year. Following modern church regulations Cardinal Shehan became the first Baltimore archbishop to resign and was in his 11th year of gracious retirement. He was a priest for more than sixty-one years, a bishop for more than thirty-eight. When he was a young priest serving in Washington, which was then still in the Baltimore archdiocese, his superior, Archbishop Michael Curley remarked: "That Father Shehan would make a good bishop some day, but his poor health will prevent that." In 1945, when Curley was in poor health, Shehan became his auxiliary bishop.

After eight years as auxiliary bishop, and eight years as the founding bishop of Bridgeport, Connecticut, he returned to his native city as coadjutor archbishop in 1961. Before the year was out, Shehan succeeded Archbishop Francis P. Keough and began thirteen crucial years as shepherd of the See of Baltimore. These were years before, during and after the Second Vatican Council, years of racial unrest, anti-war protests, and Catholic upheavals epitomized by the controversial response to Pope

234

Paul VI's encyclical maintaining the ban on artificial birth control.

Even the briefest synopsis of Cardinal Shehan's years as archbishop of Baltimore would have to underscore the importance of four things: first, his pastoral letter establishing the nation's first Catholic Ecumenical Commission in 1962; second, his lenten pastoral of 1963 calling for the end of all remnants of racial segregation in the archdiocese; third, his pastoral of July, 1966, pointing out, in the midst of the Vietnam War, Catholic teaching on the perils and moral limits of modern warfare; and, fourth, his handling of the priests under his jurisdiction when, in 1968 they signed a public dissent against Pope Paul VI's encyclical *Humanae Vitae*.

Shehan's interest in inter-faith understanding and good will was a continuation of Cardinal Gibbons' signal efforts in this regard, and led to his appointment to the Vatican's Secretariat for Christian Unity and to his role as papal delegate to Constantinople for a historic gesture of reconciliation with Eastern Orthodoxy. One of his speeches at Vatican II was on behalf of a document condemning anti-Semitism.

A flashpoint in his efforts for racial justice occurred when he was booed by some of the audience at a Baltimore City Council meeting on an anti-discrimination bill. Probably also racist in origin was a bomb threat several years later which caused a celebration in his honor to be moved from the Cathedral of Mary Our Queen to the nearby school hall.

His pastoral on the Vietnam War was the first of its kind in the United States and received international attention. It was a needed antidote to the perturbing "My country, right or wrong" statement attributed to New York's Cardinal Spellman. Atlanta's Archbishop Hallinan said that this pastoral inspired him and his auxiliary bishop (now Cardinal Bernardin) to issue their own letter on the controversial subject.

Some observers felt that the cardinal diluted the nonpartisan authority of his original pronouncement when he released a public statement two months later saying that he personally supported the U.S. position in Vietnam. By the time of Martin Luther King's death in 1968, however, he was explicitly calling for an end to U.S. troop involvement.

It has been asserted (without any denial that I know of) that the cardinal voted with the preponderant majority on the

Papal Birth Control Commission in urging a modification of the church's position. Above all else a papal loyalist, he was deeply disturbed when seventy or so of his own priests openly dissented from the encyclical *Humanae Vitae*. (On this subject his 1982 memoirs evince the most emotion.)

But, while Washington's Cardinal O'Boyle was lashing out against his own dissident priests and suspending them, Shehan quietly worked out a compromise with his. They were not required to rescind their statement, but agreed not to preach against the papal position, and to cite it dutifully when asked for the church's official teaching.

Still, he must have worried that his gentle handling of dissent might be taken as a sign of his own interior dissent, for he carried around with him for some time a letter from a Vatican authority assuring him that he had managed the crisis in an acceptable manner.

Throughout all these issues and many others, Cardinal Shehan was quintessentially the Catholic churchman. As such he was extremely dutiful, hard-working, self-sacrificing and available.

Small of stature and elegantly silver-haired, he was personally unassuming, a bit shy, unskilled at small talk, quietly unfussy about such things as meals and accommodations. He was self-reliant, preferring to drive his own car, write his own talks, make his own arrangements. He was also a workaholic, and one aide joked that after the Final Judgment he expected to hear the cardinal say: "Well, that's over. Now, back to the desk."

Though self-reliant, he was quick to seek advice from others, and genuinely sought their candid criticism of statements and actions he was contemplating. Asked to cite a noteworthy quality of the cardinal, one adviser replied: "He listens." He was also ready to delegate authority and expected the delegated person to follow through on his or her own.

On a number of public occasions the cardinal said that because he was small and seemed frail, associates were inclined to pitch in and help him to an unusual degree, and he would get the credit. Though he appeared frail, he was amazingly energetic and preferred to dash after a wanted item rather than walk after it. In his first year as archbishop he broke his thumb twice by slamming a car door too hurriedly.

Though quite amiable in his dealings with others, the cardinal did not seem to need or look for many "I-Thou" relationships. Once, while addressing seminarians at Rome's North American College, he said that an ideal priest must be ready to give up even friendships. When a delegation of students later came to his room to dispute that remark, he took their reaction in good humor.

His remarks could occasionally get him into trouble with another bishop. He once told a group of priests that a modern bishop must be more a listener and less an authority figure. Hearing of this remark, an authoritarian U.S. bishop wrote the cardinal one of the least polite letters he ever received. It was bishops of this ilk who made Baltimore priests feel so fortunate.

Cardinal Shehan had been an honor student. He had a keen mind, and was well and widely read, especially in history. (In his memoirs, though, he confesses that when he was named a bishop he was worried about his poor memory.) But he was not essentially an idea man; he did not have a theoretical cast of mind.

Disinclined to be partisan, he eventually disappointed many reform-minded U.S. Catholics who thought he was predictably on their side. The conservatives had already learned, especially during his first years as Baltimore archbishop, that they couldn't preempt him. In truth, the cardinal liked to think of himself as a mobile conservative—disposed to preserve, but open to changes that seemed sensible by conservative standards.

Whatever else may be said of Shehan as a churchman, he always strove to be a gentleman—especially, according to Cardinal Newman's "almost" definition, as one who never gives pain. No doubt his sharpest pains occurred when the claims of churchman and gentleman seemed to clash. Such was probably the case when, during a speech at St. Mary's Seminary, the cardinal felt obliged to challenge a Biblical scholar, the Rev. Raymond Brown, S.S., one of the seminary's most illustrious sons. It is not surprising to be told that under the pressure of such pains he seriously thought of resigning the See of Baltimore ahead of time.

An anecdote will demonstrate the delicacy, not to say scrupulosity, of his churchmanly conscience. In a confidential letter written during the first month of the Second Vatican Council, he mentioned in passing that St. Louis' Cardinal Ritter "has already given an admirably balanced speech on the liturgy."

Later that day he dispatched a follow-up letter. "It has come to my attention that members of the council are not supposed to mention outside the council the names of those who have spoken nor the contents of their speeches. This may seem rather strange in view of some of the reports carried by the secular press. However since it is the rule I must abide by it. Please therefore consider as if not written what I said about Cardinal Ritter."

Probably the same ecclesiastical conscience, this fear of dis-edification, kept the cardinal's memoirs from being a more weighty book historically. Important aspects of his career are either passed over in silence, or significant circumstances are scanted. For example, his book says nothing about his role on the Papal Birth Control Commission, about his Vietnam War pastoral, or about his struggles with Father Gommar De Pauw and the Catholic Traditionalist Movement.

(As for my own published memoirs: In the cool light of afterthought, and in the warm, summarizing remembrance of his manifold virtues, I now wish I had written more briefly and gently about my differences with the cardinal. When I told him as much at Mercy Hospital in early August, he replied magnanimously: "You shouldn't let things like that bother you. We are all imperfect.")

In view of his exceeding respect for the papacy, it was ironic that after being a cardinal for thirteen years he missed by a few months the chance to participate in the two papal elections of 1978. He had reached the cut-off age of eighty not long before the death of the pope who had created him a cardinal. But he retained to the end the dignity of a cardinal, and by his personal qualities kept earning the attribute of eminence.

Of Lawrence Joseph Shehan it was truer than of most people, I think, that the inner and the outer self were one. And that integrated self was one of rare goodness, humility and religious dedication.

64. The Unlicensing of Theologian Charles Curran

The Baltimore Evening Sun: March 19, 1986

RUMORS had swirled for a long time—for almost twenty years, in fact. Last week the matter became certain as well as public: One of this nation's most respected and most influential theologians, even among his non-Catholic peers, is in serious trouble with Vatican church authorities. Unless Father Charles Curran of the Catholic University of America ceases to espouse certain of his opinions, chiefly on matters of sexual morality, he will be deprived of his official status as a Catholic theologian.

Some crucial distinctions must be made at the outset: 1) Does the Vatican have the right to force such an issue? 2) In the present instance, is the Vatican acting correctly and justly?

I feel sure that Father Curran would essentially say yes to the first question. He has clearly said no to the second. Already, eminent past presidents of the Catholic Theological Society of America and the College Theology Society have agreed with him—heavyweight scholars like Walter Burghardt, Richard McCormick, and David Tracy. Curran's own bishop, Matthew Clark of Rochester, has come to his defense, calling the fifty-two-year-old theologian an exemplary priest and a moral theologian of notable competence.

Any serious religious tradition will have certain core beliefs and will have some way of determining when those core beliefs are being violated. If the authorities of the tradition empower people to teach in the name of that tradition, the same authorities can be expected to withdraw authorization from a teacher whose opinions are judged to be seriously at variance with core beliefs.

All this is simple sociology. No one would expect a board of rabbis to sanction a rabbi who wants to teach that Judaism requires belief in Jesus as the true Messiah.

The Vatican is not asking Curran to teach what he does not believe. But it is insisting that within the rules of Catholic theology (which Curran is personally free to reject in conscience), he must not expect to enjoy official status as a Catholic theologian if he continues to promote moral opinions that the Vatican guardians of orthodoxy have judged to be seriously at variance with key parts of the tradition.

Unfortunately, guardians of orthodoxy can be and have been wrong. In the case of Galileo, they were mistaken about their competency in matters of scientific theory, which clashed with their overly narrow views of the Bible. True, matters are not that simple with the Curran case, since his subject matter (Christian moral behavior) is one that of its nature pertains more to faith than to verifiable scientific fact.

Still, reputable Catholic theologians are now on record as objecting to the way Vatican authorities have handled the Curran case and to the implication that he forfeits his status as a Catholic theologian because he dissents from teachings that may be official but are not irreformably defined. As their statement notes: "The problem is . . . that there are very many Catholic theologians who do dissent from noninfallible teachings." (The presumption is that a theologian would present theologically respectable reasons for dissenting.) Finally, "the threatened action also raises serious questions about the academic integrity of Catholic institutions of higher learning."

Theology has been described as a field where "the bravest have trembled and the wisest have erred." It is not a subject matter for snap judgments, especially when what we are witnessing may well be the latest dramatic instance of the perpetual tension between "the truths we have learned" and "the truths we have yet to learn." Most thoughtful persons with open minds experience this tension within themselves, at least from time to time.

By a timely coincidence, the March 15 issue of the Jesuit magazine *America* editorializes about the church's teaching authority: ". . . the church will inevitably seem repressive and obscurantist if . . . there is disciplinary action, or the threat of it" every time scholarly speculation is in danger of being popularly confused with official church teaching. "Authority within the church can be exercised in a less than authoritarian way. Only in this way will legitimate authority ultimately be maintained."

The Vatican-Curran clash will continue to cause much soul testing in U.S. Catholicism and elsewhere. A famous saying becomes very timely: "In essential matters, unity; in doubtful matters, liberty; in all matters, charity." The strain on charity is greatest when, in the minds of some of those involved, the doubts are about what is essential. Such is the heart of the present impasse. May the truth prevail: the truth that is known and the truth that needs to become known.

Part Six

A Round of Timely Topics

65. A Troubled Abortionist Reverses His Stand

The Baltimore Evening Sun: November 29, 1979

A BOMBSHELL exploded in a magazine dated five years ago this week, November 28, 1974. The magazine was the leading U.S. medical periodical, *The New England Journal of Medicine*. The article was entitled "Deeper into Abortion." The author was a prominent New York obstetrician-gynecologist, Dr. Bernard Nathanson.

This doctor, an atheist and a humanist, had been the director of the busiest abortion clinic in the world. Previously he had been a founding director of the National Association for the Repeal of Abortion Laws. When the Supreme Court in early 1973 authorized abortion on demand during the first trimester of pregnancy, the doctor's fondest hopes were realized — though he found the court's conclusion "propped up on a misreading of obstetrics, gynecology, and embryology."

In the ensuing months, however, the doctor's doubts about what he calls "pro-abortion dogmas" began to grow. So it was a megaton shock to the whole abortion crusade when he made such statements as these in the aforementioned article:

— "I am deeply troubled by my own increasing certainty that I had in fact presided over 60,000 deaths."

— "There is no doubt in my mind that human life exists within the womb from the onset of pregnancy."

— "We must courageously face the fact — finally — that human life of a very special order is being taken . . . and the deliberate taking of life . . . is an inexpressibly serious matter."

Although at that time Dr. Nathanson still thought that abortion in the early months of pregnancy should remain unregulated by law, he has continued to develop his convictions on this whole matter. Now he has published an engrossing book on the subject, entitled *Aborting America*.

The author details his own personal and medical background, including the abortion of his first, illegitimate child. He candidly admits the lack of ethical training in his medical education and also the lack of rigorous thinking about the abortion crusade in which he became a leader. "It did not seem a time for careful analysis of the issues." As a result, "the revolution we undertook was a seductive and ultimately poisonous dream."

To make the place more medically responsible, he agreed to become medical director of New York City's Center for Reproductive and Sexual Health—"one of those ultimate euphemisms our century uses to hide the enormity of what mankind is actually doing." Its then-current roster of doctors was described by the clinic's administrator as "sadists, drunks, incompetents, sex maniacs, thieves, butchers, and lunatics."

But, under New York state's new abortion law, the clinic had become a 4.5 million dollar business, operating from 8 A.M. till midnight seven days a week, and performing 100 abortions daily at its peak. One doctor flew in from Tennessee on weekends and grossed $185,000 in eighteen months.

In the midst of all these activities, the doctor realized that something central was crumbling inside him. He gradually opened himself up to old and new data corroborating the view that the fetus, from implantation onward, was indeed an independent "intrauterine patient." "Until 1973 I was sold a bill of goods. No—let me be honest—I was selling a bill of goods."

The author devotes the latter half of his book to an examination of good and bad arguments both for and against abortion. He would regard the operation as justifiable only when the mother's life is truly at stake. For, "if we do not protect innocent non-aggressive elements in the human community, the alternative is too horrible to contemplate."

His proposal would "radically reduce the number of legal abortions to perhaps several thousand a year." As it is, abortion has become the most common of operations, out-stripping even tonsillectomies. More than a million are performed yearly in the United States—one for every 3.2 live births.

I find myself personally in agreement with most of Dr. Nathanson's current convictions, even as he reluctantly finds himself in substantial agreement with most of the principles of the right-to-life movement.

Given his unique background, he deserves to be read and pondered by every pro-abortion citizen who wishes to be honest and socially responsible. Such a person cannot afford (as Dr. Nathanson once thought he could) *not* to take time "for the luxury of contemplating the theoretical morality of abortion or the soundness of freedom of choice" in the matter.

For, among other considerations, he now sees the cogency of moralist Paul Ramsey's dictum that "every good argument for abortion is a good argument for infanticide."

66. The Sadness of Being Gay

The Baltimore Evening Sun: June 15, 1978

NEXT month will mark the tenth anniversary of Pope Paul VI's historic encyclical *Humanae Vitae*—a document that reaffirmed the traditional Roman Catholic teaching that complete sexual expression must be oriented toward life-producing possibilities. Although this teaching has problems explaining why intercourse is permissible during pregnancy and in the face of sterility, still it provides a rationale for assessing the moral significance of such nonfertile behavior as homosexuality.

One of the reasons why this encyclical is historic is that it has been massively disregarded by Catholics, both clerical and lay. In the meantime, new approaches to sexuality are being devised by Catholic philosophers and theologians all over the world.

Put in the simplest of terms, many of these new theories reject the "biologism" that links sexuality so exclusively to procreation. They prefer to ask whether a person's sexual expression helps or hinders his/her growth as a responsible, self-giving and faithful person—though they often admit the danger of self-deception in the use of these standards.

These Catholics (and other fellow Christians) often point to the relative lack of concern in the Gospels about "sex," but the great concern therein about charity, compassion, honesty, and humility. They wonder by what strange route a religion of charity becomes for many a religion of chastity.

In any case, the heavily Catholic city of St. Paul, Minnesota, recently gave witness to conflicting Catholic approaches nowadays to the "problem" of homosexuality. The question was whether that city's human rights ordinance, which explicitly included homosexuals, should be repealed. As in Anita Bryant's Dade County, Florida, the vote was yes.

While St. Paul's Catholic archbishop, John Roach, repeated the "official" Catholic position that homosexual activity is morally unacceptable, he added: "It is a matter of injustice when, due to prejudice, homosexuals must suffer violation of their basic human rights. Like all persons, they have a right to human respect, stable friendships, economic security, and social equality."

The archdiocesan priests' senate voted to support the existing ordinance. But Roach's auxiliary bishop, Paul Dudley, announced: "I am voting yes to this repeal . . . I believe that homosexual activity is immoral and contrary to the teaching of Sacred Scripture . . . Society has a right to protect itself, especially its young people, from such illness and immoral influence."

As for the biblical argument, on which Anita Bryant says she bases her fight, some recent scholarship is questioning: 1) whether the Scriptures attack homosexuality as such; and 2) whether in this case, as admittedly in others, the Scripture writers reflect cultural viewpoints based on lack of experience and of understanding. Some of this questioning may strike the non-partisan ear as special pleading.

A brief article can scarcely even sketch the outlines of this growing debate in Catholic circles and elsewhere. But after twenty-three years of counseling, I'd like to stress one point that, I think, is usually overlooked and that can humanize a thoughtful person's approach to this controversial matter.

When youngsters are told "the facts of life" they are often disgusted with all these anatomical goings on. In response, we adults often say: "But love makes all that beautiful. Being in love makes the difference."

What straight people often miss is that the homosexual's crucial problem is that he/she *falls in love* with a person of the same sex. As with straights, this instinctual, nonchosen condition means delight in the presence of the beloved, pain at separation, heightened vulnerability, energetic propulsions toward intimacy, toward pleasure-giving, toward the celebration of bodiliness—all with resultant sexual tensions clamoring for expression and release.

Love may make the world go round for straights; for others it can make the world go sour and shattering. For such others their whole nature, their vital sense of identity, and the generosities activated by love catapult them in a direction that their lawyer may say is a crime, their clergyman a sin, their doctor a disease, their families and friends a disgrace. Straights can imagine their response to a tyrant who would try to outlaw forever all affectionate intimacies between the sexes.

Granted that, as with heterosexuals, the sexual instinct in individual gay cases can express itself in ways that are cruel, selfish, seductive, promiscuous, and self-deceiving. But that, it seems to me, is a human problem, not a homosexual one.

Katherine Anne Porter, in perhaps too grim a mood, wrote of "the insoluble, stubborn mystery of sex . . . which causes us such fleeting joy and such cureless suffering." If straights keep in mind that homosexuals have the same emotional and sexual needs as they do, only more dangerously and frustratingly, they may be less eager to add to the sufferings of "the sexual minority." In the best biblical tradition, as I see it, befriending such minorities is what the best religiousness is all about.

67. A Story and a Poem for a Teacher with AIDS

The Baltimore Evening Sun: September 4, 1985

THE FIRST time I visited him I didn't know he had AIDS. The door to his hospital room bore an infection warning, but the malady wasn't specified. Though he told me as chaplain that he was seriously ill he never used the heavy word.

His first stay was for about six weeks in the summer of 1984. He was in his early thirties, taught literature, and directed plays in an out-of-town high school. We swapped stories about our teaching experiences, our favorite writers, our special books.

For his own protection he couldn't go back to teaching. So he lived with his family until he returned to the hospital this past March. As time dragged by, his eyes occasionally radiated a kind of frightened brightness. Once I tried to hold his hand, but he pulled away. "We didn't touch in our family."

One day in mid-June he suddenly blurted out: "I'm bored. Tell me a story." He had caught me by surprise, but I tried to think of a story that a lover of literature would like. Luckily, I thought of a true one of my own.

Fourteen summers ago I was visiting the Baltimore poet Josephine Jacobsen in her New Hampshire home. On the morning of my departure I discovered in my guest room a small book of her poems, which had been published in 1940 by a small press in Texas. I hadn't been aware that such a volume existed and judged that it had been a limited edition that was now out of print. The title was *Let Each Man Remember*. I asked whether I might borrow it and was graciously told to accept it as a gift.

So I said goodbye and headed down the highway. Some hours later, as my lunch hungers surfaced, I saw a *Howard*

Johnson's and thought of my favorite milky clam chowder. Parking my car, I decided to take my gift book with me.

Before long I was seated at the counter and gave my order to a young waitress. Then I began to read from the book I thought I had rather inconspicuously opened on the counter.

Another teenaged waitress passed by and casually remarked: "That's a lovely book, isn't it?"

I couldn't believe that she was talking to me or that she had recognized the discolored volume in my hands. "You mean *this* book?"

"Yes," she answered brightly. "I discovered it last summer in an old bookshop in Maine. Each night at camp I read a different poem to the kids in my cabin. My favorite is one of the sonnets up front." She leaned over the book, flipped some pages, and announced: "Yes, there it is. I know it by heart."

I gazed incredulously at that shining youngster, whose parents had probably been youngsters when this poem was published and who was now passionate with praise for these words by a stranger.

I told her I had just left the author of this book, left her standing on the steps of that "Winter Castle" which gave its name to the section of the book where the girl's favorite poem appeared.

Now it was the waitress's turn to stare in disbelief. To help convince her, I took her name and address and mailed them to the poet, who sent a loving letter to her youthful admirer . . .

My bored friend with AIDS had been listening intently. After I had finished he pursed his lips and held them that way for some thoughtful moments. Then, as a wry smile dismantled the pursing, he commented softly: "I guess there are good infections too."

Not long afterwards I came across that bridge-building book in my library. An impulse prompted me to turn to the title poem, "Let Each Man Remember":

There is a terrible hour in the early morning
When men awake and look on the day that brings
The hateful adventure, approaching with no less certainty
Than the light that grows, the untroubled bird that sings.

It does not matter what we have to consider:
Whether the difficult word, or the surgeon's knife,

The last silver goblet to pawn, or the fatal letter,
Or the prospect of going on with a particular life.

The point is, they rise; always they seem to have risen,
(They always will rise, I suppose), by courage alone.
Somehow, by this or that, they engender courage,
Courage bred in flesh that is sick to the bone.

Each in his fashion, they compass their set intent
To rout the reluctant sword from the gripping sheath,
By thinking, perhaps, upon the Blessed Sacrament,
Or perhaps by coffee, or perhaps by gritted teeth.

It is indisputable that some turn solemn or savage,
While others have found that it serves them best to be glib
When they inwardly lean and listen, listen for courage,
That bitter and curious thing beneath the rib.

With nothing to gain, perhaps, and no sane reason
To put up a fight, they grip and hang by the thread
As fierce and still as a swinging threatened spider.
They are too brave to say, It is simpler to be dead.

Let each man remember, who opens his eyes to that morning,
How many men have braced him to meet the light,
And pious or ribald, one way or another, how many
Will smile in its face, when he is at peace in the night.

Why hadn't I thought of it sooner? I had to show this poem to my friend, who believed in good infections. So I paid a hasty visit to his hospital room.

And discovered that his trials were over. But in my heart's eye I could see him: in the midst of countless, applauding, illuminating smiles, Steve was at last at peace.

68. Circling in Search of the Truth

March 7, 1979

The opposite of a true statement is a false statement. But the opposite of a profound truth may be another profound truth. Niels Bohr

JOINING a national trend, *The Evening Sun* now has an "op ed" page (opposite the editorial page), which it calls "Other Voices." Editor Bradford Jacobs's kickoff column stirred up in me other voices who agree with his point: the whole truth is very often very hard to come by.

He made me hear again the voice of philosopher Gottfried Leibniz warning that all philosophies are true in what they assert but false in what they deny. Reality is so complex, perhaps so essentially both/and, and our minds so limited, that thinkers are right when they see some basic principle at work in the world. But they are too often inclined to be blind to the claims of the other side of the cosmic coin.

Applying this wary view to history itself, I can hear again wise voices saying that history is a series of exaggerated reactions: first too much of something (like orderliness), then too much of its opposite (permissiveness).

At the theological level I hear a voice pointing out that every heresy is the revenge of a forgotten truth. The pendulum swings between human nature as all good and as all bad; between faith and good works; between letting God do everything and expecting people to do everything; between total freedom and total predestination.

I hear the man who said that he was often wrong but never in doubt. I hear TV commentator Eric Sevareid speak of dangerous certitudes afoot in the world. And wasn't certitude once wisely and wittily defined as being wrong at the top of your voice?

Yet, we have to act: and when we do, we choose one probability over other probabilities. In effect we act *as though* the other probabilities are false. And so I hear the poet Goethe assert that to act is to be unfair.

I hear another German voice at the turn of the century—that of Hans Vaihinger—who built a whole philosophy on "As Though" (*Als Ob*).

Cardinal Newman joins in with this sage observation: if a person waited to act until he were totally free of the danger of being wrong, he would most likely never act.

In spiritual and moral matters we are often required to take sides, betting our very lives on what is the ultimate truth, or the better truth, or the timelier truth, or the truth most consonant with one's most prized view of human destiny. So I hear the philosopher Kierkegaard warn that both/and is the path to hell.

He pushed for either/or. His brother was a bishop whom he regarded as wishy washy. The bishop's occasionally demented son said that his father was both/and, his uncle was either/or and he himself with neither/nor. Humor helps.

Wherefore this story: two sons were hotly debating. One made his case to the father.

"You are right!" said the father.

The other counterattacked.

"You are right!" said the father.

The overhearing mother protested: "They can't both be right."

"You are right, my dear!"

Not everyone has the right to such broadmindedness. Leaders must govern, and to govern is to decide between—unless "masterful inactivity" seems called for. (I was afraid to say "benign neglect.")

Editorialists must try to decide what is best, for now—even if they seem to make one possibility appear like the only possibility.

But in the quest for truth, the private individual must try to keep an open mind even while his hands shut doors.

The famous donkey who was paralyzed between two equally appealing hay bales starved to death. People often discover which is the wrong path by walking it awhile.

It helps if a person is honest about motives. The philosopher Descartes ascribed intellectual mistakes to the will: we *choose* to be too sure too soon, to be more certain than we ought to be.

It helps to be humble in the search for truth. If we are lucky enough to attain some of it, we need to remember that we don't have the truth, the truth has us. The word *search* comes from the word *circle*: we often travel through new falsehoods to old truths.

In a famous funeral oration, the Greek general Pericles said that some people think but don't act, others act but don't think. The Athenians were grandly special, he explained, because they both thought and acted. Pericles, he was an Athenian.

In Goethe's *Faust*, God grows fond of Faust, not because he was free from error and sin, but because he was mightily interested in what was true.

"I don't know everything. I'm not that young," said Sir James Barrie of *Peter Pan* fame. (No offense intended to our young readers.)

The truth will make you free. The search for it will make you noble, though perhaps old before your time. There are many ways to be young.

These thoughts, these voices have probably not solved any practical problems. That is another truth. Or at least a probability. And probably an appropriate place to stop.

69. Wanted: Some Jovial Friars of Courtesy

The Baltimore Evening Sun: August 24, 1979

Down through the centuries, religious orders have been founded to meet some then-current need of the human spirit. I'd like to found a modern order for the survival and/or revival of courtesy. And I'd ask a gas station attendant in the Hampden section of Baltimore to head it.

I already have a name for its members: the Jovial Friars. There was such an order in the thirteenth century, though the name was only a nickname. They were founded to protect the weak and to mediate feuds.

Their rule was rather relaxed. Maybe this made them jovial. After some decades they became so jovial they had to be suppressed.

But I like the name. The very phrase would be an antidote to these times, which are so short on joviality.

Since my childhood, for instance, I have always regarded postmen and postal clerks as bastions of courtesy. The other week though at the Post Office, I was waited on by one of the most studiously unpleasant earthlings I've ever had the pleasure of meeting. You'd never guess I was helping to pay her salary.

In the midst of finding the stamps I needed, she paused ceremoniously to take a candy, unwrap it with remarkable deliberation, and pop it into her mouth. I could have understood if she needed something sweet before licking a bitter stamp. From the look on her face, however, it must have been a sourball.

It is ironic to consider that the very word "urbanity" was coined to distinguish the refined manners of city folk from the supposed crudities of country folk. "Boorish," after all, comes from the word for farmer, and the original "villain" worked as a peasant at a country villa.

Yet nowadays city life seems to be spawning surly dispositions en mass. By contrast, a recent visit to a small Iowa town reminded me of what plain old friendliness can be like.

Still, I must be fair. Two years ago I met a man who runs an Amoco service station in the Hampden section of Baltimore city. He had lent me a gas can when I ran dry on the Jones Falls Expressway. When I returned the can with thanks, he told me he used to have seven cans. But he had trustingly lent out the six others to rescued drivers who failed to return them. And still he kept on trusting strangers with the cans that remained.

That man is a hero of our times. I'd ask him to be the abbot of my new order. If he couldn't take the job, I'd track down a man I met in a travel agency in Rome some years ago. Phones were ringing; customers were shouting madly. Yet he remained an eye of calm in the hurricane of noise.

He listened patiently to my problem and then told me where to go—in the polite sense of that phrase. But he didn't just tell me. Knowing I was a stranger, he walked out onto the street with me and courteously pointed out the direction I should take.

The Italians have a disarming phrase for "please." They say *per cortesia*. Instructively, "courtesy" originally meant the kind of behavior you'd expect from people connected with a royal court. (That's also where "curtsy" and matrimonial "courting" came from.) It's still a royal quality, but at times these days it seems as rare as royalty.

I have a candidate too for the abbess of my new order. She was a sales clerk in a Dublin five-and-dime. She didn't have the item I wanted, but she walked the whole length of the store, went out onto the sidewalk, and accompanied me to the nearby store that could help me. The Irish say that when God made time, He made plenty of it. How startling and refreshing to meet somebody who still believes that!

Now, these friars and nuns of mine: they would drive downtown every day, letting people go ahead of them in the traffic line, refusing to honk their horns right away when the light changes to green or somebody stalls. They would even let drivers in front of them take their time as they try to figure out a street address.

Having parked, they would hold open the door for people coming after them into stores, chat with beggars, pick up dropped packages (and return them to the rightful owners), and insist that waitresses take their time.

They would take solemn vows to praise five people every day at random, and say thank you at least ten times. (These numbers would be given some mystical meanings that I haven't yet decided on.)

But their main commitment would be to follow the simple advice given by the saintly Mother Teresa of Calcutta. Someone asked this heroic little woman what an ordinary person could do to make this world a little better—this "little threshing floor which makes us so fierce," as Dante saw it. She had an amazing, almost revolutionary reply: "Just smile at one another."

People might think you're pleasantly deranged or high on drugs if you started to do this on your average street in your average city. But if they knew you belonged to a religious order—I'll have to design some kind of uniform—they might indulge you. They might even smile back, especially when they read the words on the cheerfully colored holy card you distribute free of charge: "By Jove, I'm going to be more jovial." The main thing will be to take time or make time for the gift of courtesy. For as Carl Jung insisted: "Hurry is not merely of the devil. It *is* the devil."

70. Gandhi: E.T. in Loincloth

January 30, 1983

THIRTY-FIVE years ago today, Mahatma ("Great-soul") Gandhi was assassinated in New Delhi by a Hindu extremist, Nathuram Godse, who believed that the Hindu Gandhi had weakened India by befriending its Muslims. Godse was later hanged, over protests by Gandhians.

The movie *Gandhi*, now showing across the nation, will—despite its three-hour length—leave many a viewer thirsty to know more about this rare spirit, this "beacon to generations to come," as Albert Einstein called him. In his seventy-ninth year when he died, he was born on October 2, 1869, in Porbandar, now practically the westernmost city in India.

His first name, Mohandas, means "servant of the Lord [Krishna];" he took his middle name from his father, Karamchand: "believer in work"; Gandhi is said to mean "grocer," and reflects the Hindu tradesman caste. (Prime Minister Indira Gandhi is no kin.) In the movie, crowds often shout "Gandhiji," *i.e.*, "Gandhi, dear sir." "Mahatma" was an ancient title given him by popular acclaim because of his "great soul."

Mohandas married when he was thirteen; his wife, Kasturbai, died in 1944, more than six decades later. Like Lincoln, Gandhi had four sons. He himself was the sixth and youngest child of his father, who had been thrice married before he wed Mohandas's mother, a devout Hindu.

The youthful Gandhi went through a period of secret atheism, petty thefts, furtive smoking, and meat eating. His two-volume autobiography, *My Experiments with Truth* (1927–29), tells his story up until 1921. He wrote copiously—his collected works may come to eighty volumes. Tolstoy was among his many correspondents.

As early as 1918 Oxford Professor Gilbert Murray warned: "People in power should be very careful how they treat a man who cares nothing for sensual pleasure, nothing for riches, nothing for comfort or praise or promotion, but is simply determined to do what he believes to be right." That also sounds like Jesus, whose Sermon on the Mount deeply influenced Gandhi.

There are dependable biographies of Gandhi by Louis Fischer, Robert Payne, and Vincent Sheean. The last named, who was a few feet from Gandhi when he was shot, wrote a life entitled *Lead, Kindly Light*—a reference to one of the Mahatma's favorite Christian hymns.

The latest *Encyclopaedia Britannica* asserts: "Gandhi was the catalyst if not the initiator of three of the major revolutions of the 20th century: against colonialism, racism, and violence." Of himself Gandhi wrote: "What I have been striving and pining to achieve . . . is to see God face to face."

His dying words were *He Rama*—"Ah, God!"

71. But What Happened After the Movie Ended?

The Baltimore Evening Sun: November 5, 1985

THANKS to video cassettes, more people than ever are seeing golden oldies they never saw, as well as more recent but departed movies they wanted to see or want to see again. As a cultural contribution, here's a postview of three engrossing "true stories" from the movies that have left many viewers wondering.

It's Pittsburgh, 1902. The warden's wife has been falling in love with a convicted murderer, due to be hanged. She helps him and his brother escape and runs away with them. They are tracked down, the men are shot dead, she is sent to prison. End of *Mrs. Soffel*, played by Diane Keaton in a movie released within the last year and also featuring Mel Gibson.

But what happened next to the thirty-five-year-old mother of four? Maddeningly, the movie doesn't tell you. Unlike the twenty-four-year-old Ed Biddle for whom she sacrificed all, we are left hanging. Like the Pittsburgh posse, I finally did some tracking down.

Soffel served a two-year term, then lived in the Steel City area until her death six years later. She supported herself as a seamstress and by playing herself in a touring show called *The Biddle Boys*. (So magnetic were those "boys" that their caskets had to be closed to stop women from snipping locks of hair and cutting off buttons.) Her husband moved with his children to Ohio and died there in 1936.

Another true story that leaves you hanging from the emotional yardarm is *Potemkin*, often listed among the "ten best films" ever. This 1925 Soviet movie by Sergei Eisenstein dramatizes the 1905 mutiny of the Russian crew of the battleship Potemkin, the spanking new pride of the Black Sea fleet. The ship drops anchor in Odessa, itself in the throes of an anti-

Czarist revolt. The rest of the fleet follows in punitive pursuit. Join our mutiny, flashes the Potemkin. Another battleship does so. Cheers. End of movie.

What happened next? The second mutinous battleship was run aground. The Czarist ships were withdrawn in fear of the Potemkin's superior guns. (The admiral didn't know that the mutineers didn't know how to fire the guns effectively.) Puzzled as to what to do next, the mutineers sailed to Rumania, scuttled their ship, and fled inland.

Chariots of Fire celebrates the British victors in the 1924 Olympics and ends with a sentence or two about what happened later to its two track heroes. British viewers probably needed no explanation of the film's title, since it comes from a hymn that is practically England's second national anthem and is commonly known as "Jerusalem." The words are by poet William Blake (1757–1827) and the 1916 melody by Sir Charles Hubert Parry. (The popular movie theme subtly echoes the music of the hymn.)

Beginning with the question, "And did those feet in ancient time," the poet laments England's fall from grace—surely the holy Lamb of God would disapprove of the dark Satanic mills of the Industrial Revolution. But the poet plans to help fight for a redeemed future. That's why the poet cries out:

> Bring me my Bow of burning gold:
> Bring me my Arrows of desire:
> Bring me my Spear: O clouds unfold!
> Bring me my Chariot of fire.

I first heard this spellbinding hymn in another British film about a young track star, *The Loneliness of the Long Distance Runner*. ("Running time: 103 minutes," announced an unwittingly witty ad.) As viewers may recall, this hymn is sung at the conclusion of a 1978 memorial service with which *Chariots of Fire* begins and ends.

The point of the title of this worthy winner of four Academy Awards is, I suppose, that by being ablaze with a love for glory and by turning their feet into human chariot wheels, its dedicated, conscientious heroes helped in their own special way to ". . . build Jerusalem/In England's green and pleasant land." In any case, they helped to create a superlative film that will most likely be a golden oldie some day.

72. Posters and Imposters

The Baltimore Evening Sun: March 13, 1979

YOU FIRST saw it as a poster entitled, "Desiderata." It bade you "Go placidly amid the noise and the haste." Then you heard it as an inspiring song that focused on the words: "You are a child of the universe no less than the trees and the stars; you have a right to be here."

And to think that this sagacious piece of prose was found in old St. Paul's Church, Baltimore, in A.D. 1692. So at least you were told by the inscription at the bottom of the quotation.

But alas! As the poster itself warned you, "Exercise caution . . . for the world is full of trickery." It turns out that the poster should have been entitled "Desid-*errata*," and those words about Baltimore and old St. Paul's Church did not have "a right to be there." For the words were written by a Max Ehrman, copyrighted in 1927, and renewed in their copyright in 1954 by Bertha K. Ehrman.

The truth about quotations is one of life's "things to be desired," one of its *desiderata*. Stung by my betrayal by old St. Paul's, I have been on my guard about those quotes you see on so many wall posters.

Not long ago I saw these words attributed to William Shakespeare: "The world is a comedy to those that feel and a tragedy to those that think." This turned out to be a double betrayal. For the saying was turned upside down, and it was said by Horace Walpole in 1769 in a letter to Sir Horace Mann.

The quotation could have been cited correctly and the true author given credit if the poster maker had taken the time to check *Bartlett's Familiar Quotations*.

Then there was a poster seen everywhere during the Vietnam War—ours, not the Chineses'—the one quoting Hitler's complaint about students taking to the street and engaging in demonstrations.

Then I read an article in *Commonweal* by the man who edited all of Hitler's speeches and talks and various other utterances. Alas! This expert had no impression of ever reading such a statement from the German dictator. When he challenged the poster makers, they said they got it from somebody else, who in turn said they got it from somebody else, and so on.

Just the other day I saw a poster citing one of my favorite poems to friendship. "Friendship," it said, "is the comfort, the inexpressible comfort of feeling safe with a person, having neither to weigh thoughts or measure words." Some posters add a few words about how friends can be certain that "a faithful hand will take and sift . . . keep what is worth keeping, and with the breath of kindness blow the rest away."

Originally I saw these words attributed to George Eliot and probably gave her credit publicly somewhere. Then I happened to be looking through a book entitled *The Best Loved Poems of the American People*, which bears a 1936 copyright. There on page forty-three is a poem about friendship, word-for-word the same as on that poster. The author? Dinah Maria Mulock Craik.

When I saw that poster again the other day, George Eliot had been blown away, with or without a breath of kindness, and was replaced with two catchall words: Arabian Proverb.

From now on I'm going to define poster friendship as the comfort, the inexpressible comfort, of feeling safe with a quotation, knowing that the poster maker has weighed his thoughts and measured his words.

I myself was once on the other side of this quotation mess. In 1970 I published a little book called *The Christian Under Pressure*. In one of its chapters I spoke of the humble man as exemplifying "the words of philosopher Martin Heidegger: 'Growing means this: To open yourself to the breath of heaven and at the same time to sink roots into the darkness of the earth.' "

Last summer I visited a home in Pittsburgh, and on the kitchen wall I saw the following words decorating a colorful calendar and attributed to one Jos. Gallagher: "Growing means to open ourselves to the breath of heaven and to sink roots into the dark earth." Honest, Mr. Heidegger, I knew nothing about this matter.

The moral of all this is, I suppose, check your sources before a poster makes an imposter out of you. Otherwise you may end up looking like the auctioneer who asked for bids "on this lovely statue of William Shakespeare."

"That's not Shakespeare," yelled a voice from the crowd; "that's Robert Burns."

"Well," said the auctioneer with a modest blush, "that shows how much I know about the Bible."

73. My Title is Nifty; Yours is Silly

The Baltimore Evening Sun: March 11, 1980

THE LONDON TIMES made news itself lately by rejecting "Ms." as a "silly" form of address. The event is a reminder that we spend our lives addressing letters and each other with certain title—Mr., Mrs., Ma'am, Sir, etc. Some of these basics have double meanings: madam and mistress, notably. Now Ms. will endure a new round of controversy.

Most of these titles in our "address list" go back to the idea of some sort of superiority. Being the boss around the house is one common form of superiority, as husbands (housebands) used to think. *Domus* is the Latin word for house, which derives from the Greek word *demein*, which means "to build."

This *domus* gives us dominion, dominate, domestic, domicile, domain, and dome. Originally dome meant the whole house—remember Kubla Khan's "pleasure dome"? Even today a duomo is still "God's house" in the form of an Italian cathedral. And *Christus Dominus* presides over the household of the church.

The head of the household, the *dominus*, shows up in the Spanish don (as in Quixote) and in the Italian dom of Mafia and Dom Camillo fame. The Oxford don belongs in this company.

The lady of the house is the dame. In various forms she becomes the damsel, the duenna, the donna (as in prima), madonna ("my-dame" in Italian). "My-dame" in French gives us madame, whence madam, whence ma'am. "Mademoiselle" is "my little house-lady."

There was a time when being older was honored as a form of superiority. Back to our Latin, where *senior* means older or elder (as do the words priest and presbyter in their Greek roots). This word senior gives us sir, sire, senator, and senile. We all know how rank can go to your head, so it shouldn't be surprising that "surly" also comes from sir. Fancy this sentence, almost entirely from one root: "The senior senator, sir, is senile and surly."

A third set of common titles implies an unspecific superiority. Thus "master," the original form of mister and the word behind mistress, miss, Mrs., and Ms., comes from the Latin *magis*. This word simply means "greater." It is the comparative form of *magnus* (great). It gave the Romans their *magister* (teacher); it gave us magistrate and major, in addition to those "master" words just cited. It gave the Italians their *maestro*, and the Spaniards their *mayor*. Whoever calls you Mr., Mrs., Miss, or Ms. is saluting you as "O Greater One." Mr. Mayor is thus the greater greater.

So much for Latin, Greek, Spanish, Italian, and French. How about our own good old Anglo-Saxon contributions to the "address list"? Happily, two of the most picturesque titles come therefrom; namely, lord and lady. Both are the squashed results of double phrases having to do with bread.

After all, the lord of the house is the breadwinner and keeper. Change bread to loaf; add the idea of "ward" (warden, keeper), and you get "loaf-ward," which, by erosion or collapse, became "lord."

The lord's lady earned her bread by kneading it. The loaf-kneader became a "lady" by another case of erosion. (If your ears are sharp and antique enough, you might be able to hear "loaf-dough" inside the sound of "lady.") So let it never be said that no proper lady would ever soil her hands with kitchen work!

Let this verbal excursion end with the story of Mister X, who asked his son, Master X, what his teacher (magister) had taught him in school that day.

"We learned to say 'Yes, Sir' and 'No, Sir'; 'Yes, Ma'am' and 'No, Ma'am.' "

"You did?"

"Yep!"

74. Getting Your Wordsworth out of Words

ON THE recent feast of the Epiphany I mentioned to a friend the German tradition that the Three Wise Men are buried in Cologne. Quick as a flash, he inquired, "Did they run out of formaldehyde?" More recently, while discussing with another friend my piscatory preferences, I observed, "Actually my least favorite fish is unshellfish." "You mean generoush?"

I had that kind of friend even back in my school days. During a snowball battle, one of my classmates hit a bystanding Chinese student by mistake. "Ah!" quipped my buddy: "Orient hit by Occident." Speed, of course, pertains to the essence of such verbal snowballs.

Part of the fun of language is unintended ambiguity. Menus are a favorite source of such. Thus, the arresting statement: "Salads tossed at your table." (Or the etiquette admonition: "Don't break bread or roll in soup.")

Signs that try to be concise rather than precise spawn numerous doubletakes. Picture the poor paranoid who reads in his hotel room: "Your day ends at noon." Or the literalist who sees on the coffee shop door this advisement: "Shoes are required to eat here." (He might buy them at the store whose wares were advertised as being "unmatched anywhere.")

Inside the shop he encounters another sign: "Lunch will be served from 11:30 until the middle of October." Dizzy from dubiety he visits the nearby hospital and notes the warning: "Patients must not attempt to get into bed without the attending nurse." Comedienne Anna Russell has already told us about her friend who is sick in bed with the doctor.

Often the ambiguity is gentler. While visiting Georgia I saw an obituary notice that began: "Entered into rest in an Aiken Rest Home . . ." A cemetery stonecutter once wrote to me saying, "Rest assured that your wishes will be honored."

Here are some statements on which my brain did a double take:

1) He plays the piano as well as the violin.
2) I noticed how little things had changed.
3) She was against stifling uniformity.
4) We know how many of them died.
5) Pasolini's book was rejected by the judges of Italy's prestigious Strega Prize for obscenity.
6) See other side of menu for more tempting selections.

There was no humor, of course, in the treacherous headline that claimed: "Parents found murdered by adopted son." The headline meant that the victims were found by the son. Tragically, it turned out that the son was also the murderer.

Sometimes the ambiguity and humor are in the hearing rather than in the reading. A college president I know used to greet groups of visitors invariably by asserting: "You are all/most welcome."

Such ambiguity can be the friend of the writer who wants to be ambiguous. Thus the former boss who feels forced to write a letter of recommendation: "Whoever can get this man to work for him will be lucky indeed." Or the literary critic: "I shall waste no time reading your poems, which I am sure cannot be praised too highly. I have read your previous works and much like them."

Last year the national newspaper *Australian* told a story more dramatic than it knew: "He forges his only link with his rescuers by tapping on the wall of his concrete prison to assure them he is still alive . . . one for yes, two for no."

Language is one of our main escapes from the prison of self. And it won't be taps for merriment as long as words remain noticedly so creatively ambiguous in sound and sense. For, as has been pointed out, time flies like an arrow, but fruit flies like a banana.

Part Seven

Private Circles

75. The Baltimore Riots of 1968: Afterimages

The National Catholic Reporter: April 17, 1968

MARCH 30: I went to Druid Hill Park for a picnic with four white couples and their children. Just as we parked, a little Negro boy was struck by a car nearby and thrown ten feet or so. My friend Bill drove me off at once in frantic search for a phone so we could call an ambulance.

When we returned, the youngster was lying on a blanket provided by Bill's distraught wife. Somebody said he thought the boy had a broken arm and leg. Some of his teeth were broken too. His face was skinned and bleeding.

His trembling mother was kneeling beside him. A white policeman held the boy still and kept comforting him tenderly as he cried, "I want to go home."

I held his tense, restless hand and looked down into his face.

* * *

March 31: After I celebrated the 11 A.M. mass at St. Gregory's in the ghetto, a little Negro boy of five or six came up, shook my hand, looked right up into my face with his big, brown eyes, and said: "You were *great* today!"

* * *

April 4: The news of Martin Luther King's death came while I was holding an evening philosophy discussion in my seminary room. One of the assigned topics was "the problem of evil." We didn't talk much—just listened to the radio and looked at the TV.

(This was the second time in five days that President Johnson made an historic TV announcement. On March 31 he had declared that he was going to halt the bombing of North Vietnam, and that he would not run for reelection.)

George, a Negro seminarian, was in our group. When the students left later, one of them just put his hand on George's shoulder. There was no need to say anything.

The announcer said that Dr. King had been hit in the face. Memories returned of the park, the bleeding child, and the compassionate, downgazing crowd of whites and blacks.

* * *

April 5: After supper at a local restaurant, I met a middle-aged Negro, weeping in the rest room.

"Why did they have to kill that man; why did they have to kill that man?" he kept repeating. "Why didn't they kill me? I'm not questioning you, God, but why did they have to kill that man?"

He showed me a picture of his son, a major in Vietnam.

* * *

April 6: Shortly after 11 P.M. a fire broke out on Pennsylvania Avenue not too far from the seminary on North Paca Street in the inner city. The flames were plainly visible from my room. With a brisk wind blowing, they looked threatening. I walked swiftly to the site and found a junkyard ablaze. The firemen seemed to be getting the fire under control as the crowd soured out of control and began throwing things at the firemen.

I hailed a cab to take me back to the seminary. To avoid making the cab detour around several one-way streets, I wanted to get out and walk the last few blocks. "I'm taking you right to the door," said the Negro driver. "I won't let you walk down those streets tonight."

* * *

April 7: After noon mass at St. Gregory's, a young Negro woman said to me abruptly: "Please don't feel responsible. I don't blame the white people. If you blame yourself, it will make me feel worse."

At 3 P.M. I gave a lift to a white policeman who was walking home for lunch. The first thing he said was, "They didn't have any right to kill that man." For a few seconds I didn't realize what man he was talking about.

Driving past Johns Hopkins Hospital at 3:30 that afternoon, shortly before the curfew hour that had been advanced several times, I saw spreading clouds of black smoke billowing up from a nearby street. I walked down an alley to get closer to the fire.

An old Negro woman sat alone on her steps, not far from the path of the smoke and the sparks. Shaking her grey head, her eyes tearful, she spoke almost without emotion: "This didn't have to happen. If only people had listened."

Back in my car, I headed for the seminary. At a nearby intersection a group of black youths suddenly sent bricks and rocks into the windshield of a car that had stopped for a light. Glass shattering into his face, the white driver gunned the accelerator and zoomed down the street.

The youths started converging on me, shouting something about "white man." Then one of them saw my clerical collar. "Oh, you're a priest," he said. "You can go."

Tonight the announcement came that federal troops are heading for Baltimore. They're going to camp in Druid Hill Park.

76. Rasputin and Vatican II: A Ten-Year Flashback

The Baltimore Evening Sun: December 8, 1975

SHAKING the hand of a man who had shaken Rasputin's hand; talking to a man who had talked to Lenin: these were fringe benefits of a trip that took me to Rome as translation editor for *The Documents of Vatican II*, the fruit of the ecumenical council that ended ten years ago today.

In April 1965, I happened to be visiting the New York office of the Jesuit weekly magazine *America*. The editor had been asked to prepare a book of commentaries on the five council documents already released and on the eleven others that were due to be issued by the end of that year. The trouble was the poor quality of the translations already in circulation. Would I be willing to make or obtain better translations for the *America* book?

I had taken six years of Latin in the seminary, had studied six more years of Latin textbooks, and had read daily from Latin prayerbooks since my ordination. Although I was no Latin scholar, church Latin is generally easier than classical Latin. Besides, I was firmly convinced that I could do no worse than had already been done. So I took the assignment and the leap.

Between April and November, I reworked four of the five translations already published. On November 2, 1965 I arrived in Rome and was lucky enough to book a room in the celebrated *pensione* known as Villa Nova, on whose guest register were names like Hans Küng and John Courtney Murray. In a sparsely furnished room with a marble floor, a weak bulb, a reluctant radiator, no sunshine, and a rented Olivetti typewriter, I began working on the five additional texts that had just been promulgated.

I had already agreed to provide the news agency of the U.S. bishops with an immediate translation of the longest council document, *The Church in the Modern World*. This text comprised about 24,000 of the total of 103,014 words of documentation. It was still undergoing revision and would be ratified on December 7, but of course I couldn't wait till then to start translating. So I had to work from the provisional text, one that had aroused keen interest in view of its concern with family planning and modern warfare.

As it turned out, the final text became available for voting only on December 2. Some 743 lines had been wholly or partially altered, parts had been deleted or rearranged. I had less than three days to rework the translation in time for three secretaries to type it, single-spaced, on seventy-four legal-size pages, mimeograph five hundred copies of each page and staple them together in the proper order. Every English-speaking bishop and journalist in Rome wanted an instant copy.

I had planned to fly to Istanbul to witness the reconciliation ceremony of December 7 between the Patriarch Athenagoras and the pope's representative, Baltimore's Cardinal Shehan. This last-minute pressure forced me to cancel my ticket. Eventually, my right hand refused to move and I had to push it with my left hand. When I finished the last words for the waiting typists, I walked wearily but triumphantly to a *ristorante* for some spaghetti and wine. I recalled how Edward Gibbon had gone off by himself and sat quietly musing after he had completed his monumental *Decline and Fall of the Roman Empire*. In a miniature way I felt a literary kinship.

A minor crisis erupted shortly afterwards when I read over the text as released to the newsmen. The council had condemned the saturation bombing of "whole cities or of extensive areas." The typist had omitted the "or," so that the council seemed worried only about the obliteration of large cities. Some hurried phone calls headed off the error in *The New York Times* presentation of the text and elsewhere.

I returned to the United States on December 9 and continued working non-stop on the other translations until January 8. By mid-February I had corrected the last of the galleys; by mid-March several hundred thousand paperbacks were on the market: eight hundred pages of text and commentaries, with forty-three pages of small-print indexing. It was a miracle of production speed.

The scheduling was so hectic that at the very end I had to take a train to New York to deliver corrected galleys of a longish text that had arrived in Baltimore by mail the previous morning. While there I picked up the galleys of another document, read them on the train, and phoned back my corrections when I arrived in Baltimore.

The 110-day nightmare was over. (At times I actually dreamed in Latin.) The situation reminded me of a psychiatrist who had to verify the stability of a rush of draftees during World War II: "It was like checking the bolts of a jet plane as it flew past."

Sometimes during the lonely midnight hours, I had philosophic attacks about the meaning of meaning. What did more than two thousand bishops from all over the world of 1965 mean by this precise Latin word of which the dictionary tells me the meaning in Caesar's and Cicero's time? Caesar and Cicero are dead. Where do meanings go when nobody happens to be meaning them? And of all the hundreds of thousands of English words, which one means precisely what non-English bishops mean when they use an ancient Latin word?

At times the old Latin had no simple equivalent for a modern word. Thus guerilla warfare became *bella larvata*—"masked wars." Two billion people became *vicies milies centena milia hominum*—twenty times a thousand times a hundred units of a thousand men.

Not every one of these people has his/her copy of *The Documents of Vatican II*, but the book is in its thirteenth printing, with at least fifteen times a hundred units of a thousand copies in circulation.

Not long after the book appeared, *Newsweek* reported that since Walter Abbott, S.J. was its general editor, I its translation editor, Harry Costello its key sales promoter, and Cardinal Shehan the author of its introduction, the book was being called in the trade, "the Abbott and Costello, Gallagher and Shehan Act." *Deo gratias* for a touch of lightness amidst the textual heaviness.

O, yes: Rasputin and Lenin. My professional typist in Rome was an English woman with the delightful name of Pamela

Charlesworth. She lived near the Spanish Stairs and had English guests in for tea every Thursday afternoon. That's how I came to meet a certain Mr. Shelley, who was related to the great Romantic poet, and who had met these famous Russians in his traveling youth. In 1965 he worked for the British government as a Russian translator at the Geneva Arms Conference.

He told me that Lenin, wary of assassins, always sat with his back to the wall. When Shelley met the peasant "monk" Rasputin, the older man wrapped his long, black beard around Shelley's youthful hands and thus contrasted the moisture in their eyes: "The dew upon the morning grass is a rainbow of joy. But the damp upon the evening ground is the weeping of fate."

It was especially enjoyable to meet such a fellow translator. He and his fascinating stories were welcome fringe benefits in the midst of a project that was undoubtedly exciting, but occasionally seemed determined to push me beyond the fringe. Virgil's Aeneas once said to his harried companions: *Forsan et haec olim meminisse juvabit*—"Perhaps it will some day be gratifying to recall even these moments." And he was right.

77. In Defense of Nuns, Despite Sister Mary Ignatius

The Baltimore Evening Sun: May 12, 1982

I T HAS been nearly forty years since I was last taught by nuns academically. But I've continued to learn from them in other ways.

When I was chaplain at the Baltimore archdiocese's Children's Village, I saw firsthand the care and compassion shown by the sisters to their troubled charges. The sister superior had a heart condition, but when a youngster had run away and was unaccounted for, I could see her office light burning long beyond the midnight hour.

When I was chaplain for the motherhouse of the Mission Helpers on Joppa Road, I learned a lesson in tact from a sunny, elderly nun who was congratulating my younger brother on landing a job at an office building. "It's not much of a job," he said. "I just open the door." "Yes," she agreed in part, "but there are many ways to open a door."

I learned a lesson in values from another nun, who worked with lepers in Africa. A visitor watched her at work for several hours and then confessed: "I wouldn't do that for a million dollars." Replied the nun: "Neither would I."

History too has kept me learning from religious women. I've come to appreciate such women giants as Juliana of Norwich, Catherine of Siena, Teresa of Avila, and Thérèse of Lisieux. Their being nuns or nun-like did not seem to stunt their greatness. The same can be said of the contemporary Mother Teresa of Calcutta, who keeps inspiring others to "do something beautiful for God." (How that admirable Anglican priest-poet,

George Herbert, dreaded, on the other hand, to be "useless to God"—an electrifying phrase.)

These comments are occasioned by the rash of plays on and off Broadway that feature nuns, such as *Agnes of God, Catholic School Girls*, and *Sister Mary Ignatius Explains It All For You*. As drama critic Walter Kerr put it, New York theatres are being "*inun*dated." And the image that emerges is not all that flattering.

Convent life is not easy. As of 1980, it was estimated that there were forty thousand ex-nuns in the United States alone. I say, all hail to the women who had courage enough to try out the life, and courage to leave or courage to stay.

I suppose I had close contact with about seven nuns in my grammar school days. I had no sadistic or traumatic experiences at their hands. Not even once did I hear about the perilously reflective quality of patent leather shoes. Nor did I hear all that much talk from the sisters about the value of chastity or the dangers thereunto. As a preacher, I do know that you can mention God's love one hundred times and God's justice once, and there will be listeners who will remember only the reference to divine justice.

Oh yes, I had a few unpleasant moments with a few nuns. But I can't honestly claim that the sisters were more nasty or neurotic on the average than teachers in general. The fact, though, that they wore a habit made it easy for us students to think that the habit made them severe. But that would leave unexplained the warm, generous, and loving sisters I did meet in grammar school.

In any case, I gained a good education at a price that was lowered by the self-sacrifice of the nuns. And I received an education for my heart and my willpower as well as my head. James T. Farrell of *Studs Lonigan* fame said that his parochial school education gave him his most valuable conviction—that a person must learn to accept responsibility for his or her actions.

I can only say that even now I know Baltimore nuns—like the administrator of Mercy Hospital—whom I would match with anyone in the world for Olympic-size human qualities and achievements. Nobody ever promised me that I'd meet only saintly, wise, and marvelously mature nuns. I never deserved them, and they might have given me the wrong idea of how easy victory is, especially over the self.

Though sin is usually easier to dramatize than sanctity, perhaps Broadway will one day heavily feature the other side of sisterhood. I thought of this while reading an essay in a recent Broadway playbill. A woman recalled having had to stay after school and write a punishment for the nun she most feared and admired. As the girl left, the nun slipped some money into her hand and directed her to buy herself an ice cream soda. "I want you to do this and remember that after the bad stuff, there often comes the good stuff."

78. Recollections of a Home for Unwed Fathers

The Baltimore Evening Sun: July 22, 1982

THIS is the time of the year when newly ordained priests usually receive their first assignment to a rectory—those "homes for unwed fathers." Twenty years ago at this time I was leaving my first and only rectory assignment after seven years of serving at Baltimore's old cathedral—"the most beautiful church in North America," according to architectural expert Nicholas Pevsner, writing in 1936.

The rectory attached to the old cathedral has been facing Charles Street for about 150 years. Located between Mulberry and Franklin Streets, between Route 40 going one-way east and Route 40 going one-way west, it can be said to stand in the middle of a national highway. I still have sharp memories of some of the traffic I met while answering parlor calls there from 1955 to 1962. These include:

—The out-of-town couple who were on their honeymoon, so they decided to stop off in Baltimore and get married;

—The intoxicated ex-marine I spent four hours counseling one evening. He returned the next morning and had no memory of having ever seen me before;

—The man who told me he was actually dead and this was purgatory. He also confided that psychiatrists have a psychological need to be psychiatrists;

—The man who said he had escaped from Sing Sing and that I had better give him the bus fare to go back, or I would be responsible for what happened;

—The numerous shaky old men who "used to serve mass for Cardinal Gibbons" and could I spare a quarter? (The cardinal died in 1921.);

—The 13-year-old atheist who thoughtfully said *Gesundheit* when I sneezed;

—The poor family whom I invited to go through some items we had collected in a recent clothing drive. Said one delighted youngster, "This is a swell coat, Mr. Priest!";

—The barmy young lady who tried to keep her orchid fresh by massaging it with Noxzema. Once she slipped by me, invaded the butler's pantry, and tried to ride down to the kitchen on the dumbwaiter;

—Probably the most intriguing of my callers: a man who claimed he was the grandson of Czar Nicholas. The only member of the imperial family to escape Ekaterinburg alive was, he claimed, not Anastasia, but his mother Tatiana. He told me he was a hemophiliac and invited me to find a picture of the czar and compare profiles. (I did, and they compared.) He was widely read and a brilliant talker. He needed to borrow money, and his conversation was worth it.

Some of the "calls" were by telephone, summoning me to the nearby Maryland General Hospital. Once a grandmother begged me to come and bless her sick little grandchild. She hadn't told the child's father that she had called me. When I walked into the room, he yelled: "Who asked for him? He gives me the creeps!"

Another patient was apparently playing some kind of game. She would phone the rectory repeatedly for a priest, and then complain to her doctor that the priest was bothering her. So when I approached her room this sign greeted me: "No Visitors, Especially Priests."

Then there were the petty annoyances. I didn't so much mind the people who would move up and down the center aisle, making the Stations of the Cross, while I was trying to give a sermon. But the devout soul who would light a votive candle just to the side of me as I preached, and then drop into the metal box fifteen pennies, one by one . . .

Annoyance is, of course, a two-way street. I recall the time my phone rang shortly after 6 A.M. and an irate voice demanded: "How the hell do you like being waked up at 6 A.M.? Why do you ring those damned bells anyway?"

Groggily I sputtered something like, "Er, uh, they're a call to prayer."

"Oh, I didn't know that. I'm terribly sorry." And he hung up.

A classmate told me of an ingenious way to handle those silly phone calls rectories sometimes get in the middle of the night. You say, "I'm quite busy now but if you give me your phone number I'll phone you back in a couple of hours." Ideally, the caller will say, "But I'll be asleep in bed then." So you can riposte, "Where do you think I was?"

I waited for several weeks to try out this new technique. Finally at 1:30 A.M., a tipsy-sounding man phoned to ask me who was the patron saint of skydivers.

"I'm terribly sorry, but I'm tied up right now. But give me your number and I'll get back to you in an hour or two."

"Oh, don't trouble yourself, Father. I'm in a phone booth; I'll call you."

79. Chronology of a Coronary and Its Consequences

The Baltimore Sunday Sun: October 19, 1980

I T ALL began about a year ago with a routine blood test at Baltimore's Mercy Hospital. My triglyceride count proved to be four times higher than it should have been.

Since regular exercise is considered one of the remedies for this "excess-fat-in-the-blood" condition, I decided to get serious about it. Naturally I thought of jogging. So in my fifty-first year of life, I went to the extremity of buying a sweatsuit and a new pair of tennis shoes. No more joking that I get all my exercise by being pallbearer for my athletic friends.

In the crisp October air, I jogged once at an easy pace around the Druid Hill Park reservoir. A few days later, during my second circuit, I felt some occasional tightening around my neck and would pause until the discomfort subsided.

A week or so afterwards I was talking about my exercise program with a nurse friend. In view of my age, she urged me to undergo a stress test and recommended a cardiologist friend of hers at the U.S. Public Health Service Hospital near Wyman Park.

On October 10, this Dr. Robert Lange put me on a treadmill while he took repeated blood pressure readings and watched the electrocardiogram (EKG) machine attached to my chest. After nine minutes of gradually speeded-up pacing, I began to feel that neck pain. At the same time, the doctor saw some changes on the EKG.

He suspected I was experiencing angina, so he prescribed nitroglycerine tablets and advised me not to allow my pulse rate to exceed 120 when I was jogging. Angina, he explained, is a pain that results when the heart muscle is not getting enough oxygen. Though the pain is from the heart, you can feel it in other places such as the arm, the wrist, the jaw, or the neck.

The tiny nitro tablets, placed under the tongue for quick absorption, ease the angina by temporarily widening the vessels that deliver oxygenated blood to the heart. "You can carry the tablets with you when you jog," he smiled; "they won't explode."

During the following weeks, I let up on jogging and resorted instead to the kind of fast walking I had done during the stress test. I felt no need to take any nitros.

But while eating supper on Thursday, November 29, I felt some neck pain for a minute or so. This couldn't be angina, I reasoned, since I was sitting quietly. Later I learned that angina can indeed be caused by the eating-digesting process.

On Friday, the pain returned briefly several times — once while I was climbing some stairs. Saturday the pain grew somewhat more frequent and sharp. I finally took a nitro, which seemed to help.

Around bedtime, the pain returned and grew quite severe. I felt as though someone were lifting me by the neck with the kind of tongs used for hefting blocks of ice. So around midnight I drove to the emergency room of Mercy Hospital. (A cab or ambulance would have been smarter.) I had been born at Mercy and undergone tests and operations there. My record for leaving there alive was detailed and unblemished.

Three doctors decided I was experiencing "unstable angina," alias "pre-attack angina." So by 3 A.M., I was being bedded down in the coronary intensive care unit, my chest glued to monitor wires, my hands punctured by intravenous needles.

After breakfast my roommate and I were joking — "The hospital rooms may be private, but the gowns are semi-private." About 10 o'clock some neck pain returned. I called for the nurse as I had been instructed to do. She gave me a nitro and proceeded to take my blood pressure. Leaving the cuff around my arm, she dashed from the room and speedily reappeared with a doctor and several other nurses.

As a kind of dizziness and weakness overtook me, they gave

me various injections, including morphine. I don't recall feeling very much pain. My regular Mercy doctor, Nelson Sun, appeared on the scene in the midst of the emergency and told me soon afterwards that I had suffered a heart attack. I had to congratulate myself on the setting.

I stayed in the hospital seventeen days and enjoyed an "uneventful" recovery. During that time I finally learned just what a heart attack is. To begin with, it is roughly synonymous with a coronary occlusion, a coronary thrombosis, and a myocardial infarction.

When lung-freshened blood leaves the heart, some of it circles directly back to the heart by way of arteries that sit like a crown (*corona*) on the outside of the heart. These coronary arteries bring oxygen and other vital nourishment that seep back into the heart muscle.

The inner walls of these or any other arteries can gradually become coated with foreign matter. After a certain degree of clogging, angina results when the heart muscle is made to outwork its oxygen supply.

When part of an artery becomes totally blocked, a heart attack results. The area of the heart that depends on that blood supply will swiftly die. If that area is significant enough, the entire heart muscle can be fatally affected. Almost half of first heart attacks are thus fatal.

Fully instructed about the influence of diet, weight, blood pressure, exercise, smoking, stress, and family ancestry on the heart, I left Mercy to continue my convalescence elsewhere. The heart needs gentle treatment during these first twelve weeks while a scar forms on the injured area and nearby blood routes work themselves helpfully closer.

Dr. Lange had meantime invited me to join a postcoronary rehabilitation program at his hospital. On February 6, he first gave me another "sub-maximal" stress test. After a few minutes, some of the old neck pain returned. He stopped the test, prescribed some medicine, and asked me to return a week later for another stress test.

This test had the same results, so the doctor advised me to undergo a heart catheterization. In this procedure, first tried by a doctor on himself in 1929, tiny tubes are inserted into an arm vein and a groin artery. These are then guided into the heart itself, where various pressures and other data can be measured. Dye is released and films can be taken that will show precisely where and to what degree the coronary arteries are narrowed or blocked.

Two weeks later, during a three-day stay at the hospital, Dr. Lange and several other doctors performed the catheterization on me. I had to remain conscious so I could cough or turn myself when requested, so a local anesthetic was used. That allowed me to repeat the old gag, "Haven't you got anything imported?" Though I was in the chilly operating room for three hours, I didn't find the procedure particularly harrowing.

I waited a week for the report. Six out of the seven doctors who reviewed my heart films advised coronary bypass surgery. I was diagnosed as having "severe triple vessel coronary artery disease." The triple referred to the right main artery, 100 percent blocked—where I had had the heart attack—and the two branches of the left main artery. In general, these vessels were more than 70 percent blocked. Some offshoots were 95 percent blocked.

Dr. Lange recommended Dr. Robert Brawley, who was a consultant to the cardiologists at the Public Health Hospital. This Hopkins surgeon had already seen my films by the time I visited him on April 8. He was quite candid. There was a general 5 percent mortality risk and a 25 percent chance that I would be no better or even worse after surgery. That left a 70 percent chance that if I survived I would find relief from angina and other symptoms.

Statistically, he admitted, it still wasn't clear whether and to what extent such surgery prolongs life or postpones another attack. Indeed, surgery could precipitate such an attack.

My situation was curious: on the one hand I wasn't (yet) having much angina. On the other, my clogging was so pervasive that there weren't many ideal places for bypassing to. "It would be reasonable to have surgery," Dr. Brawley concluded, "and reasonable not to."

That statement threw the decision heavily back on me. True, I wasn't having many symptoms, but such was also the case up until a few days before my first attack. If I survived a second attack, the risk of surgery would then be greater and the promise of success lesser.

I spent several weeks consulting various heart specialists. By April 20, with various degrees of conviction, all but two doctors had advised me to have the operation. (The only negative advice, from two sources, was "not yet.") The next day I contacted Dr. Brawley's office and was given May 28 as my date for surgery. That would be the silver jubilee of my ordination.

As that date approached some digestive problems occurred and tests revealed blood in my intestines. So, five days before the May 28 operation, Dr. Brawley cancelled it. He wouldn't take the risk of operating and giving me necessary blood thinners when I might still be bleeding internally.

By the time I visited a specialist and took special tests, the bleeding had stopped. So on July 5, I was admitted into Hopkins and given a thorough work-up. The resident asked what medicines I was taking. Around noon the next day, Dr. Brawley arrived with bad news. By some failure of communication, I had been taking a blood-thinning medicine that I should have been told to stop one week earlier.

Therefore I was dismissed from Hopkins and asked to return (with thickened blood) the following weekend. This time all went routinely well: chest X-rays, blood tests, and a thorough shaving of the chest and groin areas and the inner legs.

This last procedure was required because it is from the inner calves and thighs that expendable veins are removed to provide the bypass material. (Whence come jocose comments about having your foot in your mouth and your leg in your chest.) The surgeon uses these "saphenous" veins to form detours for blood that is struggling to pass through narrowed heart arteries.

A catch here: If a bypass doesn't attain a good flow-through, it can collapse and prove useless. Other possible catches, which I acknowledged in a signed statement, were: "death, stroke, heart attack, kidney failure, bleeding, infection problems, and failure to improve."

By 7 A.M. on Monday, July 14, I was being wheeled to the operating room. Given several sedatives earlier that morning, I have no memory of even arriving there. A disappointment, that; I had planned to savor more deliberately what could have been my final moments of consciousness on this planet.

As those who saw the movie *All That Jazz* will vividly recall, the chest of the bypass patient is cut open, the breastbone sawed through and pushed apart, the heart exposed and eventually stopped. Then a bypass machine connected to the aorta does the work of heart and lungs while the venous bypasses are being grafted onto the arteries on the heart surface.

The next thing I knew, a relative talking near my ear was saying, "You're looking so much better." I later learned that the operation had lasted five hours, and that I heard those reassuring words on the evening of the operation, in the surgical intensive care unit. Eight years earlier my brother had died in the adjacent unit. Cousins and uncles on both sides of my family had also died in their forties and fifties from heart disease.

I don't recall feeling much pain, or having clear awareness of anything, except that I was annoyed by a respirator tube that remained down my throat until the following morning. Some chest drains were removed about the same time, and then I was transferred to an intermediate care unit for two days.

By Thursday I was back in a regular room. On the following Thursday I was released from Hopkins. The hospital bill was $9,100; the surgeon's, $3,250 and the anaesthesiologist's, $1,200 — a bargain, I'm told.

Dr. Brawley explained to me that upon examining my arteries firsthand, he had decided that two of the proposed six bypasses were not worth doing. So he did only four — three promising ones, and one of dubious value. He said the process was "tedious."

By my own counting, I had about 140 visible stitches on my right calf, right thigh and left thigh, and on the skin over my wired-up breastbone. With four feet of new incisions, I would now be easier than ever to identify.

All in all, I can say that neither the heart attack itself, nor the heart catheterization, nor the bypass surgery turned out to be as grueling as my imagination had supposed. Of course I had the good fortune to be in the hands of excellent doctors and nurses and to have had my attack in a hospital.

As I recuperate I've had various distractions to take my mind off my heart. For instance, as I waited to be taken away from Hopkins, my chauffeur failed to bypass an elevated manhole cover, which inflicted $800 worth of damage on my car.

Two months and two towings later, the car is still in the repair shop.

The heart story is good: my pep has returned and the angina hasn't. Now I wait for the end of the three-month recuperation period so I can begin again rehabilitation exercises at the Public Health Service Hospital. I'll start off with another stress test. It's about time for me to pass one.

80. The Living Room of Belva Thomas

America: April 17, 1976

THE NATIONAL magazines that told us some time ago why Johnnie can't read are now spelling out the reasons why Johnnie can't write.

The whole subject sets you to thinking about that catalyst of a woman who entered your life nearly forty years ago. Things were not going well at home, and your mother was going to have a baby around Christmas time. So you and your brothers got farmed out to relatives and friends.

You were the one who got farmed out the most literally. For Francis and Tommy went to the homes of relatives who did not live very far from that gloomy apartment in a run-down section of Calvert Street near the present location of the Baltimore *Sun-papers*.

But you were sent out to live with Mrs. Belva Thomas on Ethelbert Avenue in the suburbs. Mrs. Thomas had been a neighbor of your father before he married. Though she did not actually live on a farm, she did live in a house that was not a row house and that had flowers around it. In the back there was a chicken coop, and there were plenty of trees nearby.

Besides, Mrs. Thomas had grown up on a farm and had in her bones "the smack and tang of elemental things." They were big bones, too, fit for a tall woman of immense kindness. Thinking back, you are not sure whether she had blue eyes. But you know she had one of the cleanest, lovingest smiles you were ever to see—the kind of luminous smile that made it ridiculously unimportant that her face was plain and round and rather doughy, with a little lump down by the chin on the right side.

You stayed with her for about six months (with your own room on the second floor). Mr. Thomas was there, too—a guard for the B & O Railroad—and her grown daughter Katherine, who worked in a department store and drove the old car. Her son Gilbert stopped by now and then with his wife Bea, who was a minister's daughter. In fact, Mrs. Thomas went to that minister's church on Park Heights Avenue. They were all friendly and all Protestants and did not seem to mind your being a Catholic.

Thanks to that lady, all sorts of things happened to you during that half year when you were eight, going on nine. She got you to comb your hair straight back instead of parting it. She noticed how you were washing your food down with your milk and she got you to stop that. She impressed you by telling you that human beings are born in order to die. (And lest they die ahead of time, she stressed the importance of washing your hands after you used the bathroom.) And she let a city boy have the fun of feeding the chickens and collecting the eggs, all snowy and miraculous.

But it was inside the warm, bright, and clean wooden house that three very special things occurred. First, there was a table near the living room window that soaked in most of the sun that autumn and winter. On it, Mrs. Thomas had placed a flowering plant. Next to the plant was a pad and pencil. On the pad, with the pencil, that large lady kept a record of how many tiny blossoms bloomed on that plant, and on which day. That taught you a lot about the importance of flowers.

Near that table was a Victrola and a generous supply of records in the cabinet below it. Your own home didn't have such luxuries. Now you could sit by the hour and listen to Harry Lauder sing "I Love a Lassie" or to those nameless voices that sang "My Buddy" and "I'd Love to Fall Asleep and Wake Up in My Mammie's Arms."

But the supreme revelation of all came on the day you first played a record called "Finlandia" and discovered there were sounds in this world that could take you out of this world, could stun you with a beauty both clear and dark at the same hypnotic moment. That magic treasure box next to the counted flowers taught you the importance of music.

Mrs. Thomas was more directly involved in the third priceless revelation. People who would know you later in life would find it hard to believe that there were practically no books in your childhood home. But there was a Mrs. Thomas in your childhood. Although she wasn't a learned woman in any bookish or classroom way, she had a holy respect for knowledge. You learned that the first time you ever asked her what some word meant.

"Let's go together and find out," was her answer. So you both went into the living room (where the blossoms and the sounds were), and she took from the shelf a big book called a dictionary, and she sat on the rocking chair, and you sat on her lap while you both looked up the meaning of the word. And that's the way it happened, time and time again.

And so it was that in the same room where music flowered in your life, and flowers flowered, words and the meaning of them flowered too. That was a living room that really earned its name.

It's not surprising to you that your earliest memory of trying to write a poem goes back to that enchanted house. All that you remember now about the poem is that *down* and *town* were two of the rhyme words. You have a hunch that the subject was snow. All sorts of things got noticed when you were around Mrs. Thomas, and you wanted to keep a record.

March came, and you went back to the city. You saw Mrs. Thomas every now and then, exchanging visits. She died when you were in the seminary, but in those days you were not permitted to attend the funeral of a mere friend. (Your mother sat by her sickbed and even though Mrs. Thomas was a Protestant, she didn't mind your mother saying the rosary for her as she sat there.)

The enchanted house has been torn down, and the whole block has disappeared to make room for a junior high school— an apt substitute if there had to be one. So the house is gone, and Mrs. Thomas gone from sight. But her memory is still an oasis within you, and you keep drinking from the well of wonderment she tapped, especially whenever you sense afresh the mystery of flowers and music and words.

And you feel sorry for every Johnnie who cannot read—and not just words on a page, but in the book of life as well. And you wish for each of them in the desert of their deprivation the gift of a beautiful Belva who knows how to notice and how to savor and how to teach unforgettably.